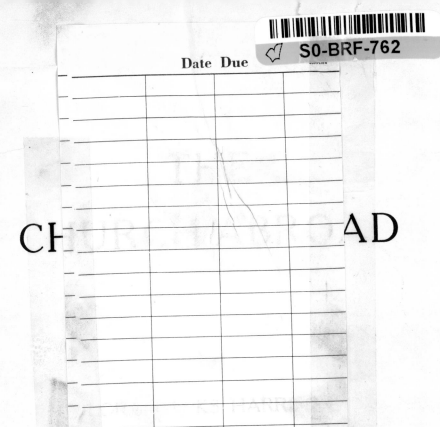

SO-BRF-762

CH̲ ̲R ̲ ̲ ̲ ̲ ̲ ̲ ̲ ̲AD

China.

Forwarding agent for Imogene Williams, missionary to Thailand.

Instructor in Missions at Ozark Bible College, Joplin, Missouri.

1

FIRST EDITION — *1957*

REVISION — *1960*

SECOND REVISION — *1969*

This book is lovingly and prayerfully dedicated to all the gallant soldiers of the cross who spend and are being spent for the cause of New Testament Christianity in the fields abroad, and to the Bible Colleges at home who seek to train them for the task.

Go Everywhere

C.E.P.

CHARLES E. PHIPPS

1. Go ev-ery-where with Je - sus, Go with Him lov - ing - ly;
2. Go ev-ery-where with Je - sus, Go when He calls—be true;
3. Go ev-ery-where with Je - sus, Go gent-ly in His name;

Go ev - ery - where He leads you, Go with Him joy-ful - ly.
Go where you'll find the lost ones, Go, and they'll wel-come you.
Go on when nights are long - est, Go as a burn-ing flame.

Go with Him up to Cal - v'ry, Go there to learn His love.
Go to the farth-est cor - ner, Go to those by your side;
Go hard to win for Je - sus, Go farth-er than you've gone,

Go with the ri - sen Sav - ior, Go with the Mas-ter a - bove.
Go to the fields of har - vest, Go preach the Word far and wide.
Go, know-ing He is with you, Go home with some-one you've won.

Used by permission

PREFACE

It is hoped that through the reading of this book you may become better acquainted with the mission fields abroad, that the knowledge thus gained may challenge you to witness "as you go", wherever you go.

It is not possible to give a comprehensive history of every work or worker, but this is an attempt to give a general survey of each field outside of the United States. Neither is this an attempt in any way to recommend, promote, or endorse any missionary whose work is herein included, nor to judge methods or means of support.

If there are any names left out it is entirely unintentional. With so many recruits leaving for the field (for which cause we rejoice) it is difficult to be positive that everyone is included. In this second revision, recruits who have definite plans to enter their chosen field by the end of the year of 1969 will be included.

ACKNOWLEDGEMENTS

To Charles Phipps for the use of his inspiring hymn *"Go Everywhere"*.

To all the missionaries and recruits, without whose cooperation the writing of this book would have been impossible.

To the editors of the *Horizons* magazine for their added source of materials.

To my "Survey of Missions" class of 1968 who helped to organize the material received from the missionaries.

To Mrs. Roy Wilson who shared in the proof-reading of the original copy.

To John and David Mehrens, young students, who spent hours in the preparation of new maps for this revision.

To my husband and our children who have been willing for me to undertake this time-consuming task.

Last, but certainly not least, to those who prayed for me in this venture.

Africa

1	Morocco	
2	Algeria	
3	Libya	
4	Egypt	
5	Span. Sahara	
6	Mauritania	
7	Mali	**29** Republic of Congo
8	Niger	**30** Rep. of the Congo
9	Chad	**31** Rwanda
10	Sudan	**32** Uganda
11	Ethiopia	**33** Kenya
12	Fr. Somliland	**34** Burundi
13	Somali Rep.	**35** Tanzania
14	Senegal	**36** Angola
15	Port. Guinea	**37** Zambia
16	Guinea	**38** Malawi
17	Sierra Leone	**39** Rhodesia
18	Liberia	**40** Mozambique
19	Ivory Coast	**41** South West Africa
20	Upper Volta	**42** Bechuanaland Prot.
21	Ghana	**43** South Africa
22	Togo	**44** Malagasy Republic
23	Dahomey	**45** Tunisia
24	Nigeria	
25	Cameroon	
26	Central African Rep.	
27	Rio Muni	
28	Gabon	

Congo

"The Land of Stanley"

THE LAND . . . .

Successor state to the former Belgian Congo, the Democratic Republic of the Congo is an independent state occupying the very heart of Africa.

Shaped like a giant basin, the Congo has a low-lying central plateau surrounded by higher land, with mountain ranges in the southeast rising to more than 6,000 feet and in the east to 16,795 feet. About half the area, mainly on the central region, is tropical rain forest, with marshes in the northwest bordering the Congo River, which drains the entire country. The Congo River is the second longest river in Africa. North and south of the forest area, the forest gives way to parklike savannas or treeless grasslands.

The natural vegetation is varied and rich. Many valuable tropical trees such as ebony and mahogany are indigenous, as are palm trees, resin-yielding trees, plantains and bananas, and in some areas, cotton and coffee plants. Nearly half of the area of the Congo is believed to contain productive or potentially productive woodland.

The animal life of the country is as profuse as its vegetation. Larger animals include lion, elephant, buffalo, rhinoceros, leopard, zebra, wildcat, wild boar, giraffe, okapi, and wild hog—a real zoo. Gorilla, chimpanzee, baboons, and many kinds of monkeys add to it. Hippopotamus and crocodile are found in the rivers. Large snakes include the python, puff adder, and tree cobra. Among insects are malaria-carrying mosquitos and the tsetse fly. Infestation by the fly hinders cattle raising in much of the country, thus meat is still a limited item in the Congolese diet.

The Congo is rich in minerals. As early as 1957 it produced about three-fourths of the world output of industrial diamonds and about three-fifths of the cobalt. Copper is the most important mineral in the Congolese economy. Mining was the one area of the economy that did not suffer a marked decline during the 1960-62 period of disruption and conflict.

In 1963, an estimated three-fourths of the African population still lived by subsistence farming, consuming all they grow and moving to a new plot of ground when the soil of the old became exhausted. The exodus of Europeans and the prolonged rebellion severely affected the production of agricultural commodities for export, especially in rubber, cotton and coffee.

Since 1960, there has been a decline in industrial activity, which includes cement, lime, soap, sugar, beer, textiles, shoes, chemicals, and cigarettes.

Most of the railroad system was damaged and put out of commission during the four years of internal conflict that followed the establishment of independent Congo. Many bridges, too, including railroad bridges, were destroyed, further disrupting the transportation system.

Until 1960 the whole of the Congo was governed directly from Belgium. When it was decided to grant independence within six months, an entire political structure had to be created, and there was insufficient time for none of the new political leaders had any governmental experience. When the Belgians were forced to flee the country at the mutiny of the army, everything collapsed. The links between the central government and the provinces were broken, and no effective control over the whole country has ever been reached since.

.... THE PEOPLE

By 1966, the population of the Congo had reached the sixteen million mark. By 1962 the non-African population, mainly Belgian, had decreased by more than sixty per cent. The density of population is low, only sixteen per square mile; the proportion of children (under 21) to adults is 45 to 55.

The original inhabitants of the Congo may well have been the pygmies who remain now in small number in the forest area. They were replaced by the Bantu who now inhabit the country.

In the rural areas the typical settlement is the village, made up of thatch-roofed houses built of bricks prepared of material from huge anthills. These are satisfactory for tropical climates.

About one-fourth of the population live in urban areas where housing is insufficient and slums surround the major city areas.

Most economic activities in the rural areas are shared by men and women according to a rigid pattern of labor division. Marriages are usually established by marriage payments. Polygyny is common. Preferential marriages and different forms of ritual marriages are permitted by some tribes.

The main common languages are Lingala in the west and Swahili in the east. French is the official, business and social language of the country.

In the years before World War II almost all education was provided for by Belgian missions (mainly Catholic) and by foreign missions (mainly Protestant). Educational effort was concentrated on the primary levels and on vocational training. An African could only obtain a higher education by entering a seminary to be a priest. By 1950 strict segregation began to break down. By 1957 elementary education was free; by 1958 two universities were opened in the Congo itself. A third university was established at the former city of Stanleyville in 1962, but its activities were halted when the rebellion spread to the northern provinces.

About one-third of the population is Christian, mostly Catholics, and about 150,000 are Muslims. Most of the rest have retained their traditional tribal animistic beliefs.

. . . . THE MISSIONARY . . . .

The doors are wide open from the Cape to the Congo, this is the opportunity of Africa. The challenge was accepted.

Nearly five years after the Guy Humphrey's family dedicated themselves to the Lord's work among the black people of Africa they found themselves in Bomili of the Congo to begin our first witness for Christ. During August, 1948, the first actual teaching was done, and five months later the first church established. Two years after the Humphrey family left America they left native huts to move on to an abandoned plantation, the first permanent home for *African Christian Mission*. They served a swampy jungle area about the size of New Hampshire within whose sphere of influence lived a hundred thousand people.

William Ransford and his family joined the Humphrey family in December, 1950 for a period of nearly two years before the Doctors ordered them to leave the tropics permanently due to the ill health of Mrs. Ransford. Robert Williams, with his wife, labored with the preacher-training school for some months in 1952.

In August, 1952, June Taylor joined the mission staff to assume office duties and direction of the elementary school program that had been established. The latter responsibility was turned over to Zola Brown on her arrival in 1953. Also that year Howard Crowl came to the field for one year for the purpose of setting up the printing press and training personnel to use it, but the Lord had other plans. A year after his arrival on the field he and June Taylor were united in marriage and they made their decision to stay with the work in Africa. After their marriage June devoted much time to translation, Howard to all phases of the work. It was in 1955 that he began to receive training to assume the leadership and responsibility of the work of *African Christian Mission,* over which he took active supervision in July 1956.

13

Having always been especially interested in the pioneer work on the mission field, the Humphreys, having prepared brother Crowl to oversee the work they had begun, left the Mission to undertake a new venture in Stanleyville, 250 miles from Bomili. Wth the help of the Lord they became self-supporting by setting up a trucking line as they launched out in this new work in the Congo.

Also in 1953 Mr. and Mrs. Clifford Schaub came to fill an emergency need. In 1954, the Olina mission station was opened at the second site, seventy miles northeast of Bomili, which had been granted to the mission some years before. An elementary school was immediately established and a training class for student preachers was transferred from Bomili. Later brother Schaub did a great deal of the printing work that was an effective tool of evangelism.

The Ronald Harshes arrived in the Congo in April 1956 to labor at the Bomili-Olina stations, where his first work was in preacher-training. Material was likewise prepared for home-study for ministers already on the field.

In the first nine years of this work of *African Christian Mission* they evangelized 4,000 square miles and were instrumental in planting thirty-three New Testament churches, approximately five thousand people were added to the Lord. But the dream and prayer of the mission to evangelize the entire area of the Congo, approximately 900,000 square miles, did not begin to be realized until after the country gained its independence in 1960 when rebellion scattered our missionaries and native Christians into other areas.

In spite of political unrest the Carl Harshes and Ron Butlers joined the work in 1961. In these troubled times Phyllis Rine came to the Congo to serve, as did the Larry Doggett family and Nancy Shewmaker. Even with the ever-present uncertainties and personal difficulties the first six months of 1964 were the best months since their independence, not only for the Congo, but for the mission activity as well. Then came the rebels!

At Stanleyville the Clifford Schaub family was miraculously saved from the rebels after weeks of imprisonment but Phyllis Rine was martyred in a rapid burst of machine-gun fire, minutes prior to the rescue of the others. "Precious in the sight of the Lord is the death of His saints". In other areas nearly all material possessions were confiscated by the rebels and the missionaries were forced to evacuate. Occasional trips have been made back into these areas of early work but most of the present missionary work is on the eastern side of the Congo in the Bukavu area, a city of 240,000. The tragedy of the

14

whole Congo situation is the slaying of the native people. Countless preachers and Christians have been tortured and killed. The whole story of these years can not be told herein.

In July 1967 when missionaries were forced to leave again the Ron Butlers went to Belgium and then on into France to begin a new work there in 1968. The Clifford Schaub family have begun a printing ministry in Canada. The Ron Harshes are engaged in new church evangelism in Ohio. But even in the dark hours, Hale Whitcomb came to assist. In the midst of evacuation he and Nancy Shewmaker were married on the airport runway. They have since worked in the Kidodobo area where as many as four hundred gather each Lord's day to worship. At present they are in the States preparing to go to Tanzania. The first Christian service camp in the Congo was held in the Kidodobo area. The elementary school operated throughout the complete absence of missionaries—without books, papers, pencils, or slates, blackboards, even without desks. Early in 1968 the Howard Crowls were granted a two-year visa by the Kenya government to live and work in Nairobi, where they are at present.

Knowing from past experiences of those on the field that "medical missions" can reach out to vast numbers of previously untouched people, Marvin and Linda Grooms joined forces with the mission, leaving for Belgium for language study in 1967, and for Nancy to take a course in the School of Tropical Medicine in Antwerp, which will prepare her to open an infirmary in the Congo or across the border in Rwanda if visas permit. She is the first medical personnel connected with the *African Christian Mission*. In 1968 they studied Swahili, (local native language) in Kenya, Africa, before entering the field. Brother Groom will give himself to the task of personal evangelism and Bible training, to the end that self-supporting, self-governing, and self-perpetuating congregations may be established. In the more recent rebellions it was found that those churches established in this manner were the ones least affected by exterior problems and pressures, and who could continue their own work of witnessing without the presence or assistance of the missionary.

The Gene Landis family reached Kenya in the fall of 1968 to establish a printing ministry that will serve the Congo until they can enter the Congo itself. Some tracts are already translated and waiting to be printed, prepared by Mrs. Crowl. This printing equipment is a memorial to Phyllis Rine.

Margaret Williams, another member of the Congo team, studied language in Kenya before coming to Bukavu. Her work will largely be in the office and in Bible classes.

15

The Larry Doggetts left for the Congo again in the fall of 1968 and in the first six months they reported a doubling of membership of churches in the Bukavu area since their earlier evacuation. There were sixty-five additions during December of 1968 in the Bukavu-Kidodobo area, one hundred seventy-two in the first four months of 1969. In this area there are ten churches established with a membership of 767 persons. The Bible Institute in the Kisangani area has been re-established with twelve students, and a new one has been started in Bukavu with fourteen students.

Larry Doggett, missionary, presenting Bibles to one of the preachers in the Kisangani area.

On a recent trip back into Stanleyville they found fifty-one churches and nearly 1,800 faithful Christians, though there has been no missionaries there for nearly five years. Efforts for regular visits are now being made.

Zola Brown will be coming home in 1969 for furlough while it is hoped that new recruits, the Harvey Waddelows, will be able to come to the field.

Since the beginning of the work in the Congo there have been 10,767 baptisms reported with an active membership of 2,567 worshiping in sixty-one congregations.

16

In the Congo the church of Christ has found one of its finest opportunities of service in a land where millions of people are struggling with the problems and temptations of a new life. Only time and prayer can tell the eventual outcome of the new freedom in the Congo. May it be to God's glory.

Ghana
"The Gold Coast"

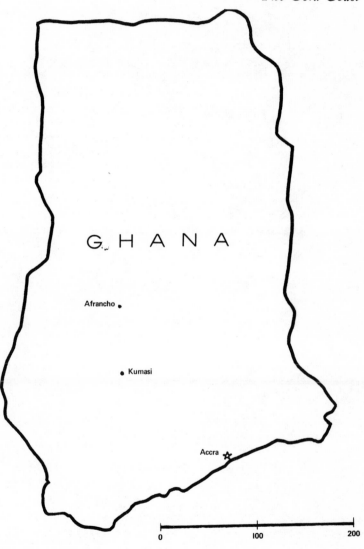

G H A N A

Afrancho •

• Kumasi

Accra ☆

0   100   200

THE LAND . . . .

On March 6, 1957 the British possession of the Gold Coast was declared the sovereign and independent state of Ghana. A new nation had been born. As modern nations go, Ghana is small. Approximately 92,000 square miles (including the former Togoland) in area, no point is more than 400 miles from the Atlantic Ocean.

Little or no wastelands exists: no mountains, no deserts, and little marsh and swampland. By far the larger part is made up of habitable plains and plateaus, ridges and valleys. In the extreme south is a mixture of grassland and scrub-looking trees more like the Texas Panhandle than the tropics.

The northern two-thirds region is much like an open parkland, covered by natural vegetation usually referred to as savanna. Though often parched, the savannas still provide pasture for several million cattle, sheep and goats. They also provide a vast amount of straw and clay for the building of huts and kralls. The indigenous West African Shorthorn is one of the oldest cattle breeds in Africa, but livestock can be raised only in the tsetse-free areas: mainly in the northern region and along the coastal plains from Accra, the capital, to eastern frontier.

Parts of the forest areas have been cut away, but they are still an important natural resource. They supply the country with its second largest export, hardwood timber. The principal money-maker, cocoa, is provided a domain in the forest.

Ghana is predominantly an agricultural country and cocoa, the most important crop. This important industry was built up entirely by African initiative. The government's agricultural program includes a further increase in cocoa production, crop diversification, the establishment of large acreages of rubber and bananas in the north west, large-scale irrigation, especially in the Volta River region, and promotion of the use of fertilizers.

Gold was the first export of the Gold Coast and is still the most valuable mineral export though output seems to have decreased, however rich deposits in the north were discovered recently. Production of manganese has likewise decreased. Diamonds are mostly of the industrial variety. Oil deposits were discovered early in 1966 which will help to decrease fuel imports.

The climate in Ghana is actually no worse than the Mississippi Valley in the heat of summer. The rainy season never lasts more than nine months, and only about half the country gets a larger annual rainfall than Boston, Mass. The whole of Ghana lies within the tropics.

The mean temperature over the greater part of the country varies between seventy-five degrees and ninety degrees, however the range is wider in the northern section.

In recent years the Ghanaians have become increasingly interested in the food resources of their fresh and salt waters. The rivers are rich in edible varieties of fish, and the coastal waters are likewise well stocked. The fishermens' seine nets are sometimes a mile in length—with one haul they may take in as much as ten tons of fish. It takes many large hauls to meet the demand, for meat protein is scarce in Ghana.

. . . . THE PEOPLE

A country's greatest resource is its people. Ninety-nine per cent of the people in Ghana are Africans, thus there are no race problems. The remainder are Lebanese, Syrians, Europeans (mainly British) and Americans. At the time of independence, the total population was forty-eight million, however by 1965 it had increased 7,740,000. Seventy percent of the population resides in the southern half of the country, especially along the coast. However there is room for growth.

Though the country is racially uncomplicated many of the Ghanaians think of themselves as members "first" of their own individual tribe. It is a man's first loyalty and the last tie he is willing to break. Most of the people are of the Sudan Negro type, of medium height and sturdy build, but there are taller and slimmer people in the north.

Education, the accumulation of private wealth through cocoa farming and trading, and in recent years, success in politics, have been the major avenues to high social status as well as sources of many conflicts. Local wealth was frequently invested in higher education abroad. The impoverished north was deprived of education as a matter of official policy. However, in 1961 the Nkrumah regime made primary and middle schooling both free and compulsory. Free secondary schooling was introduced in 1965. Adult education was provided for in five centers of the country.

Of the fifty-six indigenous languages and dialects spoken in Ghana, thirty-one are used mainly in the northern area. Most of these languages are tonal. However, English is widely spoken and is now the universal medium of instruction in schools. In 1962, the government selected nine Ghanaian languages, besides French and English, for development and use in educational institutions throughout the country.

22

A large proportion of the people, still clinging to their traditional beliefs, are animistic, worshipping the spirits that are said to reside everywhere. However, most tribes practice a form of ancestor worship and treat their chiefs as though they were more than human. Since each tribe thinks differently on such matters, religion is a separating force though there seems to be a general belief in a supreme deity. The remainder of the population consists of Christians and Mohammedans. Christianity is a symbol of status and is increasingly common among the young, owing to the spread of mission schools, especially in the south. According to a 1960 cenusu, 41.8% of the people were "Christian", in name, at least.

. . . . THE MISSIONARY . . . .

Early in December 1961 a letter was received by the Ark Valley Christian Church in Wichita, Kansas, from a young man in Ghana, West Africa. His request for a Bible was hurriedly met, as were later requests for other Bibles. News came that there was a movement in the country to preach New Testament Christianity. The movement was young. Under colonial rule, established missions formulated comity agreements who had sole religious authority for their given area. Thus prior to their political independence, the Ghanaian Christians were denied their religious freedom. However in the late 50's as many as three hundred twenty-five students were taking a correspondence course offered by Robert Mills in South Africa. With political freedom came religious freedom and through this association and study came the new movement to restore the church revealed in the New Testament. They had adopted the name "The Universal Christian Church" and numbered around 5,000, and sending out a "Macedonian call". What an opportunity!

Help came in the person of Cyril Simkins who visited at Accra, the captial, for two days, enroute to Rhodesia. In those hours he viewed what he considered "the most promising mission field in the world today". Later in 1963 Max Ward Randall and Cyril Simkins again visited Ghana for only ten days. In this second encounter they were invited to return in 1964 for a series of evangelistic services. Brother Randall answered that particular invitation and preached twenty-eight times to over 2,000 each night. His evangelistic efforts resulted in over 2,000 additions. Recruits for the field began to respond as early as 1964, however under Nkrumah's governmental regime, visas were not readily granted.

Edgar Nichols reached Ghana in mid-March 1965 on a tourist visa to be eagerly welcomed by the Christian people, whom, for the most part, he found to be sincere though they lacked in a solid foundation of Biblical fact. Because religion in Ghana appears to be more a thing of the heart than of the head, it sometimes leads to fanaticism and the rise of cults. Apparently there were some selfish desires for wanting a "missionary". It was a way of finding material gain and personal prestige for the church.

But because God had given us this opportunity to aid in and to help give direction and encouragement to this indigenous Ghanaian church, men continued to seek permission to enter the country.

The Gerald Gibson family, on leave from Minnesota Bible College, entered Ghana in mid-1966 to be a helper to the new movement. From Rhodesia, in January 1967, came the Richard Hostetter family, to be followed the next month by the Cyril Simkins, also from Rhodesia. Because they realized the great need and real value to a Christian education program, Ghana Christian College opened its doors for the first semester to train native evangelists. It is accredited as a religious school by the Ghana government, and now it also has a correspondence school.

To aid in this growing work came three other missionary families in the fall of 1967—the Kent Taylors and Ronald Rifes (with nine years of educational experience) from America, and Derrance Smaage from South Africa. The Gerald Gibson family, having accomplished their goal, returned to their teaching ministry in the States.

Students in the four-year college come from various religious backgrounds. The courses are designed to prepare men to preach, and also to help them attain positions as teachers in Ghanaian schools. In 1968, diplomas for the first two years of work were issued to twelve students. Plans are laid for permanent buildings for the College.

In April 1968 Miss Dorothy Eunson joined forces with the teachers at Ghana Christian College. She will assist in the secretarial work, and will instruct music and English in the College.

Students serve at least eight churches, and missionaries have preached in more than fifty other different churches in recent months to present the restoration plea.

This marvelous work has not been totally without its problems. Because some new men were elected to the church leadership in 1968 who desired money, rather than teaching, they attempted to have the Americans rejected from the country over visa legalities. The Lord knows the real needs of the people and made it possible for them to remain in their teaching responsibilities.

24

The Edgar Nichols, with years of missionary experience on the Tibetan border, India and Hawaii, re-entered Ghana in January 1967, and for the most part has worked separately from the College, although in the fall of 1968 he commuted 175 miles to help teach. His evangelistic work lies in the area of Kumasi. He is also in charge of the *Afrancho Christian Clinic,* seventy-five miles north of Kumasi, a cooperative project with the local government and community leaders. The staff is composed of native Christian leaders. In its first month nearly 1,000 patients were treated. Each day begins with a devotional period in which patients and staff all share. A farm project is developing and may some day add variety to the native diet.

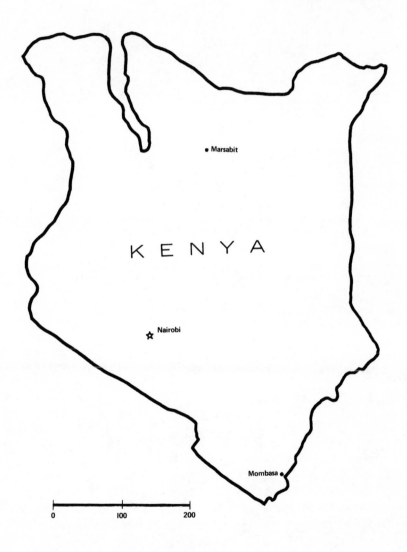

Kenya

"Land of wild-life"

● Marsabit

K E N Y A

☆ Nairobi

Mombasa ●

0   100   200

27

THE LAND . . . .

Formerly a British colony and protectorate, Kenya, lying astride the equator in East Africa, became an independent republic in 1963.

Kenya may be divided into four geographical regions: 1) the southeast coastal plains are mostly flat with little rainfall, 2) the northeast coastal and inland plains, with less than 20" of rain per year, are barren and unhospitable regions of thornbush, of little value for human occupation. Some parts of it are infested by the tsetse fly, the carrier of sleeping sickness. 3) the northwest scrubland is somewhat similar to the northeast, 4) the southwest highlands are a plateau, bisected from north to south by various mountains. This is the fertile quarter of the country in which more than three-fourths of the population—European and African—live. Here the climate is equable, the scenery one of glasslands and forests, in place of desert scrub and thorn that cover much of the country. The remarkable range of physical geography of the country is paralleled by the varieties of its landscape.

The coastal temperature averages eighty degrees and the temperature decreases slightly under three degrees with each 1,000 foot increase in altitude. The capitol, Nairobi, at 5,495 feet, has a mean annual temperature of sixty-seven degrees. Seasonal variations are distinguished by times of rainfall rather than changes of temperature, most regions having two rainy seasons.

The vegetation and animal life of Kenya reflect the variety of its topography and climate. Kenya is still rich in wild life, including many of the larger mammals, elephant, lion, giraffe, leopard, buffalo, rhinoceros, antelope, and monkeys. More than any other country in Africa, Kenya has provided generous sanctuaries for its wild life. Birds include the ostrich, pelicans, flamingos, whose flight is one of the great sights of the safari traveler, bustards, and game birds. The country has its share of poisonous and nonpoisonous African reptiles, of scorpions, and of centipedes.

The economy of the land is dependent maily upon agricultural production, although secondary industry has been spreading rapidly. In 1964 agricultural products accounted for about 90% of Kenya's exports. Coffee is the country's main source of wealth, and tourism is second in importance.

Before independence most modern farming and production for the market was limited to European and Asian farmers; however, new land has been opened to the African. Both Africans and Europeans hold large number of livestock. Meat, meat products, hides, and skins are important products.

The population figure in 1966 was 9,643,000 of which 97% were African. Though there are approximately fourteen ethnic groups they may be divided into four major cultural and linguistic groups; Bantu, Nilotic, Nilo-Hamitic, and Hamitic. While most of the land area is occupied by Hamitic and Nilo-Hamitic peoples, over 70% of the population is Bantu. The Kikuyu (a Bantu tribe), the largest tribe in the country, live to the north of the capital city and have played a major role in the political and social development of the country.

A more simple distinction among the African peoples, however, is the division between the settled agriculturalists (which include the Kikuyu) and the semi-nomadic pastoralists and hunters (which includes the Somali-speaking peoples in the north), for the ethnic compositions have been much altered by extensive intermarriage.

The Arab population is centered on the coast. The Asians, who number over one-quarter of a million, are mostly Hindus and Muslims from the subcontinent of India. They live primarily in the urban centers and are made up of at least thirty-one culturally separate groups.

The European community is primarily of British origin, although in recent years larger numbers of immigrants have come from continental Europe. This community probably numbers still less than 60,000.

Swahili, a Bantu language with a heavy Arabic admixture, widely spoken in East Africa, is an official language, as is English. However, nearly all the African tribes have their own distinct language. Among the Asian community, both Gujerati and Punjabi are widely in use.

Education in Kenya was formerly an interracial issue of great bitterness, and the contrasts in educational facilities available to the different communities were striking. In recent years African advancement has been a notable feature of Kenya education. While education for African children is not compulsory, an estimated 35% to 40% of African children of school age attend school, and probably 90% are enrolled at the primary level (first four grades). The literacy rate in 1964 was estimated at 20%. The insufficiency of funds and teachers is the main factor inhibiting a rapid expansion in educational opportunities.

The plural character of Kenya's society is very evident in religious associations. Approximately 32% of the African people are Christians, 4% are Muslims, and 64% still follow their tribal religions. About two-thirds of the so-called Christians are Protestant and one-third

Roman Catholic. Among the non-African population, some 34% are Muslims, approximately 29% are Hindus, about 24% Christians, 7% Sikhs, and 4% Jains.

. . . . THE MISSIONARY . . . .

Born of missionary parents in India, Harry Schaefer had instilled in his heart a great love for the Indian people. When no longer able to serve in India Harry Schaefer and his family found an opportunity to serve among the Indians who were working in Thailand. The high mobility of the Indian community was a difficult factor but they witnessed to them for four years before returning to the States for further graduate studies.

Challenged by the fact that nearly a million overseas Indians are resident on the continent of Africa, Harry was sent in the fall of 1967 to survey the major areas of concentration. One of these was in South Africa. The center of the second largest concentration of African Indians was in Nairobi, the capital of Kenya in East Africa. It is likewise the center of trade, commerce, and education in the three-country area of Kenya, Zambia, and Malawi. A quarter million Indians live in the capital city, owning the major businesses and commercial enterprises. Special radio and TV programs are beamed at the Indian community in their mother tongue by the government studios.

A much higher percentage of Kenya Indians still use the Indian language than do South African Indians, who now often speak English and Afrikanans. So, because the Schaefers both speak, read, and write Hindi, and because opening Kenya to Indian work would also open it to African work, they decided that Kenya was the country in which to begin.

Many Kenya citizens regard Christ's ways as the ideal way of life. The Gospel is freely preached on every side. The Bible is taught in public schools. The radio and TV have many Christian programs although it is government operated.

Early arrangements were made to present English and Hindi programs on these stations. Plans are made to open several Christian Information Centers in the heart of Indian residental concentrations.

The doors are open; the missionaries can evangelize freely. The Schaefer family left for the field immediately after the marriage of their oldest daughter in June, 1968. Two months later, Harry was called home on emergency furlough to assist in a search for this same daughter who disappeared mysteriously. No clues have helped in the search, and finally after three months without any success, they felt the deep need of the field could not be ignored, thus they returned to Nairobi in late November, 1968 to search for lost souls.

Because of the situation in the Congo, two of the families from that field are presently working in Kenya until such time as they are able to live again among the Congo people. These are the Howard Crowls in evangelism who have been granted a two-year visa, and the Gene Landis family who serve in a printing ministry.

They have found the African people in Kenya to be less responsive and less concerned about their soul's salvation than the Congo people. In the cities they have found tribal jealousy. Most of the teaching is done in the home of prospective Christians, by film strips, workbooks, and studying the Bible together. Plans are to establish two strong indigenous churches—one in English, and one in Swahili.

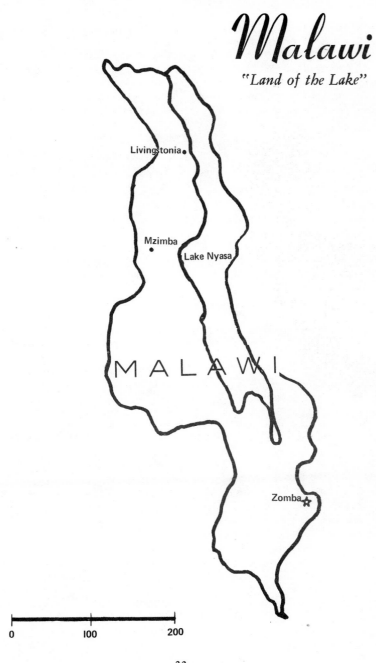

Malawi
"Land of the Lake"

Livingstonia

Mzimba

Lake Nyasa

MALAWI

Zomba

0	100	200

33

THE LAND . . . .

Formerly the British protectorate of Nyasaland, Malawi achieved its independence in 1964. It is located in East Central Africa, bounded on the north and east by Tanzania, on the south by Mozambique and on the west by Zambia. Lake Nyasa, Africa's third largest lake, lies on its eastern border. The country stretches some 560 miles from north to south, and 10 to 50 miles from east to west. The land, at the southern end of Africa's great Rift Valley, rises steeply from the swampy lakeside areas to an undulating, forested, middle plateau region at an elevation of 3,000 to 4,000 feet. Elevations rise over 8,000 feet in the Nyika Plateau in the north.

The climate varies with elevation, as well as being affected by vast water surface of the lake. The temperature generally decreases and the rainfall increases with altitude. Malawi is noted for its rapid transition from low to high rainfall. Winters are generally cool, with occasional spells of cold weather.

A thin forest occupies almost 25% of the area, and possesses a great variety of trees, both indigenous and exotic. There are a great many varieties of animal life too. Elephant, black rhinoceros, giraffe, and buffalo are found in certain areas, and hippos on the shore of the Lake. A check-list of birds records at least 609 species. Reptiles are plentiful and a wealth of fish may be found in the lake and rivers. It is also rich in insect life.

Malawi's economy is based almost entirely upon agriculture. Its money income is derived largely from the export of cotton, tobacco, tea and peanuts. The United Kingdom is the major purchaser of the country's tea. Sugar is a new crop for the local market. A large part of the population is engaged in subsistence agriculture, although surplus food crops are sold in the local markets. Corn is the staple food. Fish from Lake Nyasa supply protein for the local diet. The number of livestock is limited by a shortage of grazing land and the presence of the disease-carrying tsetse fly.

Quarrying for limestone and other building materials is the only current mining activity for mining and industry are little developed. Brick-making is a well-establshed industry, and in the mid-60's a clinker factory was established, making possible the manufacture of cement from local resources. Future industries are in the planning stages.

Land shortage and limited non-agricultural employment opportunities have led large numbers of people to work in the copper mines of Zambia, on the tobacco farms and in the factories of Rhodesia, and in the gold mines of South Africa.

. . . . THE PEOPLE

In October 1966 the population of Malawi was estimated at a little over four million, of which 7,046 were Europeans and 12,173 persons of other races, largely Asians and Coloreds (persons of mixed African and European origin). A vast majority of the African population belong to the Bantu-speaking groups, and speak a variety of those languages and dialects. However, English is the language of education, and as the official language, is being spoken by an increasing number of the Africans.

As in other parts of Africa, the period of colonial rule, which was accompanied by a demand for wage labor, and the religious and educational activities of Christian missionaries, have greatly affected traditional patterns of life, especially in the towns. Even in urban areas the African lived in tribal quarters. This served to be stepping stones to wider associations, such as political parties. Some new customs spread from town to the village but many traditional practices continue today, such as polygyny and payment of lobola (bride-price).

Christianity is widespread and has taken deep root, largely as a result of the early Scottish Presbyterian missions. However, the growth of African national sentiment has been reflected in the establishment of separatist churches which represent an adaptation of Christianity to traditional practices. There is a long-established Muslim community that includes nearly half of the total population of Malawi (63% of the Asians are Muslim). Nearly one-fourth of the Europeans and 5% of the Asians are Roman Catholic. The Methodist and Dutch Reformed congregations are small.

The development of education has been retarded by lack of revenue since it is in the hands of local government bodies. However, primary education is widespread, largely as a result of long-established missionary groups. In 1965, there were 256,219 pupils in primary schools. Secondary education is less well-developed. At the time of independence, schools for the African, Asian, and Colored were being integrated; the European communities were permitted to maintain their own schools.

Major health threats are malaria and tuberculosis. All health services are provided for Africans free of charge—if they will only accept it. So can they be "free in Christ", if they will only accept His salvation.

. . . . THE MISSIONARY . . . .

"The effectual fervent prayer of a righteous man availeth much" and when prayers did not open the door to India for the Floyd Stamm family they turned their eyes afar and tuned their ears for a Macedonian call. An urgent plea came from British brethren, via Max Ward Randall, for help in preaching the Gospel to the millions who are responsive to the Gospel in the new republic of Malawi.

The government is at least now receptive to missionaries. Time is of great importance while the door is open and the people responsive to the preaching of the good news of Christ.

The Stamms plan to enter the field as soon as sufficient funds are raised.

Nigeria

"Land of division"

Kaduna

NIGERIA

Lagos

Onitsha

Aba

0   100   200

A proud mother poses to show the handy method in which Nigerian and many other West African mothers carry their young.

THE LAND . . . .

Nigeria, ruled formerly by Great Britain, received its independence in October, 1960. It is a federation composed of the federal capital, Lagos, and of the Northern, Western, Eastern, and Mid-West regions, located in West Africa, extending northward off the eastern end of the Gulf of Guinea. It is the most populous country in all of Africa.

Most of Nigeria is a low plateau. The coast is swampy lowland, with chains of lagoons and cross creeks. Beyond the swamp forest is a zone, from fifty to one hundred miles wide, of undulating tropical rain forest. The country then rises to a plateau at a general elevation of 2,000 feet but reaching 6,000 feet to the east, and the vegetation changes from woodland to savannah. In the extreme north, the country approaches the southern part of the Sahara.

Although Nigeria lies wholly within the tropical zone the climate varies greatly in different parts of the country. Average temperatures vary little between north and south; but in the south, where humidity is higher, temperatures are fairly constant all year long and seldom exceed ninety degrees F., where as in the north there is a wide range of daily temperature during the dry season and considerable seasonal change.

The modern economy of the country is based on palm-oil trade of the 19th century, but Nigeria is by no means a one-crop economy. The palm oil trade has been supplemented by cocoa, peanuts, cotton, rubber, tin, wood, hides, and skins, and most recently by petroleum. Nigeria is the world's leading exporter of peanuts and palm nuts and kernels.

Most Nigerians are still peasant farmers, producing their own food crops and deriving an income from one or more cash crops. Food crops grown in the South and Middle Belt include yams, rice, and maize, while in the North the main subsistence crops are sorghum, millet, and sugar-cane. Of cash crops, coffee and tobacco are produced for local consumption. About 75% to 80% of the people are engaged in agriculture.

In the far north livestock raising is the main occupation. High quality meat is produced for local use. Most fishing is in the numerous rivers and streams, not the ocean, and output is not yet sufficient for local needs. Many Nigerians outside the north continue to suffer severe protein deficiency in their diet.

Weaving is the most widespread craft and locally woven cloth may be obtained anywhere in Nigeria; others are wood carving, pottery,

41

and work in leather and other skins. There is some ivory carving and goldsmithing.

Factory industries are only just beginning to develop in Nigeria, but industries are developing rapidly in an attempt to process the country's natural resources.

. . . . THE PEOPLE

According to a disputed census of 1963, the population of Nigeria was 55,671,000, a majority of nearly 30,000,000 lived in the north. The Middle Belt of central Nigeria is thinly populated and in some areas uninhabited. Although urban population is probably growing more rapidly than the rural, only 22% of the people live in towns of 5,000 or more.

The predominant racial group is the West African Negro. Although intermingled with many races of other stock, Negro characteristics have predominated in most parts of the country, however, there are over 250 different groups, each with its own language, culture and social organization. All but fourteen of these are found in the northern region. However, the official language is English, but in the north, Hausa, a mother tongue of 40% of the people there, is also an official language.

The health problem in Nigeria remains acute although great strides have been made to control smallpox and yellow fever. Malaria and pulmonary tuberculosis are the diseases of most frequent incidence. Progress is being made in the treatment of sleeping sickness and leprosy. Heretofore, the Eastern region was one of the most seriously infected areas for leprosy in the world.

The illiteracy of the country varies with the different areas. In the federal territory 43% of the population over ten years of age is illiterate; 89% of those over fourteen years of age in the north, and 53% in the western region. A major obstacle to the further advancement of education in Nigeria is the shortage of qualified teachers. Most higher education is in the hands of the federal government, which is charged with the responsibility of all institutions serving the needs of the whole federation. The advance in education in southern regions, compared with the relative lag in the north, reflects the contribution of Christian missions to Nigerian education.

About 35% of the people profess Christianity, and about 45% adhere to Islam beliefs, the remainder are classified as pagans or animists.

Throughout southern Nigeria the activity and influence of Christian missions has been strong. The Catholic Church is perhaps most influential in the East while Methodists and Anglican churches lead in the West. Other missions include the Pilgrim Baptist Church and the Sudan Inland Mission, while a number of indigenous churches have sprung up from locally led separatist movements. The northern people have retained the codes and social institutions of Islam. This division has often led to unfortunate political results.

.... THE MISSIONARY ....

Probably the first message of New Testament Christianity was offered to the Nigerian people by Robert Mills in South Africa who was publishing a monthly publication which was being mailed to sixteen African countries.

A closed door in India meant a victory for the Gospel in Nigeria. When the Roy Goldsberrys were refused visas to work in India they immediately began to investigate the possibilities of Nigeria where contacts had been made through the Mills' correspondence work. In August 1955 the mission work, known as the *West African Christian Mission*, in Nigeria was begun. At this time Nigeria was in British West Africa and she did not receive independence until the fall of 1960. Even in 1955 it was Africa's most heavily populated country with twenty-nine million people.

Several years of experience working with a Negro church in Cincinnati is perhaps the reason why the selection of Nigeria as a possible field of service was a natural one for the Don Baughman family who came to unite forces with the Goldsberry family in November of 1956. The opportunities for bringing many souls to Christ and making a Christian nation of Nigeria was the challenge to the Baughmans.

During a period when the work in the Congo could not be carried on (Oct. 61-Aug. 62) Miss Zola Brown spent time working in Nigeria. In 1963 the Goldsberry family left the work in Nigeria to begin missionary activity in Italy.

The Baughman's were relieved for furlough in 1966 by the arrival of the Lester LeMay's who had served two previous years in South Africa as "substitute missionaries". Not only did they assist with the established work but several trips were made into Eastern Nigeria where the rural folk were especially receptive to the Gospel. The secession of the Eastern Region and the eventual Civil War and extreme resultant instability of the political situation prevented the LeMays from making this a permanent place of ministry. They have since returned to the States to serve the Lord here. There is no information available as to the churches which were meeting in the Eastern Region.

43

Ordaining an elder in Owerra District in Biafra, in 1966.

Faithful preacher and family in Biafra.

44

Coming to join the Baughman work in September 1967 were the Walter Smiths who had been greatly influenced in a local ministry by the Faith-Promise idea. Kathy Bundick, from Midwest Christian College in Oklahoma City began an internship in January 1969.

The work in Nigeria is in five basic areas: new-church planting, established-church nourishing, evangelist training, radio and correspondence teaching, and medical evangelism.

This work, which is limited at the present only by resources in finance and personnel, has produced ten congregations—six in the Western area and four in the Eastern area—ten Nigerian evangelists who are presently actively preaching, and a very large number of people who have completed the correspondence course.

The radio program, which has been broadcast weekly since its beginning in October 1961 (in cooperation with the Gospel Broadcasting Mission) is a very effective means of communicating the Gospel in Nigeria. The many letters from listeners which are received each week attest to the worth of the program, which is heard over the National Broadcasting Service of Nigeria.

This sign greets all visitors on the road near the Mission home.

Christian-growth revivals are conducted in each of the churches periodically, with the missionaries and the Nigerian evangelists taking part jointly. Recently some of the Nigerian evangelists have under-

45

taken such meetings on their own, a promising step in the direction of independence in local leadership.

In addition to the congregations which meet regularly, there are a number of preaching points to which the Nigerian evangelists go for preaching and teaching, with the goal of establishing churches in those areas.

The upraised fist of these Nigerian children is a sign of the power of friendship. These children are from the nearest village to West Africa Christian Mission.

In recent communications which the missionaries have had with the government, programs have been outlined for a broadening of the work in Nigeria. For such a program more volunteers, equipped to do various jobs of teaching and evangelizing, will be needed. Future work in Nigeria could well include medical evangelism, for there is a great need in Nigeria for health services. Due to civil war in Eastern besieged Biafra, in 1968 it was reported that three hundred deaths a day was a gross understatement, though much of this was not from disease alone but from malnutrition.

It is believed that the government, which is interested in the growth and development of the country, will prove willing and helpful in an increased program carried on by the *West Africa Christian Mission* in Nigeria.

Rhodesia

"Land of opportunity"

Kariba Dam

Karoi

Chidamoyo

Sinoia

☆ Salisbury

Binga

Victoria Falls

Gokwe

R H O D E S I A

Dett

Queque

Enkeldoorn

Umtali

Gwelo

Umvuma

Gutu

Soti

Dewure

Bulawayo

Shabani

Ft. Victoria

Bikita

Dadaya

Zaka

Mashoko

Nuanetsi

Chiredzi

0   100   200

THE LAND . . . .

Rhodesia, in southern Africa, is named for the English empire-builder, Cecil Rhodes. Like neighboring South Africa, it has a predominately African population and is governed by a small white minority of European descent and culture. In 1965 the government declared its independence, against the will of both Great Britain to whom it was a dependency, and to the African nationalist movement.

Rhodesia forms a part of the great southern African plateau with over 75% of the country lying between 2,000 and 5,000 feet above sea level. Northward, towards Victoria Falls and the man-made Kariba Lake, the land falls to an elevation of less than 2,000 feet.

The greater part of the country is covered by tree-dotted gasslands, with occasional outcroppings of granite. Some evergreen forest grows in the mountains to the east.

Rhodesia's climate is generally temperate, except in the lowland areas near the rivers, where humid tropical conditions prevail. At higher elevations the air is dry and the nights are cool.

The economy of the land is still based on agriculture despite considerable industrial development, and it is heavily dependent on foreign trade. Tobacco is the principal export—from European agriculture. Other major European farm products are corn, sugar, cotton, and vegetables. African farms are mainly subsistence production in corn, sorghum, millet, beans and peanuts.

Minerals in considerable number have been found and exploited in Rhodesia. Gold was the leading mineral export for many years but since World War II production of asbestos and chrome has risen rapidly. The colony now ranks third in the world's output of chromium ore. In all, thirty-four different minerals and metals and precious or semiprecious stones are mined in Rhodesia.

. . . . THE PEOPLE

The estimated 1965 population of 4,260,000 included over four million Africans, nearly 220,000 Europeans, 12,700 Coloreds (mixed African and European origin), and 8,000 Asians. The European population is predominately urban and, in recent years, relatively static in size. South Africa and Great Britain have been the two principal sources of the European immigration to Rhodesia but political uncertainties in recent times has caused a decrease to normal immigration. The Africans in Rhodesia are mainly of various Bantu-speaking tribes with no great differences in language or customs, grouped in two large divisions, the Shona and Ndebele (Matabele). According to a 1962 census, 18% of the Africans were urban—the remainder were in rural areas. The Asian population is largely of Indian and Pakistani origins. Most of them depend on trade for their livelihood, thus they are concentrated in the towns. The Colored population is also predominately city dwellers.

Rhodesian society is separated into two major communities, European and African. At the root of the conflict between the two groups is the division of the land. The European areas include the major urban centers and the most favorable agricultural land. Africans may live in the European areas only if they are employed by Europeans, and their movements are regulated by registration certificates. Even the Asians and Coloreds are subject to residence restrictions.

Most Africans adhere to such customs as polygyny and the payment for brides. However, they also seek Western education which leads to economic and social advancement. The mission-educated elite, still a small minority, provide the leadership of the nationalist movement. Many tribal ways have been carried to the towns.

Tribal woman kneading dough, making bread out of millie meal.

Separate schools are maintained for all groups, but there is some integration at the higher levels of learning. African education at the primary level is mainly conducted by missions, which receive close cooperation and grants from the government. Secondary education and teacher training for Africans are less well developed. English is considered the official language.

Tuberculosis is the country's greatest health problem. Bilharziasis, too, remains a great problem and in some areas affects as much as 90% of the population. Malnutrition, a consequence of unbalanced diet, is also a problem in some regions.

Most of the Africans are animists. About 50,000 have become baptized Christians, and substantial numbers attend Christian services. Of the European population, about 37% are Anglicans, and 10% are of the Dutch Reformed Church. Others are Roman Catholic, Methodist, Presbyterian, and Jew. Most of the Asiatic population is Hindu or Muslim.

. . . . THE MISSIONARY . . . .

The New Zealand church came to Central Africa in 1928 to present New Testament Christianity. Though bringing about significant results, it was limited in its scope. Mashoko was a center which they had hoped to develop, but their main station at Dadaya fully taxed their resources.

Due to one of the many preliminary surveys made by Max Ward Randall the need of the Mashoko area was discovered, and a request made that American missionaries come to supervise the work in this great area.

The John Pembertons arrived in Africa in August 1956 to lead in the work which is about two hundred miles southeast of Dadaya. Working with them for the first three years were the Ladbrooks from New Zealand. Disease and lack of water made it difficult for white missionaries to live at Mashoko. It had never been done! But God provided—a new well supplied sufficient water and modern medicine helped to prevent disease.

The first need in presenting the Gospel appeared to be education—and the door was open. In 1957 there were ten village schools and one central primary school, which consisted of three grades corresponding to our 6th, 7th and 8th grades. In 1968, in Mashoko and Hippo Valley, there were twenty-three schools, with ninety-two teachers and 2,895 students. The educational program has a unique role in the total mission effort since the Rhodesian government requires that the Bible be taught every day in the classroom. The mission schools are partially government supported (teachers' salaries and annual allowance for each child) though the Christians themselves build the school buildings along with the church buildings. The schools provide a direct contact with large numbers of children at an impressionable age, many of whom accept Christ.

John Pemberton supervised the schools in the beginning but the need for one trained as an educator was quickly realized. Lester Cooper, AB and MA in education and an experienced educator, with his family, arrived on the field in September 1960. The Cooper's led in an intensive training program after their arrival, the purpose, to prepare Christian teachers for as many classrooms as possible.

Marcia Thomson reached Mashoko in 1963 to become a member of the educational team. She is in charge of all the "books". The Robert Smiths came to work with the teacher-training program in 1965. (Mrs. Smith is the sister of David Grubbs who served with Dadaya mission.) Their work includes the necessary teaching of missionary children. In mid-68, seventy students entered the third year of the secondary school, sixty-four were in the second year class. Ofttimes there are 5,000 applications a year for the 140 places in the school, but all applicants are not motivated by a desire to receive a Christian education.

Mary Grider, working through the *Faith Corps Program of Cincinnati Bible Seminary,* came in January 1968 to serve as secretary for the secondary school and assists in teaching the missionary children.

Local scout troop of Secondary students.

Mashoko Bible College actually began with one student in 1958 and was served by the Berry Kennedy family from 1959-1962 before going to the work in Bulawayo. Later efforts of the College will be included in the report from Ft. Victoria where it is presently located.

Dennis Pruett received his medical degree in June 1956. Following one year of internship the Pruett family made preparations to sail to Southern Rhodesia to join the Pembertons. They arrived in Cape Town in September 1958. Brother Pruett is the first independent medical missionary to go to the field since Dr. A. L. Shelton died on the field in China in 1922. Dr. Pruett realized the importance of helping the physical needs of the African people, but he is more concerned about their spiritual welfare. The ministry of medicine is his approach to the ultimate goal of the saving of their souls.

Sailing with the Pruetts were registered nurses: Elizabeth Morgan, Helen Doyal and Betty Iddings. Pauline Bell, from Cape Town, joined the medical staff in June of 1959. The first medical work was begun in a 10-by-12 foot tent under a huge fig tree. But, in March 1959 the government approved plans for a 130-bed hospital at Mashoko. Not only did they approve but offered to pay one-half of the building costs as well as do the actual construction which began in July 1959.

Hearts were stirred in America, lives were committed, the staff increased, nurses heard the call, doctors became concerned, technologists wrote asking for a place of service; and this hospital, like an awakening giant, became a reality in August 1961. Just prior to this, in June 1960, another government clinic fifty miles away was given to the mission for their supervision, so the outreach of the medical work is unlimited.

An excellent addition to the medical staff came in August of 1960 in the person of Madonna Burget. She was a registered nurse with a special course in midwifery. Much of her concern for the lost in the U.S. had been for the Negro people. When the hospital was in operation Madonna was put in charge of the hospital and the nursing school that was established. They had twelve graduates in its first four years. She now serves at the new hospital at Chidamoyo Mission.

As some nurses left, others came. Mary Bliffen, Sara Ann Hewitt, Sarah Stere (who gave up a promising career in Air Force nursing), and Donna Kreeger—all registered nurses—answered the call for more medical help. Gladys Jangeling came as a technologist from Oregon. Her work aids the doctor in a clinical diagnosis of diseases. She trains lab assistants as well. Sylvia Menhinick, challenged by Max Randall in South Africa, arrived to serve as a much-needed secretary.

In September 1963, to assist in the growing medical work, Dr. Jerry Smith and his family moved to Mashoko. He was trained in oral surgery and anesthesia, however he was not only a dentist, he "filled in" as physician, nurse, undertaker, teacher, and in many other areas. Realizing the great need for further medical training, they moved to Salisbury, Rhodesia, after their furlough in 1965, where this training could be received, and yet where he could still be used in mission work.

Following the Smiths, the Don Stoll family arrived in December 1963. His special training was as a pharmacist and he became responsible for all drug purchases and distribution as well as supervising the radiology department.

Late in 1963, Dr. Pruett and John Pemberton discovered another opportunity for missionary development in the Hippo Valley estates. A small hospital was established and an African clinic was served by an air commuting Dr. Pruett. By the second year of existence of the work there were five schools in operation, working as a unit with the schools in the Mashoko area. Nine preaching points were also established early in the work. It appeared as one of the most promising mission areas in Central Africa.

The Lester Van Dyke family came in 1964. Brother Van Dyke was a hospital administrator and evangelist, working both with the Hippo Valley and Mashoko hospitals. Dr. Robert Walker and family arrived in 1966 and is assisting in the medical work, especially in the six, now existing, clinics of Hippo Valley. The African has come to associate good medical care with mission hospitals, and many opportunities for witnessing are given to Mary Bliffen, R.N., and others who share in the medical work here. Dr. John Van Curen and family plan to join the work of Hippo Valley in 1969.

The Chiredzi area, in the Hippo Valley, is a highly developed agricultural area with about eight hundred European population who have a real need for Christ as well as the African population. It was to this area that the John Pembertons moved in January 1966. Marilyn Richards and Marcia Thomson moved there in January 1969 from their work in Mashoko. They will continue to have oversight of the correspondence and bookkeeping for both areas' schools and will travel to Mashoko as the need arises. A government hospital was opened in Chiredzi in July 1968 which will aid Dr. Walker who can care for complicated cases there, instead of at the 71-bed Rufaro Clinic.

The Reggie Thomas evangelistic team witnessed 318 responses in 42 services in the Chiredzi area in 1968.

A new irrigation scheme developed half way between the Mashoko-Chiredzi work, called the South-Eastern Development. Investigation uncovered a great need for medical work and a marvelous opportunity for evangelization. Both areas of work were begun in June 1968. The medical needs can be supplied by Doctors from either area.

While back at Mashoko, John E. Ross, known as the Master's Mechanic, and his wife, Sylvia, an R.N., joined the staff in October 1967 to fill a very specific need. What good is a light bulb if the generator won't work—or a faucet if the pump won't pump? The phase of John's work was a pioneer one in missions as he is classified as neither minister, doctor, or educator. He is an aircraft and auto mechanic, and a carpenter. He keeps all systems in working order, but involves himself as well in teaching Bible classes and village evangelism. Because he labors with his hands the African people are attentive to him. Sylvia's work as surgical nurse in the hospital also opens doors for witnessing.

Baby Ross carried native style.

Village school near Mashoko Mission.

In 1968 Dr. Gloria Cobb joined the staff of the Mashoko Hospital where she had had a successful three-month internship in 1965, an experience that was to challenge her to this return for her life's work. Likewise in 1968 Dr. James Frasure and wife, Joyce, (R.N.) joined the medical team at Mashoko. Also Dr. Owen and Mrs. Mary Dunlop flew to the field in September 1968 for a first tour of duty at Mashoko, before going to Salisbury in 1969. Dorothea Parker and Martha Raile, both R.N.'s, came to labor with the teaching and nursing staff at Mashoko Hospital. Kenny Messman, a med-student from Tennessee, came to serve a five-month training period in the summer of 1968 with Dr. Pruett and Dr. Walker. Along with his medical assistance he was able to preach on numerous occasions to the secondary students and to some of the African villages. His opportunities to serve and the need that he saw strengthened his desire to return to Rhodesia in 1970 when he has completed his medical training in the States.

Another one of those fields investigated by Max Randall is the Zambezi area, surveyed in 1953-54. Due to the project of the Kiariba Dam the government requested a delay in any permanent developments materially until all the valley people had been moved to new homes. The whole valley of nearly two hundred miles was flooded to become the world's largest man-made lake, an incredible project for so remote a section of Central Africa.

Batonga maiden of the Zambezi Valley.

Dr. Pruett and John Pemberton, at brother Randall's encouragement, applied for the Mission. On the 23rd of October 1958, John Pemberton and Max Randall—in Randall's airplane—surveyed and determined the head mission site for the Zambezi field. The Rod Cameron family began their labors there in early 1959, the only resident missionaries in the Zambezi Valley Binga District, the home of some 27,000 primitive

56

Batonga tribesmen. The Batonga are a simple, gentle people unlike the proud, warlike Matabele to the south. The Batonga live by fishing in the Zambezi and pasturing their herds along the great Escarpment. Most of them had never heard the name of Christ.

By September 1960 the first four schools in the Valley were in operation and each school became a preaching point. The work increased into three areas of service and was joined by the Jack Penningtons in 1962, following a year of service for them in Bulawayo.

Jack Pennington, missionary, in Batonga village.

There is the educational phrase of the work, which in 1968 had ten schools with 569 students. Some Bible is taught each day, and on Sundays the teachers conduct Bible school and church services as well. Most of the people could not read, in fact they did not have a written language until in 1964 this was accomplished and a Bible was published that would be readable for those who could read. The schools have helped to reach the older children and the teen-agers for Christ. Two-thirds of the population is under twenty-five years of age. Sewing classes are still used to reach village women and girls in some areas.

Because the government clinic was sixty miles away the second need was to assist in meeting the medical demands of the people. Though the witchdoctors are outlawed by the government, they still perform hideous rites among the people. But apart from this there is disease

57

everywhere. Due to lack of water and education, the people are very dirty and untidy. For a time, nurses Gladys Jongeling and Madonna Burget assisted in the needy medical witness.

The third, and most important phase of the work, is the evangelistic effort that is made throughout the villages in the entire area.

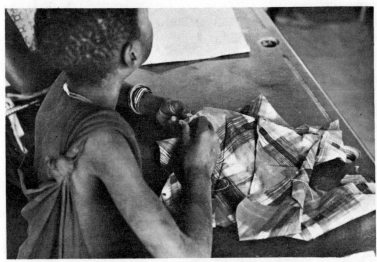

Hearing about Jesus during a sewing class.

The Camerons returned to the States for a ministry in youth camp work in 1966 and as terrorist activities increased (from across the lake) in their immediate area the Penningtons moved into Binga, a government outpost, sixty miles to the northeast. There are some advantages to this move, since they are even nearer to much of their area's work. From August 1966 to February 1967 the Wayne Unger family assisted in the work before joining the staff of the ministerial training school.

Since moving into Binga, two new preaching points have been established, as well as a Bible correspondence course. A new dimension was added in 1967-68 when twenty-five young men from the Manjolo school asked to be taught to reach their own people for Christ. In 1968 the Reggie Thomas evangelistic party conducted three services in the Zambezi area that resulted in 84 responses, thirty-three of which were baptized. Some had been taught for a period of six years.

Often the response is slow, but the missionaries take comfort in the knowledge that, through a continual sowing of the seed of the Gospel, there will come a harvest.

Dr. Erickson, from Chidamoyo, flies into Binga once a week to assist in the clinic there. And at the beginning of 1969 Dave Finney, former teacher of the high school in DeWure, came to oversee the school work of this area. Also in the new year regular services are being conducted on request of the white government people.

In 1960 American missionaries were again closely drawn to the New Zealand work for the David Grubbs family accepted the call of the Dadaya Mission, the parent of the Mashoko work. He came to have oversight of the village school work and to assist in the evangelistic program in the Native Reserve. It offered unlimited opportunity but by 1963 they could not ignore the great and urgent need for more medically trained missionaries. Thus, in the intervening years they have been diligently preparing to return to the field, and will do so, Lord willing, by the end of 1969.

Dr. and Mrs. A. C. Watters labored in India for thirteen years as missionaries of the British Churches of Christ. Then for thirty years they ministered in the field of education, the last eight as Professor of Missions at Butler University. In 1957 they went to Bulawayo, Southern Rhodesia to minister under the direction of the United Christian Missionary Society. This work began when John L. Sheriff came from New Zealand in 1896. Several African congregations were established after his arrival. The first church building was erected in 1904 and housed a multiracial congregation. The Hadfield family from New Zealand joined this work in 1906; the Walter Mansills arrived in 1912. The multiracial group separated into their various racial groups and each began to grow. It was to the European church that the Watters came in 1957, though he often ministered to the needs of the Africans and Coloured. After the first two years the Bulawayo European church withdrew connections with the UCMS so as to be able to share more aggressively in the program of evangelism of expansion with the American and New Zealand missionaries.

The Watters retired in 1967 after ten and a half years of missionary service in Bulawayo. They remained long enough to see other missionaries come to carry on, and to help build a fine Christian education plant to accommodate the 1,500 children who attended the European church, Colenbrander Avenue Church of Christ. At present they serve in their native Scotland.

Berry Kennedy and his family came in 1963 to assist, not only the European work in Bulawayo, but the existing six African churches, and the one church for the Coloured people. Bulawayo is the second largest city of Rhodesia, and three-fourths of the city are Africans.

59

In 1966 a new European congregation was started in the Hillside area of the city.

The John Vallances came to assist here in the mid-60's before going on to Gwelo. The Dave Millards served as well before going likewise to Gwelo in 1965, to help establish European work there. Others have come and gone, to witness for a season.

Judy Landrey and Rosemary Swarms came in 1967, who, as students in Lincoln Christian College, were challenged by Dr. Watters. They have many opportunities to teach Bible in the government schools, not only in the Primary Schools but in the Secondary School as well. In the Secondary School it is called a Bible Knowledge class, and is considered academic. They also work with Bible studies for a crippled children home and youth clubs for Europeans. Rosemary does some secretarial work for John Hoyt, who with his wife, came later in 1967 as the most recent co-laborers to work in the Bulawayo area. They work with the Coloured congregation, and have started Scripture classes in some of the Coloured government schools. A young man, baptized in mid-summer 1968, will begin studying for the ministry— the first Coloured minister in Rhodesia. This brings new hope for this group of people.

The need in city-evangelism is ever pressing; opportunities are unlimited. It is estimated that in recent years there is probably an average of 150-200 converts a year. The Reggie Thomas evangelistic team visited in Bulawayo for a week in June 1968, holding thirty-seven services with 103 baptisms resulting.

The Gwelo field was first opened by the Charles Gruver family when they came to the Umvama area in 1953. They found a potential but under-developed field. Their first efforts were in establishing churches in the African compounds among the European farmers and mine workers. When they could not settle permanently in Umvama they moved into Gwelo where they trained evangelists and established a primary school. When they returned to the States in 1960, super-vision of the work was turned over to Mashoko Mission. When the Ziden Nutts came to Rhodesia in 1961 to open the Sinoia-Karoi-Urungwe Reserve work, they tarried at Gwelo for a year until the Wendell Freeman family arrived in 1962.

The Gwelo work in its early years was primarily evangelistic, extending into the surrounding countryside as far as 120 miles away. The work of the Freemans in Gwelo itself is with both the African and Coloured. They supervise thirteen African grade schools and assist in over twelve outlying African churches. In their newest school, some of the grade one students were ten and eleven years old.

The David Millard family arrived in Rhodesia in 1964 and served at Bulawayo a few months before moving to Gwelo in January 1965. Brother Millard came to establish a printing ministry to meet the needs of the more than 10,000 African students and seventy-one mission churches that existed at that time. It has been said, "Christian missionaries have been teaching the Africans to read for many years, but the Communists are providing them the reading material". The printing work blesses, not only the Gwelo work where it is located, but all the Rhodesian efforts as well. David Millard also began a work among the European population. By fall of his first year Scripture classes were being held in all government-operated schools for African and Coloured, as well as the mission schools.

The Tom Thurman family and Alice Fishback came to labor for a time before setting up a printing ministry in Ft. Victoria in 1966 in conjunction with the Bible College work. The Dick Smiths also labored here on their arrival in Rhodesia.

In 1967 the John Vallance family came to the Gwelo area to assist largely with the European work. The first European convert was baptized in the summer of 1968. The European Bible school attendance is increasing, due in part to the efforts of "Holiday Bible Funtime", a counterpart to America's VBS movement. The Reggie Thomas evangelistic party held twenty services in the Gwelo area in the summer of 1968, in which forty-four souls responded to the gospel invitation. As many as 204 were present on the final night.

The Sinoia-Karoi-Urungwe Reserve area was surveyed by Ray Knapp of Dadaya Mission and Max Randall, in May of 1960. Dr. Pruett, Berry Kennedy, and David Grubbs followed up with some other surveys. The field became a possibility for evangelizing because some African people and one evangelist migrated northward to farm. Young churches were started and the opportunities were unlimited. Ziden Nutt and his family became the first resident missionaries when they moved to the Urungwe Reserve in 1962, By 1963 the first Christian Day School was opened, and hundreds were hearing the Gospel. The name "Chidamoyo" was given to the mission—meaning "the desire of the heart". In July 1963 the Bruce Ammerman family arrived to expand the work—more ladies meetings, special Scripture classes in the schools and a class for preaching recruits.

Charles Kelley and his family joined the work in 1966. Then Madonna Burget, R.N., came in January 1967 to assist with the heavy burden of medical work, but she also assists with the great work among the women. Ola Marion answered the call for a "teacher" in September 1968. Besides teaching the missionary children, she

61

likewise will engage in women's work for it is scattered throughout many villages. One of her most recent projects is teaching reading and writing to a group of teenage girls who have never been to school. Some walk as far as five miles one way.

There are about three hundred fifty women in all of their teaching groups. Besides being taught the Bible, in some cases literacy courses, they are taught sewing, and some are taught cooking.

Through the combined efforts of the missionaries in this area, there were approximately five hundred souls added in 1968. Also that year there were five hundred fifty students enrolled in the four African primary schools that were under their supervision.

Cooking crew for group meeting; menu includes, beans, meat, and sudza (basic item of African diet).

On March 11, 1965 a medical clinic was officially opened with the assistance of Dr. Pruett and Betty Iddings, R.N. Medical assistance from Mashoko (500 miles away) was made possible when an airstrip was cut out of the thick bush by volunteer labor. In 1966 a 100-bed hospital building was begun, to fulfill a promise to the government who had given them the 100-acre land plot for their mission work. But more than this, it would be an avenue never before traveled to reach the hearts of the people in the vast area around. The work of evangelizing through medical missions actually began, though, long

Two of Chidamoyo's patients.

Christian women making hospital gowns.

Chidamoyo Hospital's evangelist, Sam, baptizing young boy.

before the hospital was begun, when Ziden Nutt first started giving first aid and treating minor ailments of those who came to the mission. The nearest doctor in those days was sixty-two miles away.

The new hospital, 22,000 sq. ft. of it, was dedicated on January 20, 1968. Dr. Dale Erickson, who, with his family, had arrived three days earlier, calls it a "place where people are cared for in Christ's name". Each day the all-Christian African staff lead devotions for the patients and worship services are held each Lord's Day for patients and their families. There is nearly always a response to the Gospel invitation. One day a week Dr. Erickson flies to Binga to treat patients in a government hospital there.

The Sinoia area had been previously supervised by those laboring with the Chidamoyo Mission but the distance was 120 miles, and it soon became evident that someone could be used on the field. That someone was Dale Marshall and his family, who arrived in Sinoia in 1966.

As was mentioned earlier, the work of the New Testament church was introduced into this area by the African people themselves. There were many places where the Marshalls found churches started by native Christians who moved into a new "churchless" area. One such example is Mt. Darwin, 250 miles from Sinoia, where an African brother moved in 1965 and began preaching. There are now four churches in that area with over one hundred Christians.

Farm School in Sinoia area.

The town of Sinoia itself has an European population of 1,400 with approximately 5,000 African inhabitants, and is situated seventy-one miles northwest of Salisbury. Besides the work at Mt. Darwin, the Marshalls labor with four other African churches, not associated with schools, plus churches at twelve farm schools. Some assistance is given to the educational aspect of these schools too. There has been established an European work in Sinoia proper, with ten baptisms reported in the first year and a half. The number of baptisms among the African churches would likely number near to one thousand.

The Nuanetsi field of Southern Rhodesia was first surveyed in March 1962 by David Grubbs and Max Ward Randall. John Pemberton shared with brother Randall in further surveys of the field later in the same year. The field was voted to the churches of Christ by the African people of the area in March 1963. Already the Tom Courtney family had been contacted with reference to the field and was preparing to come. They arrived in the Nuanetsi to take up their work in early 1964, the first and only white people in an immediate area of 10,000 Africans, an area that is isolated and primitive.

Government delays kept the initial building program at a standstill but evangelism thrived and 165 converts were baptized that first year. They have since established schools for their educational work. An air strip made it possible for doctors from other areas to fly in for specific needs of their limited medical work.

The Larry Niemeyers came to serve in the Nuanetsi area early in 1967. Mrs. Niemeyer took over the Bible teaching in the school each day while Larry took charge of ministerial training.

Dan Burris and family entered the field early in 1969 to work specifically with the Shangann speaking people. Both Mr. and Mrs. Burris are accredited teachers.

Marilyn Files, a registered nurse, reached Nuanetsi in March 1969 to operate a medical clinic for the local area and provide emergency care for patients who need hospitalization. The nearest hospital is about ninety minutes away by mission plane. She will also provide medical help and spiritual teaching for the villages.

Salisbury, the capital of Rhodesia, is the largest city of the country, with 380,000 population—some 93,000 are whites—and there were no missionaries from among our New Testament churches until Dr. Jerry Smith moved to the city in the early part of 1966 to begin further medical training. However, on week-ends they work with the Umtali church, 165 miles away, and, of course, weeks days are full of medical school, thus the growing need of the actual work in Salisbury itself was not being met. But early in 1969 Dr. Owen Dunlop and

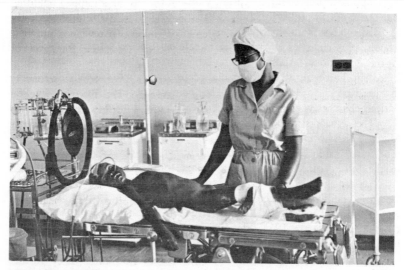

Because of neglect and witchcraft, Dr. Smith could not save this child who died of measles and pneumonia complications.

Mrs. Smith presents flannelgraph lessons at Umtali church.

his family moved to the city to help begin the needy work. Recently an opportunity has come to teach the Bible to handicapped children in a government school at Jairios Jiri. Besides the eight week-day classes, Bible School is held on Sunday afternoon. Attendance numbers around forty-five and this is the highlight of the week for most of them.

Late in 1965 the government granted a site for a secondary school in Dewure, located in the Gutu Reserve. The Douglas Johnson family moved from Zaka to open up the school in January 1966 with thirty-five boarding students. In the first month of work twenty persons were baptized into Christ. The secondary school (similar to our high school program) is the main interest of the mission, outside of the evangelizing of the people. The Lester Cooper family, David Finney and Margaret Dennis have joined this work. When the Reggie Thomas evangelistic team visited this area they held five services with thirteen baptisms reported.

The students come from all directions to study in this secondary school. Training in Christian living is an integral part of each student's education in addition to daily classes in Bible. They further their religious experience by participating in daily devotions and prayer service. Some of the students go out with the missionaries on preaching trips to help interpret, and they themselves teach Bible classes for the young children who do not speak English. (In 1968 sixty-four students were studying in the school.) There are four preaching points. The village people are beginning to see the need of sharing the Gospel and are going out to other villages to have singing and a Bible lesson.

Late in 1968 a study class was begun for a group of Europeans in the Dewure area. Some feel that only as the Europeans become concerned for the spiritual welfare of the Africans will southern Africa be evangelized.

As a means by which to help evangelize, the work of a printing ministry was set up in Ft. Victoria in 1966, taking the name CAMELS, which stands for Central African Missions Evangelistic Literature Service. Their goal is to provide all the necessary literature for the Bible schools and churches in this section of Rhodesia. Some weeks they print 6,000 Bible school papers.

The Tom Thurmans and Alice Fishback were the first to labor here in the printing work. They print in two vernaculars as well as English. The David Campbells arrived to work with CAMELS in December 1968 and will assist in the new church work among the whites in Ft. Victoria and Salisbury. Ft. Victoria is the oldest Euro-

67

pean settlement in Rhodesia, and there is both an European and an African church. A calling-teaching program seems to work best in this immediate area. When Miss Fishback returns to Rhodesia after her 1969 furlough, she plans to leave her share of the actual printing work in the hands of two African men whom she has trained and go further into the bush country to work with the women and in adult literacy classes.

Mashoko Bible College, begun in 1958 with one student, was moved to Ft. Victoria and reopened early in 1967, as Central Africa Bible College. The Dick Smiths, from Gwelo, were challenged to move to the city to oversee this phase of the Rhodesian work. More help was desperately needed in this teaching program, so when the heat of the Zambesi Valley forced the Wayne Unger family to leave they joined the Smiths in the Bible College effort. Other missionaries come in to teach some classes at various intervals, as well as those who are engaged in the printing ministry in the city.

It is the opinion of the workers in Ft. Victoria that only a lack of vision can hamper any phase of the work there. The printing ministry is unlimited in possibilities to expand, but personnel for writing, translation, drawing, set-up, editing, and printing must be available. The growth of the African congregations in assuming more leadership for the church will be in proportion to the emphasis and work done by the Central Africa Christian College.

South Africa

"Land of riches"

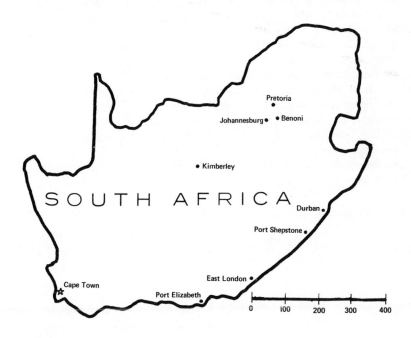

69

THE LAND . . . .

The Republic of South Africa lies in a temperate latitude at the south end of the African continent. The country consists of four provinces: Cape of Good Hope which occupies three-fifths of the southern section, Natal which only occupies 7% of the land area towards the east, Transvaal lies in the northern one quarter section, and the Orange Free State occupies the remaining 11% of the land.

Most of South Africa has elevations of over 3,000 feet; 40% has an elevation of over 4,000 feet. Resembling an inverted saucer, the land rises steadily from west to east. The coastal belt in the west and south is very fertile, producing citrus fruits and grapes. The high grass prairie of the Orange Free State and Transvaal is famous for its mineral deposits. From the Drakensberg Mountains to the east, the land falls toward the Indian Ocean in rolling hills and valleys of Natal, which are covered with rich vegetation and, near the coast, subtropical plants including sugar cane.

Being in the south temperate zone, the climate of South Africa is more equable because of its surrounding waters. Throughout the country, the mean annual temperature is just below 60 degrees F. Rainfall is unpredictable in large parts of the country, and prolonged droughts are a serious restriction on farming in such areas.

Before the arrival of the white man, South Africa had a fairly large and extremely dense animal population. Over the last two centuries the animals have been hunted with great vigor. Some species have been exterminated, and most of the larger animals have been driven into the mountain country, desert borders, or northeastern Transvaal to national park areas. Smaller animals still thrive in great number, birds number approximately 900 different kinds, and there are 200 types of snakes.

Until the end of the 19th century South Africa was almost entirely an agricultural country, the people concentrating on subsistence cultivation and stock raising. Only about 12% of the land now is arable and suffers from soil erosion and erratic rainfall. The principal crops for both whites and Africans is maize (corn), the staple diet of the Africans, which is grown mainly in the Orange Free State and the Transvaal. Potatoes are produced in large quantities on white-owned farms. European farms account for about 85% of the country's output of sugar. Tobacco, cotton, and pineapples are other profitable crops. Wine is an important export. The value of pastoral products is as great as that of the field crops. Most important is South African wool. By the end of World War II it was the fourth largest wool-producing country in the world. Since 1945, too, South Africa has become one of the ten leading fishing nations of the world; 75% to 80% of its canned fish is exported.

Towards the end of the 19th century, first diamonds, then gold deposits were discovered. The heavy investment in machinery required to exploit the gold began South Africa's industrial revolution. The sale of its gold enabled it to maintain a high level of imports, as a result the white population achieved a standard of living comparable with that of Canada and the United States. It is still the largest producer of gold in the non-Communist world. South Africa also produces uranium, copper, asbestos, manganese, and chrome. Coal outstrips in value all other mining production except gold and atomic minerals.

South African industry grew phenomenally following World War II. The major branches of private industry are metals and engineering, closely followed by food, drink, tobacco, textiles and clothing, construction, and chemicals.

. . . . THE PEOPLE

South Africa's estimated population figure of 1965 was 17,832,000, of this number 12,162,000 were native Africans; 3,395,000 were white, 60% were Afrikaans-speaking and 40% English-speaking. The Afrikaans are descended from the original Dutch, Huguenot, and German settlers who came from 1652 on. The Coloreds (mixed blood) number 1,742,000 and the Asians, nearly all Indians, 533,000. The native Africans belong to a large number of tribes with one minor and four major languages.

Among the white group, the Afrikaner majority is found everywhere except in parts of Natal. Whether in the cities or on the land, they are an unusually close-knit community. Almost all of them belong to the Dutch Reformed churches. They speak their distinguished language, Afrikaans.

The English-speaking whites are less dispersed, and far less close-knit. For the most part they live in the cities. Religiously speaking they are largely Anglican, Methodist, or Presbyterian. Most English-speaking South Africans retain a cultural and historical relationship to Great Britain, whose community is strongly rooted in South Africa.

Most of the Africans maintain tribal affiliations, but the original power of the chiefs was destroyed during the long struggle between whites and Africans. More than 2,000,000 Africans live on white-owned farms. Well over three million live in townships lying outside the

European cities. The migration to seek work in the white areas has placed a heavy strain not only on tribal but also upon family relationships. Illegitimacy runs over 70% in the African townships outside Johannesburg and represents some 30% of all births inside many of the reserves. Education is an influential force in African life . Over 80% of the African children secure some education—much of this has been through mission schools. There are a considerable number of highly educated Africans carrying on professions such as medicine, law, and teaching. The Africans are chiefly animists, but there are a considerable number of Christians. According to a 1960 census there were 1,593,939 members of the Separatist church.

The Colored speak mostly Afrikaans, but are bi-lingual in Cape Town where they occupy a middle position between the Africans, who do most of the manual labor, and the whites, who control most businesses and services. They are small tradesmen or work at various crafts or in industry. Outside the city they are laborers on many of the white-owned farms. They are largely members of the Dutch Reformed or Anglican churches.

The Asians, in contrast to the Colored, have quite a strong nationalist sentiment despite the fact that they, too, occupy a middle position between the whites and the Africans. Some are well-to-do merchants and even own real estate of considerable value. However, under zoning restrictions they cannot live in many of their own buildings. Some Indians still work on sugar plantations, others in factories, or at services. The Asians have retained their own religion, mainly Hinduism and Islam.

Each racial group in South Africa has its own system of education. Education for whites is free and compulsory to age sixteen. Both Afrikaans and English is taught in the higher grades. Virtually all Afrikaans education is in the state schools, but the English-speaking have a number of private schools. Education for the Africans began as early as 1799 in the Cape, though it is not yet compulsory and many drop out after the first four or five years. The curriculum in the schools now includes Afrikaans as well as English and African languages at the lowest levels. Since 1953 mission schools were placed under government direction, and many ceased to exist. Since 1950 most colleges have been almost completely segregated. The white population is largely literate, and nearly 70% of them are bilingual. Asians and Coloreds also have a high degree of literacy. The African literacy rate is increasing.

73

.... THE MISSIONARY ....

Thomas Bambezi Kalane was converted by W. H. Book during a visit to America, and returned to his native Africa to establish the Church of Christ Mission in Kimberley in the 1920's. The first white missionaries were brother and sister O. E. Payne, and he died after only two years on the field. C. B. Titus served for five years beginning in 1927. These were associated with the *African Christian Missionary Society*. Through the efforts of the missionaries and the African preachers, churches were started in many parts of the Union.

This was the beginning! There was little American association with the work after that until after World War II.

Melba (Palmer) Rees began her missionary service back in 1938 when she left her homeland for Tibet, to labor with the Bare and Nichols families, and Miss Gladys Schwake. Ill health forced her to return to the States in 1940, but in 1946, following the war and in good health again, she returned to Tibet. Once again ill health forced her to leave that area; this time she came out to Kunming, China. Bill Rees came to China that same year and they were married later in the year and continued to labor in association with J. Russell Morse and co-workers. When invasion by the Communists forced them to leave this field, along with the other missionaries, they chose the open door of South Africa where many of their beloved Chinese lived. It was in March 1952 that they were able to have their first service with the Chinese people in Kimberley.

Much work was done through personal evangelism supplemented by a monthly doctrinal publication that was not only mailed in the local area but to Chinese throughout South Africa and in other countries. The challenge of South Africa to the Reeses was not merely for the lost souls of the forgotten Chinese of the area, but it was the hope that some day these who were redeemed for Christ might take the gospel themselves back into China whose doors are closed to the foreigner. It was not surprising that when the door opened in Hong Kong that the Bill Rees family entered that open door in 1963, to be more closely associated to a larger group of Chinese people.

When the Bill Rees family came to the States in the summer of 1960 for furlough they were relieved on the field by Albert Hamilton and his family. Arriving in Kimberley in May 1960, the Hamiltons assumed leadership of the Chinese work and also began preaching for an European congregation. For most purposes the population is divided into three classes: 1) white people, regardless of nationality,

2) natives, all pure blacks, and 3) coloured, those of mixed black and white blood, and Asiatics.

When the work in Kimberley was placed in the hands of a locally trained evangelist in 1962 the Hamilton family moved to make Johannesburg, a city of two million, the center of their evangelistic work. According to records, a congregation was formed here as early as 1901. The present church in Johannesburg began with a racially mixed group made up of Chinese, Coloured, and white (European) members, reaching a membership of one hundred. As a result of this work two other white congregations are meeting in European sections of the city.

Youth work is expanding and a youth camp is being started. The youth of South Africa are certainly neglected by the formal churches. To assist in new church evangelism a Mobile Chapel is operated for reaching Coloured areas of the city. Six men, three European or white, two Coloured, and one Chinese, are receiving leadership training in preparation for preaching. Since 1962 there have been approximately two hundred baptisms. The Lester LeMay family came to serve as "substitute missionaries" from December 1964 to February 1966.

The Stuart Cooks, sent from a congregation they helped to establish in Casper, Wyoming, joined in the work of evangelism in Johannesburg in May 1966. The Wally Farnham and Leroy Herder families arrived in February 1968. The Herders settled in Springs, Transvaal, a city of 50,000 located thirty-five miles from downtown Johannesburg. They found the work among the whites of South Africa to be exceedingly slow since they are often connected in some way with denominational Christianity, and they are sometimes suspicious of Americans. The Wally Farnhams labor at Benoni and teach at the church that was established by Jessie Kellums back in 1925 during a great evangelistic campaign. A Holiday Bible School a (failure twenty-six years ago) was a great success in July 1968 when forty-two children were enrolled.

The Roger Vickroy family, employees of a U.S. firm, found property suitable for use as a Christian service camp, and will live there as caretakers. In their desire to witness for Christ wherever they are, they are serving in a new congregation meeting in Nigel, forty-five miles from Johannesburg, where the Herders made original contacts.

The Robert Mills family moved the work of the Church of Christ Postal Mission to Johannesburg in 1967 where better facilities were available for the expanding printing side of the work. As early as 1955 the Mills with their Postal Mission were welcomed into the

South African work, though they began their work originally in Wind-
hoek, Southwest Africa in 1952 where they found it almost impossible to
establish a growing mission work. So in 1955 they joined the workers
in Kimberley to continue the growing correspondence work and to
assist in the ministerial training school that existed there. This was
a natural combination.

A major activity of the Church of Christ Postal Mission is the
printing and distributing of the Christian message. Its original effort
was through a monthly publication that was freely distributed to
sixteen African countries and abroad to an estimated 25,000 readers.
These contacts have been valuable in opening up new areas. At one
time as many as 325 students from the Gold Coast (now Ghana)
were taking correspondence work.

Printing room of Gospel tract
center.

Local minister receiving lesson
materials.

Upon their move to Johannesburg, the Mills opened offices downtown where a tract and literature center was established. Over one
hundred different tract titles are kept in ready supply, representing
sixteen different languages in use in southern Africa. Nearly 80,000
tracts were distributed in the first year at the new location. A dozen
correspondence Bible lesson booklets are also kept in print, representing
five of these major languages. Promotion for the distribution of
these lesson books is carried in a very popular Bantu magazine which is
printed in several language editions monthly. A list of enquirers for
lessons, etc., has reached nearly 12,000.

Besides the printing, tract distribution, and correspondence lessons,
the Mills seek to give aid and oversight to the local Bantu churches
which have their own ministers. They are associated with about forty
ministers, serving 279 preaching points, reporting a total membership

of 8,000, and averaging about six hundred baptisms each year. In the fall of 1968, Dorothy Nichols, a sister-in-law, came to labor during the Mill's furlough.

Roy Coop assisted in evangelistic efforts in the Johannesburg area in the fall of 1967. Most of his efforts were centered at Benoni during his three-month stay, a city thirty miles from Johannesburg. Being convinced of the need of a strong evangelistic effort among the whites, and training them for leadership, he has made plans, with his family, to return to labor here in 1969.

Thomas P. (Pete) Jones likewise assisted in evangelistic efforts in this area in the fall of 1967 which resulted in several new congregations forming. Illness in their family prevented their early return to the field but they do plan on entering this area as early in 1970 as is possible.

The Max Randall family made their decision to serve Christ in Africa back in 1947, though hindered in their plans by the government. However, since their arrival in this great and good land of South Africa not one application for entry into this area to do mission work has been refused.

In those early years the work among the Bantu (black) races was never brighter. In those first five years the membership of the churches more than doubled. Such little work had been done on the buildings in days gone by that the Randalls, upon their arrival to the field, found it necessary to immediately launch into a program of repair and building. However a great portion of brother Randall's time was in making the contact and laying the ground work for new areas. Only those who go into new fields know the value of this advance preparation, as has proven true in all of the new areas opened in Africa in the past ten years.

Along with the days of travel, Max Randall began his Cape Town ministry on the first of January 1955. Increasingly, the missionaries realized that the only ultimate answer to the real needs of South Africa involved striking specifically at the city centers, and reaching the ruling white population in particular. His work in the European community was not without tremendous blessing, one of which was a young man who traveled to America to study for the ministry. Carrol Fulford was the first Capetown student to return to his own country for mission work.

In answer to prayer the Paul Holderman family came to the field in 1956 to relieve the Randalls for a much-needed furlough. Leaving a successful ministry here in the States, the Holdermans took over the strategic Observatory Church of Christ on Polo Road in Cape

Town for nearly two years. This church had its beginning back in the late 20's or early 30's with the Thomas mission, and was the only congregation in this area to survive the U.S. depression and denominational opposition.

In January 1960 the Al Zimmermans came to assist in the European work at Polo Road. From time to time most ministers have probably had the thought of becoming a missionary cross their minds, the Al Zimmermans had. Daily for several months they sought the will of the Lord in the matter. Having followed the development of the Amazon Valley work in Brazil from its beginning, this field appealed to the Zimmermans as well as Africa where Al served with the Navy in World War II. The final decision was left in the hands of God and the door to South Africa was opened to them.

From 1960 to 1965 they maintained a steadily productive ministry in both city and rural evangelism throughout the Cape Town region and beyond. In 1967 they returned to do African evangelism and helping in the northern suburbs.

Carroll Fulford came back home to establish a church at Wynberg and was in the process of establishing work in the capital city of Pretoria when ill health forced them to return to the States for medication. At present they are back in South Africa starting an European church and other work in Port Elizabeth, a coastal city 450 miles east of Cape Town. Medical treatment for their baby may necessitate another trip to the States.

The Gordon Nelsons replaced the Zimmermans at Polo Road church in Cape Town during their furlough in 1965 and served a year, before establishing a new and much needed congregation in the Northern Suburbs. Previous attempts to accomplish this had failed sadly, but the Nelsons were successful in maintaining this nucleus from the Observatory church for two years until the Jim Parrises were called to minister in February 1968.

In October 1965 John Fulford, a younger brother of Carroll, returned to his home city and was able to give some direction to the Wynberg church which had carried on valiantly with the help of the Observatory church. John and Louise Ladbrook (daughter of New Zealand missionaries at Dadaya, Rhodesia) were married in December 1965, the same week in which she qualified as a doctor.

In January 1967 Don and Patti Hart came to minister directly to the Wynberg church while the John Fulfords accepted the ministry of the Polo Road church. Though the concept of independent New Testament Christianity seems strange and foreign to these tradition-bound, conservative, authoritarian people and though slow to change, from this group has come many young people to serve the Lord—Charles Bell and Sandy Sinclair (Zambia), Slyvia Menhinick (Mashoko), Titus Solomon and Mr. and Mrs. James Solomon. The James Solomons returned from their USA studies in September 1967 to open up new avenues for coloured evangelism in their home city, the first American-supported efforts among the Coloured people here. Their first efforts are through Bible study and youth work in the area of Athlone, ten miles from the center of the city of Cape Town.

The work of the Harts at Wynberg has placed special emphasis upon working with the youth for they feel that here is one of the greatest avenues of growth. This work includes classes and Bible clubs for three different age groups, the oldest of which includes several young men who preach and teach already—some of whom plan to enter the ministry.

When the John Fulfords entered the ministry of the Observatory Church, often referred to as the Polo Road church due to its location, the actual effective membership was twenty-one. By the grace of God that number doubled in their first year and a half of ministry, in baptisms alone. Besides a ministry similar to a city ministry in the States, they are actively engaged in training more of the local people to lead and teach. An area Men's Fellowship is now in action to stimulate more men to take responsibility in church leadership. Training classes for teachers are being conducted also.

Part of Observatory Church congregation.

Newest arrivals in the Cape area are Darrel and Anne Stanley who came in March 1968. Darrel, son of missionary Lynn Stanley who is leading in the training school in Natal, has been accepted to study medicine at the University of Cape Town. They are thus able to share in giving valuable assistance to the churches.

When the Max Randalls returned to their beloved Africa in November 1957, they were accompanied by John and Heather Kernan and family. Perhaps this arrangement would not have been were it not for an event that took place years ago and miles away. When the S.S. Yukon ran aground in Johnstone Bay (Alaska), John Kernan, shipping home for discharge from the Air Force, began to think of his life and his relationship with God. Having made no rash promises but remembering that conversation later, he made his decision to serve Christ in Africa. After serving three years with the non-instrumental group in Rhodesia, John and Heather met on a bus in Scotland, a meeting they feel was directed of the Lord. Following their marriage they returned to Africa to labor another two years.

After a period of furlough, during which time he taught at Atlanta Christian College, they set up the Christian Literature for Southern Africa, being associated with the South Africa Church of Christ Mission. The journalism training in college, professional experience in free-lance radio and magazine writing, along with his pioneer work among the coloured people in Bulawayo and the publishing of literature (including tracts in three languages) was a good preparation for such a chosen labor.

The large percentage of the people in South Africa not only can read but do read. The Africans, particularly, read whatever they can get hold of. More people can be more easily reached through publications than in person. It can not only be a means of helping to sustain faithful New Testament congregations, but it serves as a foundation for laying new work, both worthy projects.

Major emphasis of the Literature Service is on preparation of Bible lessons, periodicals, and mission education materials. This is distributed primarily in South Africa but some items go to a number of other countries. Work is primarily in English and Xhosa, one of the main native languages, however there is some literature in at least twelve other languages or dialects. Estimates of readership indicate that every copy of a magazine has between five and ten readers, some people say as high as fifteen. Ouside of school textbooks, children's literature in African languages is practically non-existent. "Life of Christ Visualized" is printed in Zulu and Xhosa, but this isn't enough.

Xhosa grandmother.

Chief undertakings since 1960 have been a Xhosa hymnal and a Xhosa edition of "Concerning the Disciples" by P. H. Welshimer. In 1961 the Kernans moved from the Cape Town area to East London, (where they continued their literature publishing work) to labor with congregations in the Ciskei Native area (a reserve similar to American Indian reservations) and the eastern part of the Cape Province. Along with literature, their chief emphasis has been on youth work, particularly through development of Sunday schools and vacation Bible schools.

African musicians play for pennies from tourists.

The Alvin Nicholson family came to South Africa to assist in the work of the South African Church of Christ Mission in November 1953. Much of their work has been to help the natives evangelize. Thus it requires days and days of travel to visit with the different congregations, to help advise and deal with problems that do arise. And there is always the Macedonian call to "come over and help us". More men are needed to work with Bantu churches in rural and urban evangelism in Zululand, Orange Free State, northern Transvaal and central Cape.

Their early work centered around Pondoland, just south of Natal and east of Basutoland, an area inhabited by Pondos in the north and Xhosa in the south where the Kernans are now laboring. From ex-

82

perience they found it most profitable to have strong churches in the larger centers where the men come to work. Then as they returned to their homes on the Reserves they opened whole new areas with the Gospel message. This way the work more than doubled itself.

This work of evangelism also extended itself to the north to the edge of Swaziland, inhabited by the more primitive Zulus, whose language the Nicholsons learned.

As early as 1960, one thousand baptisms were being reported in a year throughout these various areas. Permits were granted for new sites. According to law, buildings must be built within a year from the time the permit is granted. Though stewardship among the natives is improving it is still insufficient many times to keep up with the opportunities for expansion, so in some cases American funds are used directly or through loan funds.

The 60's seemed to bring new hope to the native people of South Africa. In mid-year 1960 the government announced that new, less-stringent controls of Bantu movement would be applied, several industrial concerns announced increases in pay and a regular examination of the wage scale so as to assure a living wage for the employees; a more favorable educational system is being evolved and a sense of being and worth is being felt by many responsible Africans. In many areas there appears to be an awakening toward Christianity.

The church holds real hope to the Africans. If she gives that hope to this new Bantu society which is emerging, it is entirely possible that a real revival could sweep the Bantu people. The professor of Bantu languages at Natal University told a group of missionaries: "There is going to emerge a national Bantu church; it is inevitable. You men train leaders today so that when that church rises it will be Christian".

Southern Africa, in spite of its growing racial tensions and numerous problems, continues to be one of the most fruitful and promising mission fields in the world. And perhaps the Bible-training school in Port Shepstone will be the answer.

The Lynn Stanley family's decision to enter Africa for the purpose of missionary activity was not one made hurriedly. Several years before, preparation had begun for such a work. They sailed in 1953 along with the Nicholson family to take over the responsibility of the Bible-training school, while the Nicholsons labored more in the field of evangelism. Brother Stanley's desire was to serve where both teaching and preaching could be combined.

The Lord made ready the way in answer to prayer! The native-training school at Kimberley maintained four ten-week terms yearly.

At the close of the year 1956 about seventy different students had already been enrolled at one time or another. Some came for several terms, while others could only attend one term. Many of these men began preaching to local congregations, being paid by them and not by the mission. In Kimberley four new churches were started due to student effort.

The decision to erect a new school building on a different location was not a mere whim of fancy. The change was necessary. The old building was inadequate, but more important than that, the government objected to its location. South Africa is strictly segregated. There was objection to housing native students in an area designated for Europeans. The Natal area was chosen for several reasons. Port Shepstone was a boundary between the white and black areas of southern Natal. The school is located in an area declared white, where it can be adequately governed by the missionary staff, and the dormitory is on the reserve, or African side, thus fulfilling the requirements of the government. Since the move here brother Nicholson is also able to give some assistance in the teaching program.

In all, between 150-200 have had some Bible training. Nearly all of the present Bantu ministers have had their training in the school. The school now offers three years of work, though most students come for a year at a time. There are many losses due to sin or for seeking a better-paying position than the ministry. The churches are autonomous and salaries are low, discouraging many who should be in the ministry. The situation is gradually improving but far too slowly. At the local church level, education is very low and most churches have difficulty in getting a trained leadership. Work has been done with young people in camps and a start has been made to hold classes for the church leaders in the local churches, so improvement is being made.

Though our present South African work had its beginning in Kimberley for many various periods there has been no resident missionary in Kimberley itself, and none since the training school was moved to Port Shepstone.

When the Gordon Nelson family, who originally labored in the Cape Town area, returned to South Africa from furlough in April 1969 it was to Kimberley they moved, six hundred miles inland from the Cape. Here they are laboring basically with the African churches. They will be teaching these people how to preach, teach, develop Sunday schools and challenge them in a greater way to evangelize their own people—to spread the indigenous church. In addition, they will be working with the Coloured church in Kimberley. If the door is opened, an European (white) work will be started among the 25,000 whites, out of a total population of 80,000. They also plan to continue survey work into the new black nation of Botswana, formerly a Bechuanaland Protectorate, where we presently have no churches or missionaries.

Tanzania

"Land of Kilimanjaro"

THE LAND . . . .

Situated in East Africa just south of the equator is the independent African state of Tanzania which united the former states of Tanganyika and Zanzibar, off the east coast, in 1964.

Except for a coastal strip varying in width from ten to forty miles, Tanzania lies at the altitude of over 1,000 feet. A plateau, averaging 3,000 to 4,500 feet in height, makes up the greater part of the country. A third zone consists of a few isolated highlands or mountains, including Africa's highest peak, Kilimanjaro, which stands at 19,340 feet. The coastal plain is hot and humid, and poorly drained. Most of the southern plateau is poorly watered and the tsetse fly spreads sleeping sickness. Desolate and thinly populated, the area is called "the wilderness". The central and northern parts of the plateau contain sections of fertile soil and benefit from a moderate rainfall. The highland areas contain the best agricultural land, with better soils and more rainfall. Although three great rivers—the Nile, the Congo, and the Zambesi—have their origin in Tanzania, the country has few permanent rivers. The climate on the islands is tropical.

The most common form of vegetation is grasses, which are covered by thorny shrubs on much of the plateau, though this area also contains park land. Among trees, the dominant types on the coast are the native and imported mango and the imported coconut. On the sides of the higher mountains rest the cedar and podocarpus. The most useful tree of the park land is the mninga, valued in construction for its appearance and durability.

There are about 1,000 species of birds, ranging in size from ostrich to the warbler. Insect life numbers over 60,000 species, including many disease carriers. Poisonous snakes include the black mamba and puff adder. The savanna uplands are inhabited by several species of antelope, as well as the lion, leopard, zebra, elephant, and giraffe. Monkeys are plentiful. The hippopotamus and crocodile live along the rivers.

The growing of foodstuffs for local consumption and the production and export of primary produce form the basis of Tanzania's economy. The chief commercial crops are sisal (of which Tanzania is the world's largest producer), coffee, cotton, and oilseeds. The most important minerals are diamonds and gold. Rich deposits of coal, iron, and other minerals are of little commercial value yet.

With some 6% of Tanzania's area consisting of open lake waters, inland fishing occupies an important place in the economy.

Most industrial activity consists of the small-scale processing of local food and raw materials. Many towns and villages now have cottage industries that make wearing apparel, shoes, and various household items.

. . . . THE PEOPLE

The estimated population of the country in 1965 was 10,500,000. Of this number, approximately 10,170,000 were on the mainland and 330,000 on the islands of Zanzibar and Pemba. On the mainland 98.5% were Africans, largely of the Bantu stock, the great mass of which are rural and dependent on peasant agriculture. Over 75% of the non-Africans are Asians, mainly from India and Pakistan (who are urban and largely in the commerce field and increasing numbers are in the professions and public service). Other non-Africans include Arabs (whose main livelihood is in trade), Europeans (mostly employed in higher civil service, sisal and coffee plantations or in commerce), Goans, Somalis, Syrians, and a few Chinese. Because of the general lack of water and the prevalence of the tsetse fly, about two-thirds of all the people live in about 10% of the territory.

The indigenous inhabitants of Zanzibar and Pemba were probably all mainlanders who drifted over in family groups to fish and cultivate. They have been grouped into three tribes with a great deal of mixing with the Arabs who entered this area before the time of Christ. Prior to the revolution in 1964, 76% were Africans, 17% Arab, and 6% Indian, plus a few Comoriens and Europeans, though nearly three-fourths of all but the Africans re-established themselves on the east coast of the mainland.

About 94% of the mainland Africans speak one or another of the Bantu languages, though a common language has developed in Swahili, a Bantu language written in an adaptation of the Arabic script. Swahili is taught in both primary and secondary schools and is almost universally understood even on Zanzibar. It is one of the two official languages of Tanzania, the other being English, which is spoken by most foreigners. Arabic and English are also widely spoken in Zanzibar and Pemba.

About 50% of the school age children attend the first four years of primary school; approximately one-sixth go on to upper primary school, and only 4% enter secondary or trade schools. Secondary education was made free in 1964 and university grants are available. There is one University in the capital city of Tanzania, otherwise for higher education they must go out of the country to Uganda, or abroad.

At least half of the mainland people adhere to traditional animist beliefs, and religious practices vary from tribe to tribe. Ancestor worship is common. Beliefs in magic and the practice of witchcraft are widespread. Nearly two million are Muslims, on the mainland, and nearly all are Muslims on the islands. Christianity, with some two million adherents, has spread since the early 20th century, and is predominant in some districts.

. . . . THE MISSIONARY . . . .

Tanzania was chosen as the country in which the Hale Whitcombs could begin an evangelistic work, after much prayer, consideration of their experience in the Congo, and a study of the various possibilities. This country is the center of the Swahili, the most widely used language of the area. This may be used as a stepping stone for spreading the gospel to Uganda (the only major country in this part of Africa in which we have been refused permission to work).

The Whitcombs plan to enter Tanzania in September 1969 to begin a radio ministry for the Swahili-speaking people. Forty million will be able to understand the broadcasts. Correspondence courses will be offered for further teaching, and by using an airplane brother Whitcomb will be able to follow up on contacts that are made.

Zambia

"Land of the copper mines"

Kitwe
Ndola

Z A M B I A

Mumbwa

Barotseland

Kapyanga ☆ Lusaka

Livingstone

0	100	200	300	400

THE LAND . . . .

Zambia is an independent republic in central Africa, lying just south of the Republic of the Congo. It was known as Northern Rhodesia until it achieved independence in 1964 after nearly seventy-five years of British rule.

Zambia is a very large, landlocked, country, comprised mainly of a high plateau between 3,500 and 4,500 feet above sea level. Exceptions to this are the Muchinga Mts. to the northeast, which exceed 7,000 feet, and the valleys of the major river systems with some elevations below 2,000 feet.

Because of the country's elevation, the climate is mostly temperate, but tropical conditions prevail in some of the low-lying river valleys. There are wide seasonal variations in temperature and rainfall. The highest temperatures come before the rains, which come in November through April. May to September is the cool, dry season.

Dry savanna-type grasslands cover most of the southern half of the country, but tree cover increases to the north according to the increase of the rainfall. To the north and east grow a thin forest. More than half of Zambia is covered by woodland, though 7% of the country has been allocated to forest reserves. Commercial exploitation of forest land is concentrated in the Rhodesian teak forests of southern Barotseland and in the Copperbelt region.

Most of the wild animals of tropical Africa are found in Zambia. Bird life abounds; a 1957 checklist records 658 species. Over 150 species of reptiles are recorded.

Zambia's economy is based almost entirely on copper, and the country ranks with the United States and Chile as the world's leading copper producers. Mineral rights in the country were formerly owned by the British South Africa Company but following the granting of independence an agreement was reached for a transfer of these rights to the government. Production of secondary minerals, such as zinc and lead, has been increasing in recent years.

A majority of Zambia's population is engaged in subsistence agriculture. An estimated 85% of agricultural production is non-commercial. The main product is corn. Tobacco, grown mainly by European formers, is the leading export crop. Peanuts and cotton are also grown for the market, mainly by Africans. Fruit and vegetable production has developed around railheads and the major urban centers. Irrigation is used in the production of wheat, potatoes, coffee, and sugarcane.

Sleeping sickness, carried by the tsetse fly, limits cattle production in certain regions. Most of the million-plus head of cattle are an African enterprise and are largely raised in the southern provinces and Barotseland.

Zambia's inland waters are a valuable source of food, thus the fishing industry is an important part of the rural economy. Large quantities of fish, most of which are transported by rail to processing centers, are either frozen or dried.

. . . . THE PEOPLE

The 1965 estimated population included 3,698,700 Africans, 70,000 Europeans, 9,700 Asians, and 2,600 Colored (mixed African and European). The Africans, part of the Bantu-speaking population of central and southern Africa, are divided into a large number of tribal groups (73 different classifications). The Europeans are predominately British, but especially in the mining centers there are also a number of white South Africans, including Afrikaners, as well as Greek, Italians, and Portuguese. The small Asian population consists mainly of Indian and Pakistani traders.

Most of the Africans live in villages. However, some 17% of the Africans, along with 67% of the Asians and Colored, and 87% of the Europeans, live in the seven leading cities of the copper belt. At first, African immigrants to the towns lived largely within their own tribal groups, but gradually the links "back home" are placed aside for wider associations. Thus changes in the traditional African society have been effected through European rule, religious and educational activities of Christian missionaries, and the increased demand for wage labor. About one-fourth of Zambia's population live in urban areas, where over crowding and slums have plagued the housing authorities of the government.

Malaria and tuberculosis are the major health problems. Hookworm and biharziasis affect a large proportion of the African population; also widely prevalent are poliomyelitis and smallpox.

Until the end of 1963 higher education and all European education were the responsibility of the federal government. In January 1964 when the Zambian government assumed full responsibility they began a policy of racial integration. Many schools are operated by missions, but the government has pledged itself to provide eight years of free primary education for all children. By 1966, over 90% of the children, aged eight to ten, were receiving the first four years of schooling. Above this level the number decreased rapidly. The Uni-

96

versity of Zambia was established in March 1965, offering instruction in the social sciences, natural science, and education.

Nyanja, a Bantu language, is the official language of the police and Zambia Regiment. English is the official language otherwise, and its use by Africans is increasing. Afrikaans also is widely spoken.

Most Africans are animists, religiously speaking, but Christianity has made some inroads. Among the European population, the Anglican church is the leading denomination. The Dutch Reformed Church of the Afrikaans claimed slightly less than 20% of the white people. Other major groups were Roman Catholics, Presbyterian, and Methodist. Over 66% of the small Asian population is Muslim, the remainder, Hindu.

. . . . THE MISSIONARY . . . .

The city of Livingstone in Zambia has always had important historical connection with the development of Central Africa. It has traditionally been the natural gateway across the Zambezi from the southern high velt to the northern plateau. Located on the banks of the Zambezi river at the Victoria Falls, the first white man in the area was David Livingstone, after whom the town was named.

The railway reached Livingstone in 1906 and just six short years later, in 1912, the first missionaries of the Churches of Christ entered the area. These non-instrument Church of Christ missionaries have labored long and faithfully in the Livingstone and Kalomo areas.

The first visit by an American Church of Christ-Christian Church missionary, to what was then Northern Rhodesia, was made by Max Ward Randall in 1953, while he was associated with South African Church of Christ Mission. In the immediate years to follow several further trips were made with encouragement and assistance from the Dadaya Mission in Southern Rhodesia.

In 1962 Max Randall entered the area with the first work of the Central Africa Mission and settled in Livingstone where more extensive surveys were continued. When Zambia became an independent nation in 1964, Dr. Kenneth Kaunda, the son of a Christian minister, was elected its new president. In his government are dedicated, humble men, who are determined to further the political, material, educational, economic, social and spiritual good of the nation. With this opportunity in mind a decision was made in 1963 to begin work in the Mumbwa district where the government granted permission for building schools and churches. This area is very near the geographical center of the country, heavily populated by the Tonga tribespeople among whom the work was to begin. Three schools were built, without government subsidy, and four churches planted largely as a result of the evangelistic efforts of the school program.

Since Zambia gained its independence, it has taken steps to assume the full educational responsibility. A serious evaluation was made of the mission educational program, since the government has assured them that missionaries can continue to labor without the expensive school program. Beginning in January 1968 the church-sponsored schools at Mumbwa became government schools. The Zambian missionaries are unanimous in their determination to make their program evangelistic, and it was to this effort that the first missionaries, Bill and Jackie Brant, joined the work in 1964, following two and one half years of labor in Mashoko mission. After their first furlough they returned to open the work on the "fabulous copperbelt", located in the northern section of the country. In this area are some of the largest, most modern, mining operations in the world, and is served by seven beautiful, modern cities, which serve as the industrial and distribution center. Only about 1% of the seven to eight hundred thousand people have previously been touched by the Gospel.

Mildred Pace joined the work at Mumbwa in 1966 but in 1967 she began assisting the Brants at Kitwe where a printing ministry was established. Others who have come to Zambia are assisting in the writing, but the Kitwe press is turning out tracts, quarterlies, lesson material, and a Bible Correspondence Course. Although there are thirty-six distinct languages spoken in Zambia, most of these who can read can be reached by printing in four of them.

Nucleus for first congregation at Ndola.

98

In October 1967 the Dean Davises arrived in Ndola, in the Copperbelt region, to begin laying ground-work for establishing the first church there. In 1968 a new work was started in Lubato, in an area that will reach 40,000 people.

The Vernon Oakleys came to Kitwe in November 1967, and besides assisting in evangelism, they are directing the Open Bible correspondence course. It is a simplified study of the Bible and its teachings. The African people are avid readers and eager to learn, so this method is an excellent medium for teaching, especially for the new Christians. There were eighty-seven applications for the course made the first week.

In January 1968 the Charles Delaney family joined the work at Ndola. The work is new, and slow, and difficult. However, doors are now being opened and souls are being won as congregations are established in the Copperbelt cities. Some families walked five miles one way to attend a worship service, so their sincerity encourages the missionaries to be stedfast (later a church was started in their area, Twapia).

Leroy Randall, a second generation missionary, and his wife, came to the Mumbwa area in 1966 but when the government took over the schools they moved into Lusaka, the capital city, from which area they are evangelizing, not only in the city, but also in the surrounding bush country, mostly at Shakumbila.

Sitandasokwe church—30 miles from Mumbwa Mission.

99

In November 1967 the Ronald Sapp family reached Lusaka. They reside directly outside the city and work with several indigenous African churches in the compounds and also they began a new church in the Kamailo area near the city. These indigenous churches have been found to have an explicit faith in the testimony of the Scriptures.

A month after the Sapps' arrival, the Charles Bell family reached Lusaka to join in the work of evangelism. Charles was born in Southern Rhodesia and later moved to South Africa before coming to the States to study for the ministry. He realized the great need for urban evangelism, even in Africa. The city of Lusaka covers an area of thirty-six square miles. Some of the people are already Christian but need to be brought together to form an effective witness, but many of the 150,000 know nothing of Christ. The city contains many temptations and distractions which old village life does not, so the teaching must be careful and the example the best possible.

In August 1966 the Don Mechem family arrived on the field and began bush evangelism from Kapyanga, sixty-five miles west of Lusaka.

Notice similarity of chicken coop (left) to unfinished hut (right).

In 1968 some of the missionaries covered seven hundred miles in a survey trip into Zambia's eastern province to consider the possibility of witnessing in this area as well.

Another Zambia missionary comes from Africa too. Sandy Sinclair was born in Johannesburg, South Africa. When his family moved later to Cape Town, he met the Max Randall family, and through the influence of the various missionaries he became a Christian and came to America to study for the ministry and a future in missionary activity. He married his wife, Charlotte, in the States and together they came to Zambia in 1967, first to the Mumbwa station, then to Livingstone, from where they have made surveys into the Barotseland and Botswane. Scattered groups of Christians in outlying areas are being contacted, some as far as fifty-five miles north, in remote bush country. A leadership training program is being planned and Christian literature is being provided for them.

Sinclair's travel vehicle for village evangelism, attached trailer carries extra supplies.

When you reach the mission field in Zambia the lack of hospitals, orphanages, schools or colleges, is immediately noticeable. The Zambian missionaries have dedicated themselves to the primary task of direct village, city and township evangelism—for the purpose of establishing self-propogating, self-sustaining, indigenous churches after the New Testament pattern. As a result there are now approximately twenty-three churches meeting regularly. Since the inception of the work there has been an estimated 2,500 baptisms. The most significant number came during the first two weeks of August 1968. Reggie Thomas and an evangelistic team from America held services in both the bush villages and the cities and witnessed scores of people who responded to every invitation.

Asia

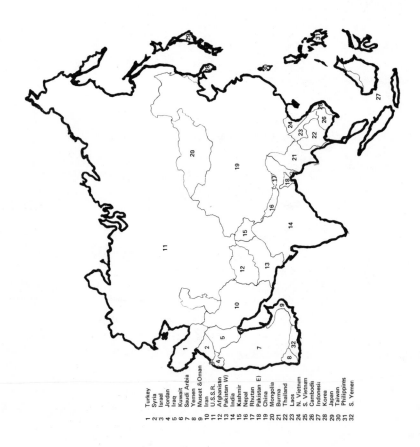

1 Turkey
2 Syria
3 Israel
4 Jordan
5 Iraq
6 Kuwait
7 Saudi Arbia
8 Yemen
9 Muscat &Oman
10 Iran
11 U.S.S.R.
12 Afghanistn
13 Pakistan W)
14 India
15 Kashmir
16 Nepal
17 Bhutan
18 Pakistan E)
19 China
20 Mongolia
21 Burma
22 Thailand
23 Laos
24 N. Vietnam
25 S. Vietnam
26 Cambodia
27 Indonesii
28 Korea
29 Japan
30 Taiwan
31 Philippines
32 S. Yemen

Burma

"*The Golden Peninsula*"

Putao
Ft. Hertz

Myitkyina

Mandalay

B U R M A

Akyab

Rangoon

River crossing in northern Burma.

THE LAND . . . .

This republic of southeast Asia is bounded on the north by Tibet, on the east by Yunnan province of China, Indochina and Thailand, on the southwest by the Andaman Sea, and the west by the Bay of Bengal, eastern Pakistan and the Indian state of Assam. Slightly smaller than Texas, it is twelve hundred miles long and more than five hundred miles wide with a tail off to the southeast.

This republic includes Burma proper, the Shan State, Karenni State and Kachin States. The population includes many different peoples: Burmese, Karens, Tai (Shans), Chins, Kachins, Chinese, Indo-Burmans, Indians, Whites and Eurasians. The estimated number living within the republic in 1965 was over twenty-four and a half-million.

Burma is separated from India and East Pakistan by a long range from Arakan Yoma to Cape Negrais. The entire area is considered largely in the tropics. The east section of Burma, including the Shan states, is occupied by a plateau which extends into the Yunnan plateau of China. Between these two sections lie the basin of the Irrawaddy and its great tributary, and the basin of the Sittang. This is for the most part lowland area with ranges of hills, and is divided into two natural regions; Upper and Lower Burma. Upper Burma includes most of the country. It is a land of mountains and thick forests. The soil is poor and the people find it hard to raise enough to eat. Lower Burma is the broad plain along the coast. The monsoon winds bring heavy rains in the summer and the long rivers carry down rich earth which is good for crops.

Burma is a country of waterways, many of which are navigable. The Irrawaddy, Sittang, and Salween (which drains the eastern plateau) are the major rivers.

Burma forms part of the great monsoon region of Asia, but its climate is modified to a great extent by the relief of the country. There are really three seasons: cool and rainless from the end of October to February, hot and rainless from March through May, rainy from June to October. By far the most oppressive factor is the monotony of the climate and the lack of a noticeable change in temperature from one day to the next.

Burma is predominately an agricultural and rural country with seventy per cent of the people directly dependent upon farming. There are only two cities, Rangoon and Mandalay, which have a population over 100,000. The latest estimated population of Rangoon (1957) was 821,800, more than four times the size of Mandalay.

About sixty per cent of the cultivated land is devoted to the raising of their most important crop, rice. Burma is first among rice-exporting countries, supplying forty per cent of the world's demand. Next in importance are peanuts, sesamum and cotton.

The area of forests exceeds 20,000,000 acres or over half of Burma, which makes timber quite an important export item. Burma teak is world famous, though teak production has declined significantly in recent years. Six thousand five hundred elephants and near a 100,000 men are used in the timber industry.

The most important mineral is petroleum, though only a small percentage of the world's output ($\frac{1}{2}$ of 1%) is produced, it is an essential item in Burmese economy. She also produces welfram, lead and tin. But perhaps the republic is best known for its rubies. Its sapphires and jade find no equal elsewhere in the world.

. . . . THE PEOPLE

Each race of people envelopes numerous tribes with many a different tongue. Burmese is one of the languages of the Burma group. About 70% of the people of Burma speak one of the Burma group of languages. Burmese is monosyllabic, agglutinative and more closely allied to the Chinese than to the Indian language. This written language is the same all over the country, its spoken variations being due to differences in pronunciation. Burmese and English are the official languages. Hindustani is widely spoken wherever Indian labor is employed.

Most of the Burmans live in the southern part of the country. The Burmese tribes live in the north. Many of these tribes follow the same pattern of living they have known for hundreds of years. Up to a few years ago headhunting and slavery were still in existence. The Burmese, somewhat more civilized than the tribes, are described as a happy, easy-going people who take life as it comes and have no great ambition, but they are quick to resent injustice and have a strong feeling of natural independence.

They have brown skins and pleasant features, and chew betel nut which reddens and slowly destroys their teeth. Though this mars the personal appearance it does not create a serious health problem as does malaria, the No. 1 problem, which causes two-fifths of the total deaths.

The typical Burmese house has side walls of bamboo matting, a thatched roof, and a floor of sawed boards. It is usually erected on posts some five feet above the ground. The homes of the wealthier people are usually of the European type construction.

The principal article of diet for these people is rice, to which is added a curry of meat, vegetables and fish paste, all highly seasoned. Fresh fruit is available at almost all seasons.

The national costume worn even by city-bred Burmans is the longyi, a piece of cloth some five yards long which is wrapped around the hips and folded over in front to form a "skirt" reaching the ankles. A jacket or blouse is worn over the upper part of the body. Shoes and stockings are seldom worn but a loose-fitting turban is worn on the head of the men and an umbrella is carried by practically everyone, men and women alike. In Burma the women are freer and have a higher status than in any other oriental country.

State primary schools which are coeducational provide free education for children from six to eleven years of age. The medium of instruction is Burmese, with English a compulsory language above the fifth grade. Buddhist monasteries which exist in almost every village likewise provide facilities for learning. Middle and high schools are available but are not free. With the exception of Japan, Burma has the highest percentage of literacy among the Oriental nations.

The government supports Buddhism, although the constitution guarantees complete freedom for other religions. However, about 85% of the Burmese people are Buddhists who know nothing of the caste system. Their religion occupies a very large part of their lives. The spiritual head of every village is the yellow-robed monk and every village has its pagoda. The chief religious principle of the Burmese is to acquire merit toward Nirvana by good works done in this life. The bestowal of alms, offerings of rice to priests, the founding of a monastery, the erection of a pagoda or the building of a rest house for travellers are all works of religious merit. Christianity progresses very slowly among the Burmese in comparison to the response made by the Karens and many of the northern tribespeople. About 3% of the population is Christian, which includes most Europeans and some of the hill people.

In addition to the Burmese people there are a number of tribespeople found in Burma. One of the largest groups is the Shan tribe, also Buddhist, and resistant to the Gospel. There are other tribes besides the Shan which have their own States, such as Karen, Chin, Wa, Kachin, etc., and in several of these states there will be found more than one tribe.

.... THE MISSIONARY ....

Had it not been that a promise made in time of stress was faithfully kept, the story of the Lisu and Rawang churches of Christ might never have been written. For the prelude to the Burma work, read the section on missionary activity in China.

The move of the entire mission staff of Yunnan-Tibetan Christian Mission (later called North Burma Christian Mission) into Burma was the beginning of an entirely new phase of the work in Lisuland. Congregations had been established within Burma at Tiliwago as early as 1933, and the work recognized by the then British government. Though the work had been visited by missionaries at various times, there had been no resident missionary permanently located on the Burma side of the work. During the winter of 1945-46 Robert Morse spent eight months touring the congregations on the Burma side and holding short-term Bible schools. It was during these months that the first requests for teaching came from the Rawang people. As a result the first Rawang congregation was established at Wuning. Then, in December 1948, Miss Dorothy Sterling made a trip into Burma to hold more schools. With her was Anzie Morse, older sister of Drema and both adopted by the Morses. Later the next year Anzie contacted typhus and died, causing a great loss to the work. In 1949, missionaries began to arrive from the China side. Of these workers only the Robert Morses, and LaVerne, and Dorothy Sterling had residence permits. The others, David Reeses, Jane Kinnett, Isabel Dittemore and Mel Byers, were granted only temporary-stay permits which the government would not extend, thus they left Burma for other fields of service. Dorothy Sterling is now serving in Thailand.

In 1950 those who were in Hong Kong (the Eugene Morses, Drema and Mrs. J. Russell Morse) effected the printing of a new edition of the Lisu primers, and other much needed material. By mid-May of that year they were able to join the others up-country. Following the release from China's prisons, and a brief furlough in the States, brother J. Russell Morse joined his family in the labor in northern Burma in 1953.

Of primary importance to fulfill the purpose of this work is the reaching of the unreached with the good news of Christ. In the early days of the work in Burma, as in China, there were no trained preachers but the Gospel message was spread by new Christians who were anxious to serve the Lord. Their joy at being released from the powers of darkness knew no bounds, and they could not keep it to themselves. One out-standing characteristic of the Lisu and Rawang Christians is

110

their complete break with the old life and habits when they become Christians. As non-Christians they are chain-smokers of strong tobacco, and habitual drunkards, and they have no respect for women, but consider them as property to be bought and sold. When they become Christians they stop smoking and drinking entirely, and begin to keep themselves clean; they no longer swear or gamble or sell their daughters in marriage, even redeeming those whom they had sold when they were non-Christians.

Baptisms in Burma-China area.

Because of the great distances involved, the language problems, and local customs and beliefs, it is often more effective for native preachers to make the first contacts among new people. This makes the educational phase of the work a very urgent and important one, and one closely connected to the evangelistic movement. Gradually, as the work grew, young men attended a series of the Bible schools and became fulltime evangelists, not supported by the mission but by each congregation or group of congregations to which they ministered.

All teaching materials, such as texts, commentaries, maps, charts, devotional materials for these three-months schools were printed by the missionaries on the field.

In 1957 some especially trained evangelists entered the Kachin area to the south with a booklet in their language containing basic Christian teaching and twelve hymns. Here they found a people previously unreached, due to the language barrier.

In 1960 the churches sent four native preacher-missionaries to open up work with the Naga tribespeople, with fifty converts in the first two years. Robert Morse worked out a written language for them that they might have some of the Gospel in written form. He also reduced to writing the Lashi and Maru languages. Always there is the need of printed material in the various languages of the people of the different tribes.

As early as 1961 various sectors of northern Burma were closed to the missionaries, emphasizing again the importance of trained native leaders. By 1963 well over two hundred churches were established and over two hundred workers were serving the Lord. In that year there was insurrection and warfare in Burma, with racial tensions and anti-foreign nationalism.

The medical and teaching program continued but in 1966 the Morse families became isolated in a pocket on the India-Burma border—and no reports of their immediate work has since been available for publication.

However, LaVerne Morse, youngest son of the J. Russell Morses, who returned from Burma in 1964 has continued to assist in the work among these tribespeople in northern Burma, the Lisu, Rawang, Naga, and Kachin. When one door is closed, God often opens another door of opportunity. In 1966 the South East Asia Evangelizing Mission was established to produce Gospel broadcasts in the native languages, plus the mailing of Christian literature to the nearly 20,000 Christians in this area of Burma. Wonderful doors are opening!

Rawang tribespeople.

112

Radio would seem, at first, to be a very unlikely way to preach the Gospel to primitive tribespeople in the remote jungles and inaccessible canyons of Southeast Asia. Yet, within the past ten years, a tremendous technological revolution has taken place through the transistor radio in every country of Southeast Asia. Battery-operated transistor radios from Japan have become the status symbol of village chiefs and witch doctors, as well as of intellectuals, in Viet Nam, Laos, Thailand, Burma and India. Thousands of illiterates can listen to radio messages in their mother tongue.

The first Lisu-language Gospel broadcasts in history were transmitted from the facilities of the Far East Broadcasting Company in Manila, Philippines, the first part of May 1968. Enthusiastic responses have flooded in from many areas of Southeast Asia. A preacher in northern Burma wrote in late summer 1968 of the Lisu-language broadcasts being received in one area alone by about 10,000 Lisu and Rawang Christians. Large crowds gather to hear from a single radio in the villages.

Preachers at a Rawang village.

There are daily broadcasts now in Lisu and one-day-a week in the Rawang and Khasi languages, which reach into Burma, northeast India and Thailand. Blue Meo broadcasts are prepared for broadcasting into Thailand, Laos, North Viet Nam, and Communist China. The

113

Lisu, Rawang, and Blue Meo Christians who are preaching for these tapes are in Thailand where they are being trained by David Filbeck and LaVerne Morse, who visits there during the summer months. Plans include broadcasts for the Lahu and Yao tribes at a later date.

LaVerne Morse, who led in the establishment of the Putao Christian School in northern Burma in 1957, indicates that these Christian schools are the main factor in the spread of the Gospel in Burma today. Teachers were scarce in those days and most of the teaching was done by missionaries, but when they were forced to leave, the school graduates became the teachers in many newly-established primary schools. A network of about twenty-five schools developed throughout the jungles and mountains, serving two hundred villages with thousands of students enrolled each year. And although American missionaries are not allowed to work in the area, the cause of Christ is going forward because national Christian leadership has been and is being trained through an early and vigorous program of Christian education. The Bible is central in the curriculum, and through their learning-by-doing system of instruction they have improved not only the evangelism program, but the health, nutrition, and literacy in the villages.

Christian Day School, northern Burma.

So it is in the hands of these thus trained to take the Gospel to those who have not yet heard. Word has been received that Lisu Bibles have gotten through to the Christians in Burma. This will

114

be a great aid to them in their witnessing. This is the first time in history that the entire Bible has been available in the Lisu language. In previous years they did have the New Testament and Psalms, and Genesis. However, by 1964 practically all stocks of the New Testaments had been used up, so until this time they had had no means of obtaining any portion of the Scriptures in their own language. Seven thousand song books and two thousand Gospel Primers have also been printed. When the first two Bibles arrived, in their great rejoicing they said, "This is not by man's strength; it is because of God that this is possible. Therefore let us first of all thank God". Let us all rejoice, and thank Him!

China

"The middle Kingdom"

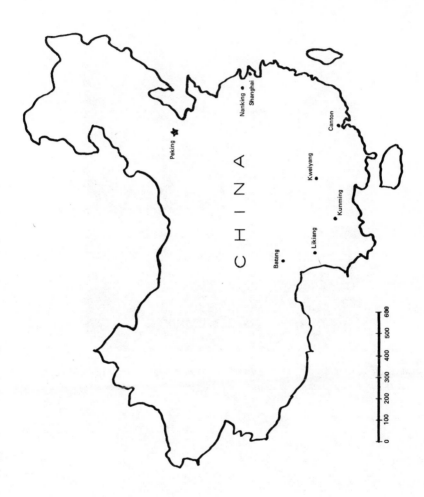

Canal water is used for washing of clothes, buckets, vegetables, and feet. Kunming, Yunnan Province.

THE LAND . . . .

The largest political sub-division of Asia, second largest of the world, China comprises the major part of the southeastern area of that continent. Its greatest length is 3,000 miles from east to west; its greatest breadth, 2,000 miles. It has been divided into three parts: (1) Outer China, which includes nine provinces of Manchuria, Inner Mongolia, the province of Sinkiang, and the special territory of Tibet; (2) The island of Formosa; (3) the area south of the great wall, or China proper. All areas but Formosa (Taiwan) had come under Communist control by 1950. China proper is only 36.5% of the whole area yet it has 86% of the entire population. It is one and a half times the size of the United States with three times the population, and more than one-fourth of the world's population. The Communist Chinese census of 1953 reported a population of near 580 million, excluding Taiwan. Estimates now place the figure over 700 million, with 41% of them under eighteen years of age.

The coastline of China, forming a somewhat irregular curve to the south, extends some 5,362 miles from the Yalu River to Tunghing. The coast is washed by three inner seas; the Yellow, the East and South China Seas, and is cut off from the Pacific by Japan, Ryukyu Islands and the Philippines.

The general slope of the land is from the high mountains of Sinkiang, Tibet and Mongolia in the west to the low coastal areas in the east. Tibet, "the roof of the world", has the highest area, a plateau with an average altitude of 13,000 to 14,000 feet. Sixty per cent of Greater China is over 6,000 feet elevation. Southern China, in contrast to the north, is a very mountainous and rugged region. Yunnan Province in the southwest of China proper is a plateau with an elevation of over 6,000 feet whose mountain ranges, contrary to the others, run in a north and south direction. In a general way this region corresponds to the Colorado Springs district of the United States. Translated, Yunnan means "south of the clouds". Kunming, its capital, enjoys one of the few flat areas in the province.

China lies almost entirely in the temperate zone but due to its position it enjoys the coolest climate for its latitude in the world. The size alone would indicate the many differences in climate and temperatures, that would occur. In the winter, days are bright and cloudless in the north and west but in the Yangtze Valley and the south the winters are warm and oftimes humid, with heavy rainfall on the southeast coastline. In Yunnan Province where the elevation is high, snow falls a few days out of the year and winds are strong. The

119

heat and high humidity makes China south of the Yangtze uncomfortable in summer and even the north has hot but short summers.

China has always been an agricultural country. Three-fourths of the population are farmers. Most of the land before Communist invasion was parcelled out among small peasant proprietors. By 1965, 99% of the peasant households had been collectivized into "communes", which averaged 5,000 households each. Almost all the cultivable land is now tilled, even the hillsides are often terraced to the hilltops. Chinese farming is highly intensive, much like our gardening. Most of the land is worked with broad hoes. The size of the population gives plenty of workers for every menial task for men cost less than draft animals. However, water buffalo, found extensively in south and central China, are used for heavy labor. A small-type variety of horse is likewise used in several of the southern provinces.

As many crops are raised as the climate will permit; in the south, three a year, but only one in the north. Crop-growing season varies from a year in the south to eight to nine months in the Yangtze Valley, while only four months in Tibet. Some crop rotation is practiced but the Chinese farmer largely relies on continuous manuring, using human excrement, canal mud, burned lime, and almost any sort of organic material that is obtainable. Even with the long growing seasons and the production they do have, China cannot produce enough to feed her multiplying millions. Rice is the important crop in the south, wheat in the north. In Yunnan Province excellent peaches, pears, apricots and persimmons are grown. The Yangtze and Yellow River valleys are the chief producers of cotton which ranked third among the world's cotton growers.

Only three domesticated animals are of importance: pigs, sheep and goats. Cattle are raised in small number for Moslems and foreigners to eat.

China is a land of flowers. Those derived from the country itself are azaleas, camellias, gardenias, peonies and "mums".

For centuries waterways have been a leading means of transportation in China. It is covered by a network of roads, many amounting to little more than footpaths. In 1948 China had 81,966 miles of roads and about 75,000 non-military vehicles. There was likewise at this time 8,120 miles of railways in operation which is a poor supply for the size of the country. Since Communist occupation much formerly unused track was placed back in use. At this same time there were ninety-seven airplanes for civil aviation with air routes covering 55,000 miles. But perhaps a truer picture of China's means of travel would be in the horse and man-drawn carts, rickshaws, junks and sampans.

Generally it may be said that the Chinese are a round-headed race, with a rather low forehead, a broad and flat nose, large mouth, small chin and prominent cheekbones. The hair is invariably black and lank. The iris of the eye is more or less black, and the eye itself is narrow and almond-shaped in appearance due to the eye-fold. The average stature is short except in the north. The hands and feet are generally small. The color of the skin varies from pale yellow to dark brown.

The Chinese are tops in practical ability and shrewd common sense, but are inferior in logic and abstract reasoning. The faculty of memory is highly developed. Their temperament is high strung and excitable but they have unusual ability to control outward expression, and are extremely polite. They are largely thrifty and industrious and respectful of authority. They are a people who like to laugh and be happy and play games at which they are very adept. Home life is important and families are closely bound together. However, it is quite certain that these latter conditions will have been changed considerably under Communist rule.

There is a general similarity of dress in all of China. Men's dress consists of a loose-fitting jacket and loose pair of trousers. Over this a long coat fastened down the side may be worn. Women's dress is similar to men's, especially for the laboring class. The practice of footbinding, which indicated the mother's authority and supreme rule over her daughter, is dying out. Hats are worn by the working class to protect them from the sun.

There are two principal meals in the day and except in the north rice is the staple at each, served with a little pork or fish and vegetables. Bean curd is a very common food while delicacies are bird's nest soup, bamboo shoots, and preserved eggs. Green tea, without cream or sugar, is the universal drink. It is not uncommon to see a business man drink from the spout of his own little individual teapot.

There is a large "floating" population who make their homes on boats along the coasts and larger navigable rivers. A well-to-do Chinese dwelling consists of about four buildings enclosing a courtyard. As a rule they are one-storied with walls of wood except for the outer wall which is made of bricks. Shops are open to the streets and are closed at night by shutter doors. However, the great masses live in dire poverty and in time of famine die by the millions, unnoticed but by a few. They live in homes of wattle daubed with clay or of sun-baked bricks which when exposed to the elements for a period of time will crumble and fall, only to be replaced again. Floors are merely pounded earth. Windows are scarce and usually covered with paper.

Chinese is one of the major languages and the oldest living one of the world. The Chinese syllable has a simple phonetic structure but speaking or understanding the language is made more difficult by the four tones normally used. Mandarin is the official language but the dialects vary with every section even though they are written identically the same.

The Chinese have always held learning in great respect, yet teaching and the upkeep of schools were left largely to private initiative thus China was slow to educate the mass of its people. The influence of Christian missionaries, the example of Japan, and reports from Chinese who studied abroad made themselves felt. In 1905 a new government school system was planned. Many advancements were made until in 1951 when the Communists took over private institutions of higher learning and reorganized them under the State. Emphasis was placed on elementary schools, training of political workers and technical education. College programs were shortened to supply the demand for administrators and technicians.

It is said that China has three main religions: Confucianism, Taoism, and Buddhism, but little distinction is drawn between them for they ofttimes combine several systems without being aware of doing it. Most Chinese believe in the animation of the universe with evil and good spirits, and in ancestor worship which was the oldest source of their philosophy of life, and in many gods, some imported.

Popular Taoism is now a system of demonology and magic while Confucianism can hardly be regarded as a religion at all, but rather as a code of morals and political wisdom derived from the writings of Confucius and his followers. Since the Communists took power, Confucianism has been virtually wiped out on the mainland. Taoism is of Chinese origin but influenced greatly by Buddhism which reached China from India during the first century and was more powerful than Taoism but began to decline at the close of the T'ang dynasty. Mohammedanism has around 50,000,000 adherents, found mostly in the northwest and southwest (Kansu and Yunnan). Of the non-Chinese people, the Tibetans and Mongols are almost solidly Buddhists, adherents of one or another of the Lamaistic forms of that faith. Most of the people of Sinkiang are Moslems. Christianity was introduced by Nestorian missionaries under the T'ang dynasty (618-907). The Jesuits reached Canton in the 16th century while Protestant missions date back to 1807. Before the Communists came into power Roman Catholicism had an estimated 4,000,000 followers, and Protestantism, 1,000,000. As early as 1949 foreigners began to leave and in 1951 six hundred missionaries left. Those remaining were forcibly held and often persecuted, among them J. Russell Morse who was in Yunnan Province.

Many churches and temples were converted into museums and exhibition halls as Communism began an attempt to destroy Christianity and the Confucian culture whose emphasis was on the family system with its ancestral worship.

A new China is beginning to come out of the ancient ways and conditions of old China. Only the tomorrows will tell what her future will be.

. . . . THE MISSIONARY . . . .

The story of direct-support missions in China begins back in October 1926 when Brother and Sister J. Russell Morse severed their connections with the *United Christian Missionary Society,* under which they had first come to the China-Tibetan border in 1921. Having completed their 5-year term which had been agreed upon, they stepped out on faith, trusting the Lord to supply all their needs, hoping to begin a new work among Tibetans. But their new venture soon met with what to some people might have seemed failure, for, because of political conditions, all Americans were ordered out of that part of China by the American government in the spring of 1927.

In early May, 1927, the Morse family (now with two sons) and two other families started the long walk across the "Hump" to Burma, a journey which was to take them seventy days through trackless jungle. Clearing their trails as they went and facing numerous dangers, they trusted the Lord to bring them safely to their destination. The area through which they passed was inhabited by primitive, ignorant, unlovely tribespeople; the Lisu and Daru. But unattractive as they appeared, still their need for Christ was so great that the Morses were greatly burdened for them. So they prayed, promising the Lord that if He would bring them safely through their hazardous journey they would return to the mission field.

They did return to the mission field in 1929, still hoping to work among the Tibetans, but once again political troubles kept them from the work they planned. Instead, they settled in the Chinese-Tibetan village of Yea Chi, in the Mekong Valley of Northwest Yunnan Province. There they engaged in language study and evangelistic work, and also started a Christian school. Attention was called again to the Lisu in 1930 when a Lisu Christian came to the Morses requesting literature to use in teaching his own people about Christ.

The Lisu people responded eagerly and soon the requests for literature and teaching were coming in more rapidly than could be met. Congregations of Lisu Christian were established not only in the Mekong Valley but also over the mountain pass in the Salween Valley. By 1933 the gospel had been carried into still a third valley, this time in Burma. The gospel message was not carried by trained preachers or evangelists, for there were none at this time. Instead, it was new Christians who carried the message everywhere when visiting, trading or working.

The increased number of Christians needed more teaching and the Morses met the need as best they could while carrying on the work at Yea Chi. They were reluctant to leave the work but due to Tibetan invasion in early 1939 they were forced to leave, so they settled in the Lisu village of Tobalo, still in the Mekong Valley. However, having made one move that year they did not feel they could move all their belongings again so soon. But in the fall of that year a flood destroyed their home and most of their belongings. So they did move again, this time into the Salween Valley.

They were laboring here when the war with Japan came, and were cut off from the outside world, both as to communications and supplies. Those war years were a time of physical hardship and sacrifice, but of great spiritual blessings. All their sacrifices were more than repaid by the joy of seeing the number of Christians grow from 2,000 in 1940 to more than 6,000 in 1946.

During those years also, the size of the mission staff had been increased by the coming of several associates. When the Morses returned to the field after their furlough in 1937, they were accompanied by new recruits, Harold Taylor and Isabel Maxey. In 1944, in spite of the war, it was possible for Miss Dorothy Sterling to join them on the field. This was largely due to the great medical needs and the fact that Miss Sterling was a registered nurse. In 1945 Isabel (Maxey) Dittemore returned to the field with her husband, Warren, little thinking that in less than a year he would lay down his life in the Master's work. He contracted typhus and died in July 1946, and was buried in the Salween Valley, the land of the people he so dearly loved. In 1946, also, Miss Jane Kinnett and the David Reeses arrived in Kunming, Yunnan Province, remaining there for language study before going on up to the Lisuland work.

When the Morse family left the United States in the fall of 1948 to return once again to China, they had added two new members, in the persons of the brides of Eugene and Robert Morse, both of whom had married that year. In addition, there were two other new workers,

Miss Imogene Williams and Miss Lora Banks, coming out for their first term of service.

The Harold Taylors, with the Harry Randolphs and Mel Byers, were working in the central portion of the main city of Kunming. The C. W. Callaway family, not able to enter Burma on a permanent visa, were laboring near the Morse family in the village of Shang Hsipa, while Bill and Melba Rees were conducting classes and services in the village to the east.

Flannelgraph used in village evangelism.

Other workers have included the Edgar Nichols, Norton Bares, Vernon Newlands, Ellis Backs, and Miss Gladys Schwake who have labored at various periods among the tribes along the Tibetan border.

Outside those in Yunnan Province and along the Tibetan border there was only one other family spreading New Testament Christianity in China. The Rolland Sjodins were in Kweichan Province carrying the saving message of a loving Lord.

The year 1949 was a fateful one for China, for it was that year that the Communists took over the whole of the great country of China. Of the group that sailed in the fall of 1948 only the Robert Morses reached the mission station in Lisuland. The Eugene Morses were turned back by the Communists and went out to Hong Kong with Mrs. J. Russell Morse and Drema, Morses' adopted Tibetan daughter. The Harry Randolphs and the Harold Taylors left the work in central Kunming, Miss Williams and Miss Banks also left Kunming, the former going with the Callaways to open a new field in Thailand, the latter to the States where she became Imogene Williams' forwarding secretary and with her interest still in missions, the author of this book. The Bill Reeses entered the open door of Africa to continue work among the Chinese people.

That year also LaVerne Morse and Mel Byers went from Kunming up to and across a portion of Tibet, and thence southward into the Salween Valley, hoping to be of some assistance to the other workers there. Finding that all the others had safely made their way over into Burma, the two young men made the long trek across the mountains, reaching the mission station in Burma in the spring of 1950.

Chinese evangelists, James (left) and brother Yin (right).

Remaining in Kunming with the Chinese Christians, Brother J. Russell Morse saw a great ingathering of souls. In the first year following the exodus of the missionaries there were 220 converts baptized, one new congregation established and thriving, and a fifth congregation well started. Brother Morse ministered as best he could to the medical and spiritual needs of all the Christians there, with the assistance of some of the Chinese leaders. He was imprisoned March 22, 1951 and held under punishment and solitary confinement for 14 months before his final release in June 1952, a release that many believe to be in direct answer to prayer.

Rolland Sjodin also remained at his post until imprisoned by the Communists, and was released in 1953 after being under three years of Red rule.

And thus it was that the doors of China were closed. Chinese Christians are being persecuted for their faith, and writing a testimony of "suffering as a Christian" that will be a thrilling story when known.

Hong Kong

"Fragrant Harbor"

THE LAND . . . .

Hong Kong is a British colony on the southeast coast of China. It consists of three parts. One, the island of Hong Kong, with 29 square miles on which is situated the colony's capital, Victoria, was ceded to Great Britain in 1841. The second part, Kowloon Peninsula, a low-lying tip of the mainland, was ceded in 1860. In 1898 Britain leased the third section for 99 years—the New Territories are a largely mountainous extension of China's Kwangtung Province.

About 80% of the colony's total area is wasteland; 14% is cultivated, leaving 6% to contain one of the world's highest population densities. Hong Kong's population passed three million in 1960 and continues to rise. The estimated population in 1965 was 3,804,000.

Hong Kong's greatest natural asset is its deep water harbor, sheltered from typhoons and capable of accommodating the largest ships. Hong Kong originally owed its prosperity to its function as a center for the collection and distribution of goods, and it was highly dependent on its trade with China. However, now domestic manufacturers furnish the bulk of the colony's exports. In 1963 the U.S. bought 26% by value of the total exports. After textile manufacturing the colony's biggest money-maker was tourism. Visitors throng to this "floating market" in increasing numbers.

The climate of Hong Kong is subtropical, governed by the monsoons. The average temperature is 72 degrees F—annual rainfall, 85 inches. The mean relative humidity exceeds 80% in the summer.

Apart from snakes, lizards, frogs and a few wild deer, monkeys, boars, and an occasional tiger or leopard on the mainland, the animal life of the colony is domestic, comprised principally of poultry, pigeons, pigs and cattle.

. . . . THE PEOPLE

Hong Kong's setting is often breathtakingly beautiful. Luxurious homes and apartment buildings jut out from the Island's steep green sides. However, most of its people, probably 80%, live in or around the colony's two downtown sections. Hong Kong has always been a haven for Chinese seeking refuge from poverty, war, or political unrest; thus well over one million have entered the area since the Communist conquest of China in 1949. For years the refugees were not only living in long-standing slums, but on sidewalks, in doorways, on stairways, in tiny hovels in alleys or on steep hillsides, and on tenement roofs. From 1954-1964 the government built low-cost housing for more than 700,000, with plans to resettle others through the forthcoming years. Meanwhile this overflow of people presents all kinds of problems. Rents are higher than in most other places in the world, the average workman pays from 25-45% of his wages in rent.

Education, for instance, is neither free, compulsory, nor adequate, but it is expanding. More than half of the 2,184 schools of 1964 were without government aid. Low-cost medical services, although insufficient, are increasing. Charitable and missionary institutions operate twenty-five private hospitals. The island's most serious social problem is narcotics, particularly heroin. In the low-income group, it is estimated that one-third of the male population over the age of fifteen is addicted.

Ninety-eight percent of the Colony's people are of Chinese descent; thus a great variety of Chinese languages and dialects is spoken but the Cantonese dialect is universally understood. A large number of fishing families live on their boats; in 1961 the boat population was 138,320.

The main religion is Buddhism, but Christian denominations are well represented and there are small groups of Muslims.

. . . . THE MISSIONARY . . . .

Through the years missionaries came and went through Hong Kong and impressions were made by the witness given, but no one stayed long enough to leave a lasting work until the Bill Rees family came to begin a work in Kowloon in 1963. Their earlier years of missionary experience took them from the China mainland, when the Communists came in, to South Africa where they witnessed to Chinese and others in Kimberley. With these years of experience in the language and customs of the Chinese people it was only natural that they would see the open door of Hong Kong.

Schools appear to be the best method of reaching people for Christ in Hong Kong. Daily Bible teaching is not only allowed but encouraged in the schools. Homes that are otherwise closed to the missionary are friendly when the children are enrolled in the mission school. Teachers also learn through required attendance at services.

The Education Department of the government, unable to provide adequate schooling for Hong Kong's growing population, continues to offer assistance and encouragement to those interested in starting schools. There are opportunities for opening schools in newly developed areas with an 80% loan from the government. The schools become self-supporting even though the tuition fees charged are quite small.

Shu Chen Li, a native Chinese, began a primary school in the Wong Tai Sin Resettlement Area that has over seven hundred pupils now, and is greatly in need of permanent quarters. Brother Li formed the Christian Education Association of the Orient in an effort to get more Christian Day Schools started in Hong Kong. Effort is also being made to establish a Secondary School when funds and helpers are available. Such a school is needed to counteract the influence of the Communist and Catholic schools. Hong Kong's young people are more interested in a good education than perhaps anything else. English is the key to better jobs or entrance into a University. A six-story, 24-classroom building, by using two sessions, could handle 2,000 students in such a school.

In April 1968 brother Li became very seriously ill and following tests his condition was listed as cancer of the liver. The Reeses assumed responsibility for the school work in the weeks he was unable to be at work. However, the Lord had need of brother Li, for a time at least, and by July 1968 he was back at work. The Doctors have since changed their diagnosis but life expectancy is still poor due to his diseased heart and lungs.

Besides assisting in the school program, the Reeses are doing personal evangelism and conducting an English service, working partly among the children of the British military and other official families. Though this latter part of the work is small, the list of contacts grow and new classes are being planned. Their son, Ben, will go to Hong Kong in the summer of 1969, for a year, so that they may leave their work for a furlough in the States.

The Wayfull Jew family arrived in Hong Kong in February 1969 to assist in the school program. They are finding a place of service as they learn the language.

India

"Land of the Himalayas"

THE LAND . . . .

Like a giant kite undivided India lies open for flight in Southern Asia, occupying more than 1,500,000 square miles, equal in area and population to the whole of Europe, excluding the U.S.S.R. The largest majority of the population lives within the arc enclosed by the mountain wall; one fifth of the world's population. The 1966 census showed that over four hundred and eighty million people exist in this country. More than 80% of the people in 1961 still lived in villages, averaging one hundred families per village.

South of the mountain wall, across whose borders no railways go, lie the east and west sections of the Hindustan Plain with the dividing zone near Delhi, and the penisular India which is sub-divided into the coastal plains and the plateau. Most of the area is under a tropical regime except for the mountain country and the extreme northwest region. Practically all the subcontinent's rainfall comes from the monsoon, whose occasional failure causes periodical famines to which the country is liable. The total amount of rainfall varies from 20 to 457 inches per year; but most of the desert areas receive less, having to irrigate to support any crop agriculture at all. India is predominately dependent upon agriculture for its economic existence. Government programs, which include bringing unused land under cultivation and expanding irrigation, increased farmland by 1963 to 45% of India's total land area.

One-third of the world's rice is grown in India. It is the second largest producer of cotton. The world's supply of jute is derived almost wholly from the two Bengals. Tea, found largely in the eastern state of Assam, has become the chief product of European capital. The oil fields of India are likewise found in the most-eastern State. With all of this, and more, India should be the richest country in the world, and yet the average yearly income of the Indian wage-earner only a few years ago was from eighteen to twenty-four U.S. dollars.

Much of the natural vegetation is no longer evident due to intensive cultivation, however brushwood jungles occupy portions of central Bengal, while west of Calcutta is a region of scrub jungle. Tropical forests cover much of the highland country and coconut palms are typical on the coastal dunes of Malabar. Various wild animals abound. The leopard is found in all parts of India. Elephants are found only in remote hill sections, in greatest numbers at the Assam-Burma border. It is interesting to note that all salt water fish are poisonous.

There is actually no single description that will fit all of India, for each individual section has its own remarkable story to unfold.

. . . . THE PEOPLE

Four language families are represented here, two of which are found outside of India (Indo-European and Tibeto-Burman) and two that are unknown elsewhere (Dravidian and Mundo).

The modern Indo-Aryan of the Indo-European family includes a large number of languages, most of them with many dialects which run into one another without well-marked boundaries. Perhaps the one spoken by the largest number of people would be Hindi, which became a literary language in the 17th century. As Hindi, in its Devanagan written form, (High Hindi) it is an official language of the Republic of India. As Urdu, written in Persian script, it is an official language of Pakistan. But as spoken by many it is simply called the Hindustani.

The Dravidian family of languages prevails in the peninsula south of the above family. The Mundo family is spoken by five million of the economically primitive people throughout Central India. The Tibeto-Burman is represented by several hundred languages, each with a small number of speakers, in the Himalayan ranges and hills of Assam. The Naga dialect is spoken most widely in Assam, though the isolated language of Khasis is also spoken there by more than 230,000 people. And with this variety of languages comes distinct varieties of people and habits.

The inhabitants of northwestern India are very different from those of the south or east. Those dwelling in the northwest are tall and straight in body and warlike in character, and from this group comes about 80% of the volunteer army of India. The plainsmen of Bengal are peace-loving and industrious and from this area and that to the south come the leaders of Indian art, literature and politics.

Most of the people of India are poor, and their clothing, food and home comforts are of the simplest nature. It is impossible to give any general description of the dress of the country, so widely does it vary, but for the most part it is picturesque and fitted for a hot climate. White is a favorite color. Though many of India's women remain veiled, much of the seclusion of women is being foregone for greater freedom.

Vegetables are grown everywhere and are used widely in the ordinary diet. Cultivated fruits are prevalent and spices are an essential element in the Indian diet. Tumeric and chillies are in universal use and cultivated everywhere. Throughout the whole of India horned cattle are the only beasts used for ploughing.

The chief means of travel, especially during the rainy season, is by bullock cart. The ekka, a two-wheeled cart drawn by pony, is used yet even in large cities to augment street cars, automobiles and buses.

One thing held in common by the masses of the Indian population is poor health facilities and a high rate of illiteracy. Because of the death-killing famines and the health conditions the average life expectancy was twenty-seven years, however, due to new controls on epidemic diseases, this rate has now gone up to fifty years (1965). Few doctors are available for the bulk of the population living outside city limits. The establishment of mother-and-child health centers, maternity wards, and nurses' training centers have been given priority in the health programs set up by the government.

Free and compulsory education has been virtually nonexistent. However, during the early sixties free universal education was introduced for the age group, six-eleven years, and the total number of pupils attending schools is expected to rise to about 65 million. In 1966 nearly 70% of the total population was still illiterate, though the British established Universities and the government supported hundreds of high schools as well as elementary schools. Among the principal changes in the educational system were: the introduction of education through work in the elementary stages; vocational courses and improved teaching of science in the secondary stages; the establishment of multi-purpose secondary schools and the expansion of science teaching facilities at the University level. The missions also have a large number of primary, elementary and approximately one hundred fifty secondary schools, as well as schools for special training in the technical fields.

Though divorce is legalized it is seldom practiced. Marriage ordinarily occurs early, betrothals arranged even earlier, and is for life.

Like its people and its languages, the religions of India present the utmost variety. According to legend, Christianity was brought to India by the apostle Thomas. By the 4th and 5th century a Syrian sect existed in Cochin. Protestant missionaries came in the 17th century.

Over 300,000,000 of the people are Hindus; the Moslems number around 95,000,000, the largest percentage of which are in Pakistan, northwest and eastern Bengal. Those embracing Christianity number more than eight million, of which two-fifths are Roman Catholic.

The remainder of the population are Sikhs, Jains, Buddhists, Parsis, Jews, animists and other various groups. Over one and a half million are following tribal religions. The oldest of these smaller groups is animism which represents the beginning of religion in India.

Because Hinduism affects the life of the major portion of the subcontinent of India we shall describe it briefly here. It is a total way of life, including social order, law, science, literature and art. It has no formal creed, no standardized cult practice, no controlling ecclesiastical organization. Conceptions of deity vary, largely due to the intellectual level of the people. Worship is usually individual, not congregational. They believe in rebirth, the state of which is determined by the person's deeds in his earlier life. Escape from this cycle constitutes salvation. Hindus use images freely in their worship as comprehensible symbols of a deity which has no form apprehensible by human senses. The most obvious characteristics of the ordinary Hindu are that he worships a plurality of gods, looks upon a cow as a sacred animal, regards certain rivers as holy, and accepts Brahmanical supremacy and the caste system. The classes most receptive to Christianity are those who are outside the Hindu system, or whom Hinduism regards as degraded.

Despite the poverty and misery to be seen on every hand, India keeps its romantic aspect as a land veiled, withdrawn, never to be wholly understood by the people of the West.

. . . . THE MISSIONARY . . . .

Assam is a strategic mission field in free India. It is politically important to the countries it borders—Bhutan, Burma, China, India, Pakistan and Tibet. The boundaries are not fixed, and the population varies. There could be no greater challenge to a Christian than to make the Gospel known to so great a representation of the world's people as this.

A glance back in the history of the work in Assam shows how a man with vision and courage went out to start a movement that changed the thoughts and lives of people who, before this time, had no knowledge of Christianity in all its purity. This man, Rajani Roy Kharkhongir, a Khasi tribesman, learned that a person does not have to have the creeds of men to worship the Lord. He learned that sprinkling is not baptism, and that the early church had the Lord's Supper every Lord's Day, though he was taught differently by other religious groups. Other fellow-ministers would not join him in this position, but believing that others should know of the "new light", he set out on his mission. That was some forty years ago.

Others did come and follow the Word of God and it only. After years of lonely living and preaching, missionaries came; men like Ben

140

Schiller, then a missionary in Bilaspur, India, and Edgar Nichols, a refugee from Tibet and the Communists. There were eleven congregations with about 1,000 Christians when the Nichols reached the field. Finally the Archie Fairbrother family came in November 1951, followed by the David Rees family in 1953. The latter two families formed the Assam Indian Mission Churches of Christ.

Brother Kharkhongir's desire to reach the Khasi people first, then out to others has been partially fulfilled in Assam itself, because in the church in Assam you can find Nepalese, Chinese, Tibetans, Mikir, Hindustans, and Karens, as well as the Khasis, who have the greatest number of Christians.

When the Fairbrothers came to the Khasi Hills they explained that they did not have the ability to cure the sick, nor the money to feed the poor and the orphans. One of the leading men answered, "We did not ask you to come here to do these things for us, we want to know more about the Word of God".

Chances for all to learn were presented to young and old alike. A Christian Day School was started in Mawlai, a suburb of Shillong, the capital. Similar schools were soon started in other villages. In them the Bible is taught each day as well as other subjects which are recognized by the government of India.

When the Reeses arrived in the Khasi Hills they immediately went to work assisting the Fairbrothers in the school and evangelistic work. Because of the extreme ill health of Mrs. Fairbrother, she and the family returned to the States in 1954 for medical help. (Mrs. Fairbrother is the daughter of Dr. and Mrs. N. H. Bare who spent over a decade in West China on the Tibetan border.)

Manual training classes were added by David Rees to the class work in the school at Mawlai. Eventually this day school was recognized by the Indian government, though it receives no money since it was to remain a Christian Day School. Besides the regular school work, worker-training schools were held periodically for teachers and workers. Gospel teams, under the Reeses' direction, helped in village evangelism.

In answer to the needs of more definite training, a Bible college was started in 1958. The beginning enrollment was five, but two students dropped out; one for more language study, the other to support his family. Of the other three, one was the daughter of the early pastor, brother Kharkhongir, who worked among her own people, the Khasi. The second was a Naga boy who resigned a government position to study at the school. The third student was Philip J. Ho, who had been on the field the longest, having come in about 1950.

He is Tibetan-Chinese, having been educated earlier by Gladys Schwake in Tibet and in Kunming, China. He helped Mel Byers and LaVerne Morse on part of their trek across the "hump", and assisted the Ellis Back family in their awful flight from Communism.

Phillip became an invaluable aid to the mission. He spoke both Tibetan and Chinese fluently, with fair English and some Hindi. He also had good command of the Khasi language for his medical work that he began in 1953. He passed his compounders exam in January 1956 and worked for several years with the government hospital in Shillong. The mission dispensary is a good instrument for winning the friendship of the people and showing them the way to the Great Physician.

Recovering from illnesses that forced them to leave the field in 1954, the Archie Fairbrother family flew back to work in the summer of 1957. Because of an old knee injury, brother Fairbrother was advised to avoid any situations which involved any climbing or much walking, so they settled in a new location on the plains at the base of the Khasi Hills. Much of their work then was in translating materials for use in their teaching program, while the Reeses assumed the major portion of village evangelism.

Teachers of the Middle English and High School.

In 1965 the Middle English School began expanding into a high school. The Reeses pioneered in a new "walking Bible School" in

142

the spring of 1967, assisted by the Bible students. On the three week-ends it was conducted they reached nine villages, with a total of eleven baptisms in five of the villages. Three new churches were to be established. Workers were challenged to give more of themselves in service; discouraged church members reconsecrated their lives. Also working in this venture was Joy Evans, a niece of Lois Rees, who labored in Assam for one year while David was on furlough. In this area where they served there are at least forty-five congregations meeting regularly and there have been approximately 3,000 baptisms since 1951.

In late January of 1968 the Fairbrothers and Reeses were given a 30-day notice to leave Assam, being falsely accused of "political activity". Due to the immediate educational needs of their children, the Fairbrothers returned to the States. They are now engaged in teaching duties at Kakota Bible College. The Rees family was granted a 30-day extension in which to get everything ready for their departure and prepare the people for the seeming necessary separation. They were able to clear the missionaries of all charges of political action before their extension ran out. They were granted permission to go to Madras, India where they are now assisting the Art Morris family in training local leadership for the indigenous churches in southern India.

In late August of 1968 Warren Rees, son of David and Lois Rees, was able to visit the Assam churches to confer with them concerning Gospel music and sermons in the native language to be aired from the Philippines. These Khasi broadcasts began near the end of 1968 and will be a powerful instrument in winning to Christ many others of the 295,000 Khasi tribes-people. This is in connection with the *Southeast Asia Evangelizing Mission* operated by LaVerne Morse. Emrys Rees and Bnasan Uriah do much of the taping at Minnesota Bible College where they are presently students. This means of teaching and strengthening the nationals is all the more urgent if Indian government policy continues to order missionaries out of the country.

Phillip Ho, who in the mid-60's came to the States to further his education, met and married Margaret Cook in 1966. They arrived back on the field in December 1966. They were not affected by the government's order to leave since Phillip re-entered India on a Compounder's visa. Thus his major work must be with the medical dispensary. However, they assist as needed in the work of the youth and teaching. Margaret has been teaching in the preacher-training school. At least for a year they were attempting to keep the primary and secondary schools open. Most of the 40-some churches of the

143

Khasi and Jaintia Hills are carrying on, a few with some progress. No one knows what the future holds but the Lord will make possible for His Word to be continued to be spread, by some means, among the Khasi.

The *Central Provinces India Mission of Churches of Christ* is a mission of evangelism. Its aim since the beginning in 1928 has been to establish churches after the New Testament pattern through the conversion of non-believers, and the leading of those who imperfectly believe by expounding to them the way of the Lord more perfectly.

Harry and Mrs. Emma Schaefer (who were missionaries first under the *Christian Women's Board of Missions,* then the *United Christian Missionary Society,* from 1913-1927 in India) stepped out on faith in 1928, returning to India to begin work at the railway area of Bilaspur. This became the center of their work, and the base from which later expansion began.

In 1935 the Bilaspur Children's Home was started for destitute and needy children. By 1956 it had grown to the extent that it had three hostels, two for girls and one for boys, housing over two hundred children. The effectiveness of the Home is seen in the many leaders in the churches who were once in the Home.

In 1937 a middle school, which later became a full-fledged High School accredited by the government, and two primary schools were started. Over 1,000 students were taught in the mission schools in 1957. In 1937 also the Bible Seminary enrolled its first students.

Efforts in the first ten years were concentrated on village itinerant evangelism, using the center at Rantanpur, or tents pitched elsewhere, to preach the Gospel to hundreds of surrounding villages. Each year the Lord added to the church.

In 1939, Marion Schaefer, daughter of the Harry Schaefers, completed her education in the States and came to Bilaspur. In 1941, Harry, Jr. came to the field for a period of service.

On April 20, 1946, Harry Schaefer, Sr. was called home from the battle fronts of the mission field and was laid to rest in Calcutta. Later that year, Harry Schaefer, Jr. returned again to the field. With him this time was his bride, Lillie Belle.

Mission expansion necessitated more missionary personnel, so for six months while in language study and six months on the field itself (1946-47), O. D. Johnson, Mrs. Leah Moshier and Miss Dolly Chitwood were affiliated with the Mission.

In the spring of 1948 Bernel and Joan Getter arrived and after language studies they moved to Katni and led the work there. In August 1948, the Ben Schillers arrived at Bilaspur to be president of the Bible Seminary. He also had charge of the schools and hostels while the Harry Schaefers were on furlough. In the spring of 1951, their particular mission fulfilled, the Schillers returned to a ministry in the States.

In 1950 Laurabel Samson came to India to take charge of the office work and do children's work. Eventually she managed the Children's Home for many years in the absence of Mrs. Emma Schaefer.

Don and Eleanor Davis arrived in India in May 1954. After language school, which is essential for every foreign worker, they came to Bilaspur and, while continuing Hindi study, began leading in the English-speaking church services among the Anglo-Indians and teaching in the Bible Seminary. In 1956 Don was elected chairman of the new work of New Testament Publications, which was an effort to have more printed helps available for the churches. This type of work is found advantageous in this field. Until their furlough in 1959, Don directed the High School and Primary School program, as well as manage the home for orphans and under-privileged boarding students.

The Ben Schillers were denied a re-entry permit to come and take over leadership in the High School, and the Davies could not re-enter in 1960 either.

Having served for five years at Maudha (India), the William Rolands came to Bilaspur on their return from furlough in 1954. The school for preachers at Maudha and the Bilaspur Seminary combined into the Central Bible Seminary and William Roland became the President. The school has since re-opened in Madras, in south India. In the 1960 school year the Rolands worked with the Woodstock School in Landour, Mussoorie. At present they are in the States furthering their education.

Two of the newer fields to be opened in the area are the Sarguja and Orissa District. In 1951, while living in Katni, the Bernel Getters went to the Sarguja area. With ten preachers, they entered the previously forbidden territory of Sarguja and proclaimed, for the first time in this area, God's plan for the redemption of mankind. It was one of the more backward areas of the whole of India, and reports of human sacrifice were not uncommon. Their religious background is entirely different from the Hindu and Muslims, for they are animists and do not believe in life after death. On the Getters' return from furlough in 1954 they moved into the city of Sitapur, in the Sarguja District. From that time until their new bungalow was completed in 1956 they lived out of trunks, in tents, most of the time. This enabled them to carry on the evangelistic efforts in this area. The

145

Tom Rashes, from the Kulpahar area, assisted in the Sarguja District evangelism in 1959.

In 1952 a Macedonian call came from Orissa that could not be resisted by the Harry Schaefers. Their time was so full with supervising the evangelism of the countless number of villages and the middle and primary schools at the home base that it seemed impossible to expand in yet another section. But nine months after the "call" was received, they went to preach. The Lord supplied every need as they took advantage of this glorious opportunity. The Schaefers settled at Bargarh in the midst of the Orissa churches to make it easier for them to work in this area that begins 215 miles from Bilaspur. Within a little less than four years there were five evangelistic centers and eighty fulltime workers. In their efforts they reached over one hundred miles from where it began at the border of Orissa. The Harry Schaefers returned to the States on furlough in 1958. After five major attempts to gain re-entry into India it was apparent the door was closed to them. However, the Schaefer's witness to the Hindu is not over. In August 1960 they entered Bangkok, Thailand to open a complete new area in the witnessing to the Hindi there. They served there for four years. In 1968 they began a new work in Kenya, Africa, especially witnessing to the Hindi.

After forty-three years of faithful service in Bilaspur, Mrs. Emma Schaefer returned to the States, following a thrombosis in 1957. She is now living in the Mt. Healthy Home in Cincinnati, Ohio. Her thoughts and prayers will continue with those in India who push forward across new borders for Christ's cause.

When the Harry Schaefers could not return to India, the Bernel Getters assumed as much oversight of the Bilaspur and Orissa work as possible. Thus a program of evangelism has been carried on in the five primary schools and one middle school, where there was an enrollment of over one thousand students in 1968. The Sitapur and Bilaspur Hostels housed 150 children, affording the Indian an opportunity for an education in a Christian atmosphere. The orphanage at Bilaspur, however, had to be closed. The Getters are related to seventy-five congregations, financially. At least twenty-five congregations are conducting services through the guidance of elders or by preachers engaged in secular work to support themselves. There have been approximately seven thousand baptisms over the past twenty years.

An Anti-Conversion Bill was passed in the province where the Getters reside. It emphasizes the illegality in converting an individual "from one religion to another by the use of force or allurement or by fraudulent means and for matters incidental thereto". Bernel Getter appeared in court in February 19, 1969 and was cleared of charges. At present they are free to carry on with their work of teaching and evangelism.

On January 22, 1965, Dr. Zoena Rothermel completed fifty years in India. She has faithfully served her living Lord throughout these years in the land where her husband and son died.

Dr. Rothermel and her husband were the second missionary family to go to the mission field as direct-support or "faith" missionaries, returning to India only about two months after the Wolfes returned to the Philippines. Both had first served under the *United Christian Missionary Society.*

In 1928, only two years after the beginning of their new work in the Hamirpur District, Dr. Rothermel's husband passed to his reward and her son died an accidental death seven months later, leaving Dr. Rothermel to carry on alone with her daughter, Jean.

In 1930 the Fred Smiths came out to help in the work and supervised mission activity during Dr. Rothermel's furlough (1933-35). When she returned to the field the Smiths went back to the States to work. Dr. Rothermel served loyally all through World War II, delaying her furlough until the fall of 1943. On her return in 1945 she was accompanied by the Tom Rashes and Miss Edna Hunt who stayed with her until they had learned the language. At that time they moved to Kulpahar to take over the old *United Christian Missionary Society* station there.

Dr. Rothermel's daughter, Jean, married William Roland and they came out to India in 1947 to labor until brother Roland's health made it imperative that they return to the States for medical treatment. When they were able to come back to India in 1954 they settled at Bilaspur to supervise the Bible Seminary where the Ragual Bible Seminary had consolidated with the Bilaspur Bible Seminary.

In August 1947 Ralph Harter came out to work with Dr. Rothermel, though later he set up his work independent of the Christian Mission to India. His work will be discussed later in this section.

Miss Gladys Hoppe returned with Dr. Rothermel from her furlough in May 1952. She was an excellent language student, but ill health prevented her from remaining more than two years.

So for her remaining years in India, Dr. Rothermel served alone in the Ragual District. She gave free medical care to all who came— using this method to obtain a hearing for the Gospel of Christ. A primary mission school was conducted for children of the Christians. Several fine young men were partially trained before going to Bible College to complete their Bible education. Due to the lack of a man

147

to supervise the evangelistic efforts much of the time, the fruits of the field were not what they could have been otherwise, however, well over two hundred people accepted Christ through the efforts of the Christian Mission to India. Dr. Rothermel retired in 1965 and will reside at the Mt. Healthy Home in Cincinnati, Ohio until the Lord calls her to her heavenly home.

The Kulpahar mission was first built by the forerunners of the *United Christian Missionary Society* some forty years ago, but due to the policy of retrenchment, the U.C.M.S. closed down this work in the United Provinces. It was national Christians who first acquainted the "faith" missionaries in the Province with Kulpahar's need and who urged that someone should save the dying witness.

In June of 1947 the Tom Rashes, who had labored with Dr. Rothermel since 1945, and Leah Moshier and Dolly Chitwood, who had been associated with the Schaefers in Central Provinces for one year, decided to join their efforts to begin a work for the Master. With most of their language study behind them, they contacted the officials of the Kulaphar property, and upon agreement of terms, these four missionaries moved to Kulpahar in October in answer to the national's requests.

In April of 1949 Frank and Marie Rempel arrived from Canada to add their efforts to the growing witness of the mission. In November of the same year Edna Hunt, having labored with the Rashes earlier, joined them in the Kulpahar work.

In December 1949, Ruth Lincoln set up the medical work at the Kulpahar mission where she remained until 1952. At that time it seemed best that she go to a more healthful climate in the south of India. In April of 1953 Helen Doyal arrived from the States to take up the medical work of the area. Helen had prepared to enter China as a missionary but the doors of the land closed before she could enter. While waiting for the Lord's guidance she took nurses' training, and when she was ready the Lord opened the door to India.

The missionaries count it providential that Kulpahar Mission was established in the same year that India became a free nation. This has made it easier for them to adopt the new methods and new attitudes for which the new age called. The national brethren have been and are accepted as equals in every way, and in turn they have accepted the missionary. To prevent a system top-heavy with missionary organization, the "project system" was adopted, whereby each missionary was completely responsible for the policies and finances of one phase of the work. By training a national leadership for the church and its various avenues of witness, it is possible for the missionaries to stay in the background.

148

Upon arriving in Kulpahar in the fall of 1947, the missionaries immediately saw the need of a school. There were a few children who had learned to read and write earlier, but for the lack of facilities they were not continuing to "increase in wisdom". Late in that year a mere handful of youngsters and one persevering teacher gathered together for the beginning of Kulpahar Christian School, the project of Dolly Chitwood. Slowly the school began to grow until in 1950 Junior High School classes were added. The total enrollment was thirty with three teachers handling all the classes. The enrollment swelled to ninety in 1954, and it was that year the provincial government granted official recognition to the school.

The door of a new field of service was opened in January 1948 when the first sick, opium-fed baby was brought to the mission. By the end of the year a dozen children were being cared for at Kulpahar Kid's Home under the direction of Leah Moshier. At the end of a building program in 1953, eighty children were living in the orphanage. These children come from various backgrounds; a goodly number are orphans, some are from broken homes, some where a father has been unable to care for the children after the death of the mother, others just unwanted. Because of the nature of the work, much of Leah's time is spent in providing the things necessary for physical growth that boys and girls entrusted into her care may "increase in stature". But in providing for their physical welfare, their spiritual needs are met as well. Each year some of these boys and girls make their decisions for Christ, many of them during the yearly camp program.

Upon coming to Kulpahar, Edna Hunt assumed a variety of responsibilities ranging from teaching in the Bible College and witnessing to the village women, to supervising the building of the dispensary. Perhaps her greatest love was the project of the Kulpahar women's work. She directed a home that operated as long as its occupants lived, and carried on work among the village women.

It was a joy for Miss Hunt to see the women serve quietly and faithfully, day and night, counseling with other women, teaching children and helping wherever possible. The work of the orphanage and school, as well as other phases of the work, could not be continued were it not for the host of Indian Christian women who share the heavier burdens of tedious daily tasks. "To hear the cries of distress, to lift up the fallen, to comfort the sorrowing and to minister unto the sick—for these needs God has given us women with hearts of compassion." Kulpahar has no shortage of these great souls!

Following the example of the Master who had compassion of the sick and afflicted, the Kulpahar medical work was, from the beginning, a means of opening both doors and hearts to the Gospel. This was the project of Helen Doyal, R.N., until she left the field in 1956. In the summer of 1954 a small dispensary was opened in one of the rooms of the Bible College. These quarters were very insufficient so in 1955 a five-room dispensary was completed, and immediately put to use. It was a needy center, since the nearest hospital is fifty-five miles away over roads impassable during the rainy season. To carry out the work of the dispensary Vida Stewart came from Canada in February 1957. This she did, along with language study. In 1959, Vida took a mid-wifery course in Bilaspur to better enable her to serve Christ through the field of medicine. Because of the Indian drug laws it was urgent that some Doctor could back the work and order the drugs. Dr. Grace Singh was located and she came the fifty miles one day a week to be of service to the Lord.

By Vida's furlough time in 1960 the work had been built up until an average of 540 patients were treated each month. On Doctor's day an average of forty-five patients came for treatment. After her furlough, Vida did not return to India. She married Lew Cass and entered the field of Brazil. Edna Hunt took over as manager of the dispensary until her departure from Kulpahar. Dr. Singh still comes one day a week for clinic and especially to treat the children who live at the mission. A nurse and pharmacist carry out the doctor's orders between clinic days.

The church of the Lord is nothing if it is not permanent. To make sure that this permanency should exist, the missionaries followed Paul's direction to Timothy to "commit to faithful men, who shall be able to teach others also". It was to this purpose that India Bible College was dedicated when founded by the Tom Rashes in their early days of service in India. Leadership of the college shifted to the Rempels on their arrival in 1949. They were aided by Edna Hunt and several young Indian men in the teaching program, which was designed to fit the need of the Indian field. Both short courses and advanced courses were provided. The first five couples were graduated in 1950. By 1956, twenty-eight men and women had graduated and a number of others had received training. At this time formal training in the Bible College was discontinued.

In understaking a "publications ministry", the Rempels merely changed to a new medium of instruction—the printed instead of the spoken Word; and to a different group of students—the potential elders and deacons of the local church instead of the evangelists. These are the potential workers who simply cannot be reached through classroom instruction, yet they are the core of any local church and need especially to be grounded in the truth if the churches are ever to become self-sufficient. Thus vital Christian books were made available to them in their vernacular as well as special correspondence courses and pamphlets written to meet local conditions and problems.

Contacts made through New Testament Publications were not limited to Christians. In an increasingly literate India, the demand for reading material affords an open door for witnessing to interested non-Christians. The Rempels moved to Kanpur in 1959 to facilitate their publication work, and labor in conjunction with Ralph Harter.

Although Kulpahar has been the center of the work, efforts were always channeled to reach out to other areas. Since November 1948 when the mission truck and trailer, piled high with students and camping equipment, left for its first preaching tour, the Mission has been regarded as home base for an active program of evangelism. This work of evangelism was a challenge to Tom and Leota Rash, and one they continued in until they returned to Canada in 1963 where they are presently serving.

When the Rashes and Edna Hunt left this area of work, only Leah Moshier and Dolly Chitwood remained to continue their labors with the "Kid's Home" and the "School". One hundred seventy-six now live in the home. Since 1948 altogether three hundred thirty-three children have found the comfort of being wanted. In a country where the government takes no concern for its orphan or abandoned children, and non-Christian religions do very little, the Home is an outstanding witness to Christian love and compassion. Its existence and work are known to people for hundreds of miles around, from highest government official to humblest peasant. Dedicated to the glory of God and the saving of homeless and unfortunate children, its purpose is being realized more fully each year. Many, once unfortunate and unwanted, are now respected, admired Christian young men and women, taking places of responsibility in the life of the Church and the community.

Since 1948 the School has enrolled nearly eight hundred students from the Home, the Christian community, and the nearby village. The staff and facilities are adequate for the 1968 enrollment of about two hundred, from kindergarten through junior high school. The District Board of Education, which granted them accreditation in 1955 and maintains regular inspection of their total program, congratulated them in 1968 on attaining the highest academic standard among the eighty-seven junior high schools in their district.

Day by day in the school room not only are the foundations of knowledge built upon, but the foundations of character are laid. Continually it is emphasized that secular knowledge without spiritual character is worthless. The School has earned a reputation in their District for competent instruction, but more important than that, the honesty and fair play which characterizes the student body and faculty has gained for it the respect of all in the area. For this is a country where cheating in school is the general practice, often abetted by the teachers.

If mission schools did not exist the program of evangelism among young people would be greatly retarded, since no time for Bible instruction would be permitted in the school day. Without the mission schools, all Christian young people would have to attend the government schools where Hindu teachings would not be discredited but taught as true. Moreover, the children recognize that getting an education is a privilege in a country that cannot provide schools for all. Through daily devotions in the Home, Bible classes in School, and gospel preaching in the Church, all the children on reaching an age of spiritual understanding, have accepted Jesus as Lord. Those who have grown up are taking places of leadership in the church at Kulpahar and in other congregations in that Province.

Harvesters preparing noon meal in Kerala.

In 1952 when Ruth Lincoln had to choose a more healthful location for herself, she traveled further south to the state of Travancore, now called Kerala. Though this state was for a time under Communist rule, it was not allowed to pass any laws unless the central government of India agreed. The authorities were interested in medical work, so

152

did not question the work of the Church of Christ Mission Hospital that Miss Lincoln set up in Thalavady. (The people have since voted Communist rule out.)

Mission Dispensary.

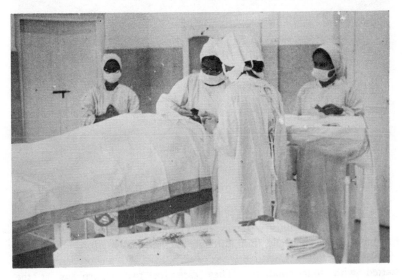

Operating room.

A mission dispensary was opened in December 1952. The following year a 16-bed hospital ward was built and in 1955 an operating theatre, delivery room, laboratory and more ward rooms were added.

A village hospital is much different from an American hospital. Though beds are provided for each patient, they must bring their own bed linen. Also because they are very particular from whose hand they eat food, each patient brings his own servant to cook. For every patient there is usually one relative besides the servant so it makes for crowded conditions in all the rooms. Christians and Hindus are both admitted, thus Christians have much opportunity to witness as they have their daily Bible study and prayers in their rooms.

In 1957, two new doctors joined the staff to assist Dr. Oomen who began working with Miss Lincoln in earlier years. With their coming they were able to develop a Public Health Service that was greatly needed due to ignorance and superstition of the poor village people. They also were able to train young ladies in nurses' training who could help them in the hospital and in village work.

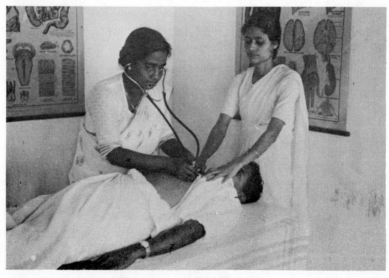

Dr. Oomen examining patient.

The medical ministry serves thirty villages in the area not only for their physical needs, but through the mission's efforts they hear of New Testament Christiantiy as well. In 1956 an orphanage was started with four children. They care for twenty orphans at the present time, and these are given Bible training daily.

Ralph Harter labored many years alone in Kanpur, India, devoting much of his time to publication work. For nearly twenty years he has published a monthly magazine in the Hindi language, much of the material printed is written by Christian natives. The copies of this magazine serve as native 'evangelists'. A Bible Book Store was begun in 1954, not only selling religious books and Bibles but they own a press which is used to print some books in Hindi. Some 8,000 copies of the Hindi edition of "Life of Christ Visualized" were distributed through these efforts.

The Rempels moved to Kanpur from Kulpahar in 1959 to labor in connection with this printing work. He became editor and publisher of the 'Christasian' magazine in English.

About 1960 brother Harter established a free-lending library containing nearly 3,800 religious books. In 1966 a reading room was added which enlarges the service possibilities. Midget libraries (approximately seven books each) have been opened in private homes about the town.

Brother Harter also provides a home for young men, mostly from rural areas who come to the city to attend school or to learn a trade. They are required to attend church services and to read the Bible daily, over which they are tested. This number of boys varies from four to eleven.

When India Bible Institute opened in Kanpur in 1953, the Tom Rashes came as principals, though much of their effort was upon Home Study Bible courses that reached over 3,000 students. In 1949 only one out of ten people could read and write, by 1963, four out of ten could.

Ghandi's grandson once said "the missionaries taught us to read, but the Communists gave us the books". That is one reason why the missionaries in Kanpur have placed so much emphasis on providing religious material for them to read. Ralph Harter now serves alone in Kanpur as he did in the beginning of his work in India.

The work of the Lord in South India started with the conversion of one man by brother Fred Smith and Mrs. Zoena Rothermel in 1936. Through the witness of this first convert, three others were won to Christ. These three men began to preach and lay the groundwork. In the fourteen years before active missionary help arrived, Dr. Rothermel kept the spark alive. When the Arthur Morrises arrived on the field at Madrappakkam village in 1950 they found one preacher serving two small churches.

In their first year of service, the Morrises operated seven village schools. This effort is an effective means of village evangelism, since

155

the Bible is taught in all the schools and the native evangelists serve as the teachers. By 1960 there were forty-two village schools. Night classes were provided for many of the children of the very poor families by voluntary preachers and teachers who themselves made sacrifice to make it possible. The Morrises at first had a boarding home for student boys, but this developed into a home for orphan boys. They had one hundred thirty-five residents in 1968.

The medical work was started by Mrs. Morris in August of 1950 with a two-fold purpose: to care for the sick Christians, and to win friends for Christ from the Hindus by healing their bodies while preaching Christ to them in the process. It was difficult to keep a doctor in the village hospital but by 1957 a native male doctor labored part-time. Over 1,000 patients were treated that first year after the hospital re-opened in the fall of 1956 (following a furlough). In 1960 the hospital was recognized by the *Christian Medical Association of India.* A sixteen-bed in-patient wing was added to and approved by the Mission to Lepers, making this the first leper hospital to be operated by our missionaries. Now there are thirty-two beds for the lepers, plus a maternity ward. Thousands of lepers receive treatment both in the hospital and as out-patients.

The medical work has proven very valuable to their witnessing in South India. Dr. Frank Gnananadan, an army doctor under the British, works in the hospital now, assisted by a couple of medics. To further eleviate suffering, a famine relief program was set up for 1966, 67, 68. Fifty thousand meals a day were fed during this three year period.

The South India Christian College was opened in October 1951 with twenty-two students enrolled. In 1953 Bill and Ethel Gulick came to be in charge of the Bible College work. Teaching in a school with an average of fifty students was a full-time job when all material had to be translated into both the Tamil and Telegu languages. Classes were set up for four years for full-time evangelists and one year courses for those in the Trade School. By 1957 twenty-nine men and women had completed their year in the Trade School. This program was set up to teach the Bible fours hours a day, and a trade four hours a day. This way a trained leadership would be self-supporting, enabling the missionaries to train a greater number of workers in a shorter period of time. The trained evangelists of the Bible College worked with these men of the Trade School and further taught them as they lived and preached the Word in their various areas.

At the present time the Bible College, reformed, is called South Asia Christian College. It is the only Bible College on the continent of Asia. The David Rees family, when ordered out of Assam, received permission to work in Madras, thus relieving the Art Morrises for furlough in late 1968. The school, as did its earlier counterpart, still seeks to train adequate leadership for the indigenous churches. Their number has increased from 130 to 250 in the last nine years. Since 1950 there have been 12,500 baptisms reported; 1,900 were reported for the year 1968 alone. Approximately four hundred have been baptized since the Rees' arrival. Some of these were due to village evangelism done by the Bible College boys and a few others. In one eight-day period they reached eight villages with a harvest of sixty-seven reaped. Two churches were established where no one had ever worked before, and two in other villages. Hostel boys, on another village tour, baptized sixty-six. The Reeses also have charge now of three youth hostels which appear to be most effective. Cheating, lying, and stealing are common, and not frowned on unless one is caught. The character of the hostel boys is so superior that the time, effort, and money spent on the hostels are worthwhile.

Late in 1957 the Gulicks formed a new work legally incorporated as Christ Nagar Institute and located on a two-acre site eleven miles outside the city of Madras. Following a furlough and a year of Tamil study their work centered in the teaching program of the Institute. Boys who are studying in the eight Standard through the last year of high school were accepted as students. In 1962 there were fifty-six students. They received their secular education by attending the nearby government schools, but study the Bible one hour daily at the Institute. The secular classes are casual and teachers inadequate. English, a required subject, is most difficult for them. The students hold their own devotional services on campus each evening. Their daily Bible studies prepare them to teach in the five near-by villages on the Lord's Day. These communities are almost completely Hindu.

The goal of the Institute is to work with the younger generation and to establish them in the faith. College educated ministers sometimes lose their touch with the village people for most of them are very poor and uneducated. The village churches are usually so poor that they cannot afford to pay a minister's salary, thus their leadership must often come from within the church itself.

The area in which the Gulicks are living is rapidly becoming industrialized, thus each passing day brings further opportunities to reach the new increasing middle class of India. Along with other work brother Gulick has written a correspondence course covering sixteen basic subjects, available in Tamil. Whether teaching, preaching or healing the sick, the end goal of all the efforts of the Art Morrises,

157

Bill Gulicks, and now the David Reeses, is to win souls into the Kingdom of God in South India.

Over a century ago a Christian Boarding School was built in Landour, Mussoorie, India, called the Woodstock School. This is an interdenominational school established for the purpose of teaching missionaries' children. Set up on systems similar to Britian and the U.S., classes are held for kindergarten through high school.

Missionaries of the Churches of Christ (Christian) in India formed an affiliation group for closer ties with the school. The forming of this group gives many advantages, one of which is the lowering of school fees nearly half. This group is responsible for furnishing a teacher or teachers for the school, or for the physical development of the school. Our teachers have been the William Rolands, Velma Held (for three years), and the latest, Miss Pendley.

In conjunction with the Wycliffe Bible Translators, the Richard Hugoniots came to Araku Valley early in 1966. This area is in the central eastern hills seventy-two miles west of the sea coast city of Visakhapatnam. Their work was with the Khonda Dora people who are rather primitive. Their first efforts were to listen and record the language, that eventually the Gospel might be shared with them. This work was shortened when the government reversed a decision to allow the Translators to remain in this state of Andhra Pradesh. They were forced to leave the area, thus they returned to the States in April 1969.

Indonesia

"Land of volcanoes"

THE LAND . . . .

Comprised of five large islands and more than three thousand small ones, Indonesia forms an arc between Asia and Australia. They were formerly known as the Dutch East Indies but gained their independence in 1945, though they did not become self-governing until 1949. In 1965 Indonesia was the fifth largest country in the world in population. It is also a country with a wide variety of natural resources and a good potential for economic development.

The large islands all have a central mountain range rising from more or less extensive lowlands and coastal plains. Many inactive and scores of active volcanos dot the islands, accounting for the predominantly rich volcanic soil that is carried down by the rivers to the plains and lowlands.

Straddling the equator, Indonesia has a tropical climate. Though the temperature in this equator land seldom goes over 90 degrees (in the shade) it is difficult to remain in the shade, nor can you escape the high humidity, neither do the seasons change except by the amount of rainfall. Actually altitude rather than season affects the temperature. The climate has other irritating results, too. Skin rash and fatigue are common; mosquitoes, flies, bugs, and ants are year-round companions. Frequent care must be given to your possessions to protect them from mildew and rust.

Four out of five Indonesians depend on agriculture to make a living; three-fifths of the cultivated land is on the island of Java. There are two types of farming: small farms owned by Indonesians who engage in some rubber and other export crop production but chiefly in subsistence forming, and large foreign-owned enterprises producing export crops. Because the population is rapidly increasing, the government seeks to achieve food self-sufficiency through expansion or arable acreage, improved farm techniques (including training of farmers), and moving of Javanese to the Outer Islands.

Indonesia is the world's third largest producer of natural rubber and tin. More than 70% of all exports are produced by Sumatra and about 14% by Java. Industrial development is still small in comparison with the size of the population and the national income.

Petroleum is by far the most important mineral resource there. Sumatra, the richest oil area, produces 70% of the Indonesian oil. Tin is second to petroleum in value of production. In addition to iron ore, mineral resources that may ultimately be successfully developed seem to be nickel and copper, in that order.

. . . . THE PEOPLE

Indonesian society is full of diversity, and much of it is also in the process of change. Great efforts are being made to stress national identity by means of the national language and by political exhortations. Many still are traditional peasants whose horizons are limited to their village and the nearby town. Schools have increased those horizons in some families—and the larger cities have more than doubled in recent years. Among city groups, foreign shirts, fountain pens, motorcycles, and automobiles are the new status symbols.

The Indonesian people are basically of the "Malaysian" race, which include the Javanese, Sudanese, and Madurese, and many other smaller groups. They are characterized by smallness of stature, light to dark brown pigmentation, thick, sleek black hair, broad formation of head, wide nose and thick lips. There is a self-contained minority group of Chinese on the islands, plus Arabs and some Europeans. The estimated 1965 population was 104,500,000 people.

All Indonesians except the Papuans and the people living in certain parts of the Moluicas speak Malayo-Polynesian languages. All the many branches are related. Pasar (Bazaar) Malay is understood by all Indonesians engaged in business and commerce. A version of Malay, called Basha Indonesia, is the official language. It contains words from many dialects as well as from Dutch, English, Arabic, Sanskrit, and others. English, now the second language of the country, is a compulsory subject in secondary schools.

Vigorous efforts are being made to advance education and reduce illiteracy which was estimated in 1961 to still be 53%. However at the end of 1964, President Sukarno announced that the republic was free from illiteracy. The constitution states that education is to be non-discriminatory and that primary education is to be free and compulsory. Schools are coeducational except for certain vocational and religious schools. The school system is patterned much like the Dutch system. Institutions of higher learning have sprung up in amazing numbers, however the training of teachers in sufficient numbers and in quality of education are major problems.

Although nearly 90% of the people are nominally Muslim, freedom of religion is guaranteed by the constitution. Balinese, who number nearly one million, have remained Hindu in religion and culture. The nearly two million Chinese are largely a combination of Buddhist-Confucianist. Of the three million or more who profess Christianity, 70% are Protestant. In a few areas, as in central Kalimantan (Borneo) the people are still pagan.

. . . . THE MISSIONARY . . . .

A flood tide of reports coming from Indonesia tells of an unprecedented response to the Gospel, not only by individuals, but by entire communities. Apparently the key event to this dynamic change was the abortive Communist coup of September 1965, which left a great spiritual vacuum, fraught with insecurity and bewilderment, thus providing an open door for the Gospel of Christ. In the twenty months that followed Roman and Protestant churches won an estimated quarter of a million converts—about equal to the number won to Christianity in the preceding four hundred years. The supply of Bibles and New Testaments was quickly exhausted and the American Bible Society's new press in Java could not keep up with the demand. People by the thousands wait to be taught, wait for teaching to be báptized, wait for someone to aid them in finding Christ.

Max Ward Randall (veteran missionary among our churches in Africa and surveyor of the world's mission fields), along with LaVerne Morse and Harry Schaefer, visited Indonesia in 1967, and reported, "What we do for Christ in Indonesia will have a greater effect on Southeast Asia than what our country is doing, militarily, in Viet Nam". The door was wide open!

Being greatly challenged by this opportunity for witnessing, the Lew Cass family, veterans of Brazil missions, arrived in Indonesia in 1968. They have settled in Bandung, approximately ninety miles east of Djakarta, where they hope to be able to establish a work of evangelism. Permanent papers have not been issued and mail is censored. Many invitations have come from preaching, some from denominational churches. In the summer of 1968, brother Cass was able to work in a youth camp in eastern Java.

Because of the great challenge presented by the need of Indonesia, two other families will join the work in 1969. The Orient will not seem strange to Carl and Grace Fish for they served seven and one-half years in Okinawa and Japan, until a critical illness in the family forced their return to the States. The Charles Winegarner family will be new to missionary service, but not to serving Christ. Mrs. Nance Winegarner is a registered nurse and Charles is experienced in business management, advertising and public relations. In addition, he was engaged in Christian and governmental research, speaking often on issues relating to the Christian and his country. The Winegarners will be producing two educational films for use in the churches in the United States—the first, "Eternal Life and Indonesia", will be completed as soon as on-location photography can be completed in Indonesia. The second film, geared for younger people, will be entitled "God, Life, People and You". This will cover World Evangelism at home and abroad.

Two families of our non-instrumental brethren entered the country in late 1967 and early 1968. Truly the field is wide open. The only problem is that only those approved, invited, and/or accepted by some recognized church group in Indonesia can obtain entry.

*K*orea

*"Land of high mountains
and sparkling streams"*

K O R E A

Seoul

Kangnung ●

● Taejon

Pusan ●

| | | |
0   100   200

THE LAND . . . .

One of the most ancient nations of the world, Korea is a peninsula extending southward from Manchuria lying between the Yellow Sea and the Sea of Japan. It borders the U.S.S.R. on a twenty mile line, and is separated from Japan by only 110 miles of water.

Korean's greatest length is five hundred and twenty miles and its greatest width is two hundred and nineteen miles, which makes it a little larger than the state of Utah. Before the war there was an estimated population of over twenty-nine million, 97% of whom were Koreans, the remainder were mostly Japanese and Chinese. In mid-1965 the population numbered over thrity-nine million, of which twenty-eight million lived in South Korea.

Since 1945 the peninsula has been divided. North Korea comprises the northern 54.8% of the peninsula—South Korea is the remaining 487 square miles. Although Korea is divided by an artificial political barrier, there are geographic differences between north and south. North Korea is more mountainous and its climate more continental than peninsular South Korea. Cold winter temperatures and a short growing season make double cropping of fields impossible. South Korea is a land of more extensive plains and milder winter climates. The plains and valleys are generally fertile for farming. However, to the Korean farmer, with his often primitive methods, the danger of flood or drought is always present. Flood-control and irrigation works are badly needed.

Korea has one of the healthiest and finest climates in the world. In summer the heat is tempered by sea breezes, and winter skies are always blue and bright, with a crisp, dry atmosphere. Only during the wet and sticky rainy season is it uncomfortable.

Eighty per cent of all South Koreans are members of farm households. Even the townspeople have small gardens, chickens and fishponds. It is truly a nation of villages. Only 15% of the people live in urban centers of 10,000 or more, of which number Seoul is the Capital (South Korea) and cultural center.

In the south the chief product is rice which is planted in 27% of the cultivated land. Double cropping is possible also, due to eight frost-free months. Millet and barley are the chief rice substitutes for other areas. Native cattle supply good meat and fine-grained hides, but the number is small since crop-land is developed to raising grain for human consumption. The north is richest in timber and minerals. Mulberry trees are plentiful so that area is well-situated for raising silkworms. Many gold and iron mines were opened during Japanese occupation.

In resources and economic development, Korea is roughly divided by the 38th parallel. We see that the north produces most of the country's mineral output, while the south produces most of the textiles and has most of the food processing plants. Thus they are dependent upon each other.

.... THE PEOPLE

The Korean people are of the Mongol family, yet different from the Chinese and Japanese stock. The age of the nation is perhaps realized when we understand that they were scholars, artists, and craftsmen at a time when Europeans were still barbarians.

They are a strong and well-built race. They have straight black hair, slanting dark eyes, and olive-brown skins. Their cheek bones are high and their noses rather flat. They are usually taller than the average Mongolian.

Although some Koreans have adopted Western dress, the majority still wear at home the characteristic white or sky blue dress of the Yi Dynasty (which ended in 1910). Children wear very brilliant colors; their jackets often resembling a rainbow. All men wear jackets and voluminous trousers; the women, jackets and skirts. One of the most important parts of feminine dress is the waist band, worn between the jacket and skirt. Shoes are never worn indoors.

The Korean women marry early and work hard, and are considered inferior to men.

The traditional house of the well-to-do Korean is a high one-story building with a tiled roof and a double gateway. The grounds are surrounded by ten-foot walls. Humbler houses have smaller windows and lower roofs made of straw rather than tile. They usually have four to five rooms, with partitions of paper, in addition to inner rooms. The floors are paved with flat bricks under which is tunnelled the heat from the kitchen to the main chimney. These bricks are usually covered with a thick oiled paper and sometimes with a matting or woven carpet. They do not use chairs or beds, but sit and sleep on the floor. At night mattresses with blankets or quilts are brought out. The most prominent pieces of furniture are the heavy, brassbound clothes chests, usually one for each member of the household.

Worse off of all are the pack carriers, the street-stall keepers, the itinerant vendors, and those who have no means of support, such as northern refugees, war widows, etc. In extreme cases these people live in caves scratched from the hillsides around Seoul, while others dwell in patchwork shacks made of discarded planks and tenting of corrugated iron. A majority of the common people live in wretchedly dark, dirty, and vermin-infested dwellings. The government in 1966 began setting aside funds to help alleviate the shortage of one million homes.

Though the spoken language is unrelated to Chinese (some words are borrowed from them) until the 15th century Koreans wrote exclusively in Chinese characters. At that time a completely phonetic alphabet of twenty-five letters was introduced. It is so simple that a foreigner can master it in a day. The language is soft with a natural lift, no deep nasal tones, little accent and no difficult slurring. They have their own manner of singing, which is largely spontaneous and difficult for Westerners to appreciate.

Before the Japanese conquest only the upper-class Koreans were educated. Then the Japanese provided schools for about four out of ten children but for the purpose of producing loyalty to Japan. Since the war allied occupation forces introduced new educational methods. Education in South Korea today is almost a national passion. By 1960 about 95% of school-age children were receiving the compulsory six years of schooling, though theoretically free, parents must pay many fees and costs. Secondary education is not compulsory and is highly competitive.

The Koreans are very superstitious so it is not surprising that ancestor worship and other practices associated with Confucianism were known in Korea centuries before the time of Confucious and still are practiced today. Buddhism was introduced in the 4th century but the Koreans are Taoists at heart though the religion as such never has been active. Shamanism, which has a mixture of demonology, magic and astrology, has a strong hold on the common people. Protestant missions began their work in 1884 and Korea is more "Christianized" than either China or Japan. In South Korea today those following some form of "Christianity" number about two million, one-fourth of which are Catholics.

. . . . THE MISSIONARY . . . .

The first churches of Christ were planted in Korea by Koreans from Japan who came back to Korea under the leadership of the Cunningham Mission of Tokyo, Japan. Through the years this work was without the help of foreign missionaries most of the time. However, for short periods of time it had, in turn, the services of J. Michael

Shelley, T. G. Hitch, and Owen Still. These churches numbered about twelve, but only one of them survived World War II, and even it did not survive the Korean War.

The present work in Korea was started by the John Chases in 1936, in which work they continued until the spring of 1940. They first served in Japan in 1927. The John Hills joined the work in June of 1939, remaining until November 1940 when the threat of war necessitated their return home.

During the pre-war period seven churches were established, all in or near Seoul, except for one at Chaw Do Ri in north Korea. Seoul Bible Seminary was started in 1949 and grew rapidly in size until there were seventy students. Several hundred Koreans were baptized and fine mission property was purchased. Brother Chase made several short trips to Korea in 1941, 46, 48, and 1954. Though he never returned permanently, he did conduct a successful campaign in an attempt to raise $50,000. for new Korean chapels.

The John Hill family returned to Korea for their second term in February of 1949 and worked until June 1950 when the Korean War suddenly forced them to evacuate to Japan. In this era the greatest number of baptisms in any one twelve-month period was from May 1, 1949 to April 30, 1950, when 768 known immersions took place. Later in the fall of 1950, brother Hill was able to return for a five-week period, and from June 1951 on he was able to remain most of the time in Korea. He left the field for America in July 1955, after the loss of his wife in April of that year.

Paul Ingram arrived in Korea in January of 1953 and labored until January 1955, even though his family was forced to spend most of their time in Japan. Brother Ingram had the privilege and joy of having one entire audience (41 Korean war veterans) respond to the gospel invitation. This is some indication of the open door at that time.

In April of 1953 Robert West came over from Japan to help John Hill and Paul Ingram in the Bible Seminary, the work with the churches (which then numbered forty-four) and the four hundred fifty homeless children. By 1954 the number of Korean churches and preaching points had increased to sixty-seven and over one thousand children were being cared for in eight orphanages; one of which was directly operated by the Korean churches, but assisted financially by the missionaries.

Other help in the Seminary was received from Alex Bills (then in Japan), Jane Kinnett, Howard Davis, and Lila Thompson. Mary Louise Barnhill came later in 1954 to assist in the children's work, but severe ill health, brought on by an attack of jaundice, forced her to return to the States in the fall of 1955.

A new era of mission work began when the Harold Taylors (veterans of nearly twenty years with service in two Oriental countries —China and Japan) accepted the plea of Christian brethren to take over the then unsupervised work in Korea. In the fall of 1955 only Mrs. (Lila Thompson) Hiller remained, and she left with her husband in the early days of 1956.

When the Taylors arrived in Korea in November of 1955, they were surprised to find so much of the work had remained intact. It was a testimony to the commendable work done by those who had been there and to the faith of the churches established. Nevertheless the needs were many and varied. The Taylors began visiting two or three churches each week and established contact with them all through correspondence. District rallies were planned to help strengthen the various areas. Most of the churches were rural. They were also poor and small. In February 1956 it was reported that there were 1,379 baptized believers in the Korean churches, but attendance was often ten times the actual number of Christians in some of the churches. Building programs were set up to actually begin the "chapels for Korea". In some instances buildings needed only to be repaired but in most cases groups were meeting in tents, rented halls, or school buildings. On March 31, 1956, the first chapel was dedicated, and to make the event even more memorable, four responded to the Gospel.

When the Taylors arrived in Korea they were offered the responsibility of taking over the leadership of a Middle School. Since that time they have shared in helping three such schools. These schools presented a grand opportunity to train boys under a Christian influence. Teachers are trained at the Seminary to help in such schools, and in turn many of these student boys will enter the Seminary for preacher-training later.

When Mrs. Lila Hiller left, the work of the orphanages also became the responsibility of the Taylors, a responsibility they gladly accepted. In the orphanages they saw human lives salvaged and bodies healed, but most of all they saw the opportunity of teaching Christ to the children of Korea. Many of these children have "outgrown" the orphanages but have returned to assist the missionary in the cause of Christ. Only recently one orphanage was closed by the government. They apparently intend to eliminate many of the orphanages altogether. The children were transferred to either a nearby orphange or placed in the homes of relatives.

Because of strong denominational influence among many of the churches, the Taylors found that more Bible teaching was needed. In 1957 many of the churches had no regular preachers and most of them met in homes or improvised church houses. In the 1955-56 school year, thirty-six students were being taught by six faculty members at the Seminary. Of all the responsibilities, the Seoul Bible Seminary was felt to really be the most important of all, for from it the greatest need could be met. That is the need of developing leadership capable of working in the cities and with people who can become pillars of the church in Korea.

A new campus was built for the Seminary in 1961. In 1962 the Gordon Pattens arrived in Korea to join the work of the Mission. March 1963 was the date for the opening of the Seminary and the beginning of its first four-year program. The new four-year term that started in March 1968 had thirty fine students enrolled. In the spring of 1968 a new Middle School began meeting in the Seminary buildings in the evening.

In connection with their teaching ministry, the Pattens assist in printing and distributing tracts. They also have a college-level correspondence school that presently reaches 650 students. A magazine, printed six times a year in the Korean language, numbers 2,500 copies, 1,000 of these are given to the Republic of Korea Army Chaplains for distribution to troops. The missionaries' homes are always open to American servicemen too, and they occasionally help sponsor week-end retreats for them at a U.S. Army Retreat Center. Gordon Patten preaches and teaches twice each week to about four hundred men in a government-sponsored camp for wayward men. There have been forty-five baptisms there, largely due to the evangelistic efforts of visiting Joe Garman in 1967.

To help fill the need in Korea the Richard Lashes were led to change their vision for service from Okinawa to Korea. Both Richard and his wife, Melba, had long desired to have some part in the foreign advance of the Church. Their contact with the Korean work began upon meeting Harold Taylor. Their interst continued as they did the mailing for Korean Christian Mission. By that time, however, they were deep in their plans for serving Christ in Okinawa. Though they had chosen to serve in Okinawa, the Lord chose to have them serve Him in Korea. So it was that they came to Korea in June 1957 to be associated with the Harold Taylors in the work of Korean Christian Mission. Most of their first year was spent in language study in Seoul. In the spring of 1958 they moved to Kangnung, a large country town on the east coast, 150 miles across country from Seoul.

172

Kangnung Christian Church building.

The Lashes labored in Kangnung for four years, leaving four village churches, comprising a total membership of about one hundred fifty. These groups worship in good cement block buildings and have native leaders. In the fall of 1963 the Lashes moved to Pusan, a port in southeast Korea, the country's second largest city. After another year of language study, they began an educational venture, in conjunction with a Korean minister, known as the Far East Christian Vocational

New church project.

Far East Christian Vocational College.

College. This is a two-year junior college, with a Bible school plus vocational work added as a sideline, with a view to helping make young men capable of self-support as they go out to preach. In their third year they enrolled seventy students. They graduated fifteen students in December 1968, making a total ot forty-four graduates thus far. Of this number eight are classified as Christian workers and preachers. Whether this type of work will be completely effective has yet to be established. They also have a project of helping congregations build adequate buildings, largely through gifts of other Korean themselves.

Students and friends of the Vocational College.

Christian Radio Mission came into existence in 1947 because of the determination of Alex and Betty Bills to use radio in spreading New Testament Christianity to the mission fields of the world. Their first plan was to set up a missionary radio station in West China, but the Communist victory in China made that impossible. Then they heard that Japan would be granting permits to new commercial radio stations, so they went to Japan only to find that the government would not grant their station a permit. However, they did find opportunities to produce radio programs and release them over various radio stations already in Japan. Besides the broadcasts in Japan they were able to produce programs for short wave stations in Manila to release on stations beamed toward Japan. Their next opportunity was to prepare the English language program for release on Radio Luxembourg in Europe. They were assisted in this by Martin Clark, who served as soloist and announcer, and Exie Fultz, who took over the responsibility of the follow-up program and the Bible correspondence course.

While doing this work the goal of Christian Radio Mission was to

174

have a transmitter of its own. Then, instead of a few minutes once a week at great expense, the Gospel could be on the air several hours in several languages of the Orient each and every day.

Pusan, Korea is a perfect location for reaching the Orient. Besides the millions of people in South Korea, programs could be beamed through the Bamboo Curtain to those in Communist slavery in North Korea and to those on the China mainland. In China the government requires every family to have access to a radio receiver so that all government propaganda can reach them quickly. Programs could be sent out in Mandarin and Cantonese for the millions in the great coastal cities who would be able to hear the station easily. In Japan there are fifteen million radio receivers, all within potential range.

The Alex Bills family came to Pusan in December 1956 to attempt to make this dream a reality. Finally after seven months of constant searching, a tract of land was chosen in 1957, located about five miles from the main part of Pusan, near the edge of the ocean (for overseas transmitting). Not one, but many different programs were presented on various radio stations, including a Chinese language program that was set up late in 1959. However their dream of having their own transmitter was never realized.

Early in 1960, services were begun in the Bills' home in the village of Kwang An Dong. Some who attended had never heard the gospel story before. Flora Mae Guernsey was the first of several recruits to join the Bills in the work of Christian Radio Mission. She arrived on the field in October of 1957 to take charge of the secretarial duties and assist in the music on the programs, as well as teach Bible classes in Pusan.

The Joe Seggelke family arrived on the field in February 1958. This family came with a wide range of experience and talents, all of which could be used in radio work. But most specifically brother Seggelke was to be the Traffic Manager of the station. This is probably the most important functional job in a radio station.

Next to arrive was the Bert Ellis family. His previous radio experience included participation in the direction and production of local and network programs, as well as considerable broadcasting during almost eighteen years of fulltime ministry. As program director, brother Ellis had the general oversight of the music standards of all the programs.

In January 1959, the Korean Broadcasting Mission was formed, of which the Ellis and Seggelke families became a part. At that time Flora Mae Guernsey returned to the States and became associated with Mission Services, Joliet, Illinois. In April 1959 they began daily broadcasts over station HLKU, the first commercial radio station in Korea. The Ellises were associated with this station since its beginning, as official advisors. Through this outreach many enrolled for a correspondence Bible study course (prepared by Harold Taylor in Seoul).

In June 1960 the Seggelkes moved to Seoul to supervise the work of the Taylors (orphanage, construction of Seminary building, weekly Bible classes) leaving the Ellises in complete charge of the work. When the Taylors returned from furlough the Seggelkes returned to Christian service in the States.

Besides the radio programs, the Ellises formed student Bible clubs with one hundred fifty high school and college students. A Sunday School for children reached an average attendance of 300-400 students. Other classes for various age groups were held weekly. Study materials were prepared for all these activities in the Korean language. Because the activities were so many and varied an adjustment had to be made, thus the radio program was terminated before the end of their first term of service. Following an extended furlough period due to illness and surgery, they returned in 1964. A new opportunity was presented to them to teach in Pusan Union Seminary, an independent school started by a Presbyterian minister. Brother Ellis teaches nearly all of the New Testament courses. Mrs. Ellis uses specially prepared Christian material in her English classes. In addition to his teaching, Bert Ellis is preparing various books .for publication. The first is a series of four volumes on the Life of Christ. One of the Epistles of John is complete; a series of Acts is being written. These will all be in the Korean language. Korean ministers are laboring in the area of direct evangelism, but more help is needed with this phase of the work.

In 1959 a new mission was set up, called The Christian Mission to South Korea, when John Hill returned to Korea again (Jane Kinnett, formerly a missionary to Burma, China and Japan was married to John Hill in 1956).

The Hill family arrived in Korea in August of 1959 and picked Taejon as the center for their new work. This is a big railroad crossroads and a central location in South Korea, about 125 miles south of Seoul. That same year Korea Bible Seminary was begun, evangelistic meetings held and the Gospel preached at every opportunity. They have helped since to establish four Christian Junior High schools (the newest is being built in Pusan) and a school for blind children. They are helping financially with four orphanages. From the Bible Seminary have come over fifty graduates, many of whom are preaching regularly. They have 173 students now studying, plus a correspondence course that is offered to those who cannot attend the Seminary.

Korea Bible Seminary.

Bible School and Church at Tal Chuŋ Church—1968.

In 1966, Virginia Hill, a daughter, joined in the work of her father. She teaches some classes in the Bible Seminary, conducts English Bible classes outside the classroom, some for student nurses, others for University students. Besides this, she now has an orphanage for seventeen small children.

Monthly women's meeting in area church in Taejon.

Some children and staff members at Eden Orphanage.

Soon to join the work at Taejon will be Mrs. Eline Williamson, whose husband is in the Air Force in Korea. Others (Koreans in the United States training) will be returning as some already have in other areas of Korea.

There is a very real need for an American teacher to come to Seoul Foreign School to make it financially feasible for our missionaries' children to attend.

Korea, "the land of the morning calm", is far from calm, politically or spiritually. It is a divided country, politically. It is a needy country, spiritually. Christianity has been known in Korea since 1884, but each new generation must be challenged with the Gospel as it comes to an age of understanding. The time is far too short; the task too large for normal means. Modern technology lends a helping hand in mass communication through radio. The Gospel Broadcasting Mission began a "Search the Scriptures", 15-minute program, late in 1967 which continues to be produced by a Korean Christian teacher and minister. He also supervises the follow-up program of calling and teaching.

For the remarkable growth of the Korean churches, from five in 1939 to nearly one hundred twenty in late 1968, much credit must go to the Korean preachers, especially to Eun Suk Kim (now deceased) and Chaplain Hal Martin, now retired from the U.S. Air Force. Because of the indigenous nature of much of the work in Korea, and due to wars and numerous missionaries who have served in varying lengths of time, (besides the fact that there is very little cooperation among the various areas) it is almost impossible to determine the number of converts. Since honesty seems a very rare virtue, there are ofttimes many Christians in name who are not so in life. But it is evident that the Koreans often seek after spiritual things. When

Evangelistic band and Joe Garman at Taejon.

179

Joe Garman came to Korea in 1967 for a two-months evangelistic effort, hundreds responded to the Gospel invitation and over 1,000 were baptized into Christ. There were prison inmates, atheists, Buddhists—people from all walks of life, in all areas of the country, and all in need of a Saviour.

$\mathcal{P}$akistan

"Land of Islam"

THE LAND . . . .

The very reason for Pakistan's existence today is its devotion to Islam. The new nation formed within the Commonwealth and in 1947 won its independence as a dominion. It is the fifth most populous nation on earth.

The land is divided into two sections—1,000 miles apart: the western wing is in the former provinces of Baluchistan, Sind and the North-West Frontier, part of Punjab, and the States of Khaerpur and Bahawalpur; the eastern wing is in the eastern part of Bengal and part of Assam. The western province is twice the size of California, the eastern is about as big as Iowa or Illinois. Kashmir is claimed by India and Pakistan, and is the occasion for violence, even a full-scale warfare in the summer of 1965. The two sections differ widely in language, terrain and density of puplation.

In the West a desert and a semi-arid plain rise to mountains much as in the American far-west. East Pakistan's flat, fertile delta was built by three rivers, the Ganges, the Brahmaputra, and the Meghna. During monsoon months thousands of square miles lie flooded and much of the pedestrian traffic must move by boat. Controlling the monsoon floods is beyond Pakistan's power, for 98% of the catchment basins, where flood control would be most effective, lies in India, Nepal, China, and Tibet.

The country is pre-dominantly agricultural: their problem centering around water—too little, too much, or too salty. West Pakistan is distinctly arid, the soil usually sandy and is generally fertile where water can be brought to it. East Pakistan is a typical monsoon climate; the soil is very fertile. The major agricultural differences between the West and the East may be summed up by saying, the former is the land of the camel, the latter the water buffalo.

Rice is the chief crop. "Luxury" quality rice is exported to India while larger quantities of ordinary rice are imported from Burma. They also grow wheat, sugar cane, and cotton. The eastern section is the world's largest exporter of raw jute. Fish and fish products are likewise important exports. The main manufactured products are paper, burlap, and cotton textiles. The only fuel or mineral produced on a larger scale is natural gas. There is some poor-quality coal. The country's known iron ore deposits are either in difficult locations or of poor quality.

A Mexican dwarf wheat is being tested on experimental farms in hopes of doubling wheat production, which is a major source of food in the west. The Western people eat more meat, the Eastern rely heavily on their fish for protein intake.

. . . . THE PEOPLE

The Western area is peopled by a dozen races that numbers approximately 53,000,000. They are of all sizes and complexions. These people speak Urdu, a mixture of Hindi and Persian with heavy borrowing from religious Arabic. On the other hand, the people in the East speak Bengali, a tongue written in a thousand year-old alphabet, totally unlike Urdu. Small, dark-skinned, and fine featured, the Eastern people excel in the gentle arts of painting and poetry, music and dance. These people number 63,000,000, thus having over half of the population with 15% of the nation's land area. East Pakistan is one of the most densely populated areas in the world. Though West and East are separated by many things, they share the problem of over-crowding. If growth rate is not checked their present population will have doubled by 1985.

The family takes precedence over all other loyalties, with those to the tribe, the religious sect, and the district, following. A sense of nationality is gradually evolving.

Pakistan, like other Asian countries, is gravely beset with problems of public health aggravated by extremes of climate and widespread malnutrition. The great menace is malaria, though efforts are being made to eradicate this disease, as well as tuberculosis and smallpox.

The literacy rate when Pakistan began as a nation was below 18.9% but they are trying to improve this with new schools, adult training centers, etc. Compulsory education is a goal not yet attained. Girls attend separate schools at both primary and secondary levels.

The English language will be used for all official purposes until 1976, and beyond if it proves expedient. It is the only language common to both wings (West and East). There are several other local languages in use in various sections.

Because Pakistan was formed as a refuge and home for the Moslems of the India subcontinent, it is religiously overwhelmingly Moslem, with some Hindus, Buddhists, Christians, animists, and Parsis. The Hindus are concentrated in East Pakistan and constitute about 20% of that province's population. Most of the Christians are primarily in West Pakistan.

184

. . . . THE MISSIONARY . . . .

Our first missionaries to Pakistan arrived in 1960, the Lee Turner family of Oregon. In those early days brother Lee studied at Punjab University, did linguistic research, and made contacts for Christ wherever possible. The mastery of this language (in the West) requires a new way of thinking as well as mastery of the difficult Persian alphabet and of various phonetical characteristics not encountered in English.

Soon after their arrival the Turners began to teach in various villages around Lahore. By November 1961 Lee was translating the New Testament into Urdu with the aid of Professor William James. Progress is, of necessity, quite slow. Various religious groups have set up schools and offered scholarships to those who affiliate with their groups. Often times church affiliation means nothing more to a Pakistani than an opportunity to gain an education or some other material benefit. Care must be taken to show these people the true meaning of following Jesus.

The year 1963 was a very significant year for the Turners. They witnessed their first four conversions which so perfectly represents the broad appeal of the Gospel. The first convert holds a M.A. degree, another one was a high school graduate and a government employee. A third one is completely illiterate. The fourth one reads simple Urdu and is a bricklayer. Yet in Christ they are all one, for Christ died for all. Another event in 1963 was the arrival of Muriel Oberst. She soon began work at the United Christian Hospital in Lahore, and within two years she was also practicing midwifery in Lahore and several surrounding villages.

The Pakistan-Indian war of 1965 broke out while the missionaries were on furlough but when they returned in 1966 they found that the native Christians had carried on very well. Attendance in the village of Shah Jawal reached seventy. They increased evangelism in the villages, stressed teaching programs for women as well as the men. In 1967 they translated VBS materials and adapted them for use in the villages. The women missionaries hope to be able to teach the Pakistani people simple sanitary measures, child care, and hygiene, and to administer medication and treat various diseases.

In 1969 brother Lee started using recording equipment to teach the people how to read and write, for the purpose of sharing with them the privilege of reading God's Word in their own language. This knowledge and ability will enable them to become better established in the faith. This is especially important as there is an increasing bitterness of the Muslim people toward Christianity.

186

Syria

"Land of the Bedouins"

S Y R I A

● Aleppo

● Hama

Damascus

THE LAND . . . .

Syria is an independent state in Southwest Asia. Once a part of the United Arab Republic it seceded at the end of September 1961. Syria has remained an ardent proponent of Arab unity though a practical union with Egypt proved unsuccessful. Syria, along with other Arab countries, is an implacable foe of Israel. In the renewed Arab-Israeli hostilities of 1967, Israel troops crossed the 1949 armistice line and occupied the southwestern corner of Syria. Changes of boundary lines occurred even as early as Bible times.

An over-all deficiency of moisture and a marked seasonal distribution of precipitation characterize the climate of Syria. Most rain falls in winter; summer is generally dry. Temperatures in the desert areas tend to be somewhat more extreme than those of the Mediterranean coastlands. The average July temperature for Damascus, the capital, on the western edge of the "steppe" is 82 degrees F. Frost and snow are common in the northern steepe areas.

The rivers of Syria are important because of the vital need of irrigation water. However, only the Euphrates to the northeast and the Orontes on the west are capable of supplying sufficient water to irrigate large tracts of land. Irrigation is retarded by difficult engineering and political problems. Only about 35% of Syria's land is arable, and the best soils, where a wide variety of crops can be grown, represent only about 10% of the surface area, yet 65% of the people are rural. The steppes and deserts, which account for more than half the area of Syria, have low rainfall and extreme temperatures which limit economic activity to grazing, carried on by nomads, much as it was done in Bible times. Animal production accounts for about one-third of the value of the agricultural output; cultivated crops, such as wheat, cotton, fruits, and barley, account for the remaining two-thirds.

Modern manufacturing is very recent in Syria. By far the most important industry is textile manufacturing. The leading industrial center is Alappa, with textile, cement, match and other factories, closely followed by Damascus, with textile, cement, glassware, cardboard, rubber boots and shoes, match and canning factories.

Syria's traditional ports were Haifa, Beirut, and Tripoli in the south, and Alexandretta in the north, but all these cities now lie outside Syrian territory. Since 1950 a new port has been built at Latakia to handle the tons of import-export items.

. . . . THE PEOPLE

Life for the more than five million Arabic-speaking Syrians is characterized by the conflict between a small, highly educated, Westernized upper-class minority and a large and illiterate (or barely literate) majority whose forms of life, dress and customs have hardly changed in centuries. Women in the rural districts are still veiled, though women of the cities have placed their veil aside to participate in the literary, social, and political life of the country.

Organized in tribes, the nomads still roam the deserts wherever pastureage for their herds is found. The majority of the population eke out an existence as tenent farmers or sharecroppers. Their villages of mud-brick huts dot the countryside.

Illiteracy is high, in 1960 it was almost 60% of the non-Bedouin (nomads) population over ten years of age. However this is being reduced by expanding educational facilities and the use of new tools, as radio, for mass education. Elementary education, for five years, is free and compulsory, but it seems impossible to provide it in every village.

Arabic is the literary language, but European languages, especially French, are often used for scholarly publications. Syria's intellectual life is well developed, especially influenced by the French, and is concentrated in Damascus. Damascus is reputed to be the oldest continuously inhabited city in the world.

About 70% of the total population are Muslims, most of them adhering to a monotheistic creed and traditions set by the majority sect, the Sunnis. The Alawis constitute an important minority in Syria. Although they consider themselves Muslims, they combine their avowed creed with Christian rituals and esoteric cults. Among the dozen or more different Christian communities the largest are the Greek Orthodox and the Armenian Gregorian. The Protestants and Jews are small in number, and a very small number of Yazidis are devil worshippers. Under the constitution, the president of Syria must be a Muslim, and Islamic law is recognized as being a major source of legislation, but freedom of belief and worship and the rites of the several religious communities are guaranteed.

. . . . THE MISSIONARY . . . .

For nearly nine years, Sammy Brake, a young Syrian convert, studied in the United States in preparation for returning to his homeland. In January 1963 he reentered Syria, recognized by the government as an ordained minister of the Christian faith. This makes him exempt from military service, but by the same token he is not allowed to make a living by any other means than his service as a minister.

He has been able to speak occasionally at some established church gatherings, but more in line with the intention of his ministry, he has been able to meet regularly for quite some time now with a group of young University men who are interested in the study of the Scriptures and prayer. Included in this group is a Roman Catholic and an Orthodox. The Syrian University of Damascus in 1964 had a membership of nearly eight hundred students of Christian background and four thousand Muslims.

Syria is only mildly tolerant of Christians, and governed by leaders who have great distaste for the political powers of the West, feeling they are responsible for the presence of the state of Israel. Thus as Christ's servant in Damascus, Sammy Brake does most of his work through individual personal witnessing. To evangelize directly among Muslims is forbidden by law.

Thailand

"Land of the Yellow-Robe"

THE LAND . . . .

Bounded on the north by Burma and Indochina; on the east by Indochina; on the south by Indochina, the Gulf of Siam and the Federation of Malaya; and on the west by the Bay of Bengal and Burma, is Thailand, the land that is named for freedom.

Formerly known as Siam, in 1939 Thailand was proclaimed the official title of the country. Not being free under Japanese occupation it was called Siam again, only to resume its "free" name when their independence was restored.

It is about four-fifths the size of Texas, with a 1966 estimated population of 31,508,000. Geographically it may be divided into four great natural regions: 1) Northern Thailand, the mountainous region between the Salween and Mekong rivers; 2) Eastern Thailand, which is a part of the Mekong drainage system; 3) Central Thailand, the basin of the Chao Phya River; 4) and Peninsular Thailand, the northern two-thirds of the Malay Peninsula.

The mountains of Northern Thailand form a series of parallel ranges divided by cultivated valleys. They vary in height from low hills in the southeast to five to eight thousand feet peaks in the northwest. Approximately seven percent of the land is under cultivation.

Eastern Thailand, a poor and sparsely populated area, slopes eastward to the Mekong River from a height of 1,000 feet. For the most part it is a high, dry plain. The raising of cattle, hogs, buffaloes and horses is more important than crop agriculture. What little is grown is consumed locally. It is a region of tropical scrub, thorn trees and high grass.

The richest section of the country, and the most densely populated, is Central Thailand. Consisting of a flat river valley flooded in the rainy season and irrigated by artificial means in dry weather, it is an area of high grass, bamboo and palms. Here it is that Thailand's main-stay and great crop, rice, is produced. Where once 97% of the arable land was devoted to rice growing, now some sixty per cent is planted in rice and the remaining cultivated land is used for rubber trees, crops from which oil may be produced, and for secondary food crops. Bangkok, the capital, is located in this central section. Both modern and oriental, it presents an interesting picture to the many tourists who travel there.

The chain of mountains along the Burmese frontier extends into the Malay Peninsula, dividing peninsular Thailand lengthwise. This strip which is forty to one hundred miles wide contains the bulk of the country's mineral wealth, of which tin is the most important. Rubber plantations are extensive. There are likewise rubies, sapphires, and other precious and semiprecious stones. Less than four percent of the working population in 1960 was engaged in industry.

About 55% of the total area is forested. In the north, forests of hardwood, especially teak, are found, as well as pines. About one-third of the world's supply of teak is furnished by Thailand. In the central region, bamboo trees and coconut and betel palms abound. Mangroves and rattans are plentiful in the coastal lowlands. A wide variety of tropical fruits also abound, such as mango, durian, pomegranate and pineapple.

Thailand's wild life is the most extensive in the world. The forests are full of big game animals such as tigers, leopards, honey-bears, and single-horned rhinoceroses. Several species of deer, sheep, goats, oxen and water buffalo are found, and the ordinary gray elephant is used to haul teak. The white elephant, actually pale gray, is considered sacred. The Siamese cat is the most unusual of the domesticated animals. Birds of a thousand varieties are found throughout Thailand; the forests harbor peacocks, pheasants, and pigeons. Fish are abundant in the rivers and coastal waters. There are fifty-six varieties of snakes of which only twelve are poisonous.

Except for the area around Bangkok, and through roads running to Indochina, there is, properly speaking, no adequate highway system in Thailand. In some of the outlying areas roads have been drastically improved due to the battles of border wars. Until recent years, the elephant, the coolie, and the oxcart were the chief means of transportation, and still are in remote sections. Today modern railroads have generally replaced these primitive methods of transportation. Rivers are important highways of trade; three-fourths of the freight traffic are carried on inland waterways.

Thailand is tropical and has a high degree of humidity. The weather is generally rainy from May to October during the southwest monsoon, except on the Malay peninsula where heavy rains fall even during the northeast monsoon (October-February), and is dry the remainder of the year. November to February is considered the "cold" season. For most of the year the weather is hot. The greatest extremes of temperature are in eastern Thailand; the most equable, on the Peninsula. Except in the elevated interior, the northern section's minimum temperature seldom goes below sixty-five degrees and maximum temperatures above one-hundred degrees are rare.

. . . . THE PEOPLE

Except for a few Negritos living in the mountains, almost all the people of Thailand are of Mongoloid stock, having originally come from south China. The Chinese, one of the larger minority groups, have retained their own language and customs. They are the business men of the country. Moslem Malayans live on the peninsula. Cambodians, Annamese, Shans and Burmese represent a part of the population. Numerous but small remnant groups of tribes that possibly entered Thailand from the north inhabit the remote hill sections of the north and west. Among these are the Lisu, Yao, Lao, Sgaw Pwo Karen, Lahu, Akha, and the Blue and White Mao.

In general the northern Thai resemble Chinese; they tend to be taller and lighter skinned than the southern Thai or Siamese. Their eyes are well shaped, slightly inclined to the oblique. Noses are broad and flat and lips are prominent. The face is wide across the cheekbones and the chin short. Hair is coarse and black.

The typical Siamese is gentle and good natured, patient and hospitable. They are intelligent and courageous, and lovers of freedom from which cause they effected the change of name. They are likewise industrious, but not commercial. They are tolerant and have no caste distinction among their own people, but they do look down upon the tribespeople.

Health is generally good except when there are epidemics of malaria, cholera and plague. Vaccinations for such were made compulsory in 1914, though this did not affect the large tribal population. Male life expectancy at birth is forty-nine years, female is slightly higher. The tribes who dwell in the remote parts have a natural death rate uninfluenced by modern medicine. However in more recent years missionaries have been able to treat some of the tribal people.

Thailand is an overwhelmingly rural country, and the lives of the people are governed by the seasons of planting and harvesting. It is estimated that 88% of the population still lives in small villages. The peasants in eastern Thailand are largely self-sufficient, weaving their own cloth and buying few manufactured goods. In other parts of the country, surplus rice is normally exchanged for the few things the people cannot make themselves.

Housing in the rural area is simple. Because of the warm weather, a simple bamboo structure built in a day or two is usually sufficient. In Bangkok and a few other cities some Western-style houses have been built, although these are not always suited to the heat and humidity.

Each village has a wat, the name for the Buddhist temple. Traditionally, Thai boys have been educated in Buddhist monasteries, and more than 77% of the local public schools and 23% of the government schools were located in monasteries, but more and more children are being educated in public schools. In 1921 education was made compulsory for all children between the ages of seven and fifteen. Primary education lasts four years, secondary six years, and university preparation two years. About 35% of the people remain illiterate.

การคัดเลือกไข่, การบรรจุน้ำผึ้ง จากสวนผึ้งลงขวดหรือการ
ตัดขนแกะ ที่ตกหนาจากแกะตัวอ้วน ๆ นั้น เป็นความ สบายใจและ
ยั่วให้เด็กชายหญิงทำงานช่วยเหลือ งานประเภทนี้ช่งตนเองได้คลก
คล้อยู่ในต่างประเทศโดยการอาศัยอยู่ตาม ครอบครัวต่าง ๆ ในชน
บท อันมีวิถีชีวิตแปลกกว่าทางบ้านเกิดของตนโดยสิ้นเชิง.

Sample of Thai script.

The Thai language is an Indo-Chinese language of monosyllabic and tonal nature. There are forty-four consonants, divided into three classes, and thirty-two vowels. The vowels are expressed by signs placed around the consonants. There are also accents to indicate the five tones. The tribes speak their own language, of which three at least have never been reduced to writing. Many of the tribespeople are bilingual, however, so can be reached through the language of another tribe.

Buddhism is the state religion with 90% of the population nominally Buddhists. Quite naturally Thailand has been called the Land of the Yellow Robe since that is the characteristic dress of the Buddhist monks. Naturally most of the people are orthodox Buddhists, though many Brahmanic characteristics are found which are of ancient Indian origin. There are also many Moslems, Confucians, and some Christians, including both Catholic and Protestant missions. Of animistic origin are the charms and talismans popular in northern Thailand. Each Buddhist temple bears the image of the elephant, portraying the importance of the sacred white elephant, which, legend tells us, was one of the seven gifts made to the infant Buddha.

Though this is the "land of the free" they are a people under bondage to the heathen gods.

. . . . THE MISSIONARY . . . .

At daybreak October 18, 1949 the little ship Hoi Wong lifted anchor and sailed thirty miles up the Chao Phya River to dock in Bangkok. Among the passengers were the first undenominational missionaries from America to Thailand. Down the gangplank went the C. W. Callaway family and Miss Imogene Williams. Due to the advance of Communism these had only recently flown from Kunming, West China to Hong Kong. Still desiring to be used of the Lord in the Orient, they prayed that He might guide to the place of His choosing. The Lord at the appropriate time provided information regarding Thailand and the knowledge that the door to this land stood ajar. From this point, He led them to make Thailand their new field of service.

There had been no time to gain a background knowledge of the country and of conditions which they would meet. They had, however, learned that there were mountain tribespeople in at least the northern-most sector of the country. They purposed to go to that area as soon as possible inasmuch as they had previously been preparing for tribal work, feeling that opportunities for conversions would be greater among the tribes than with the Buddhist plainspeople. Of necessity they spent a little more than six months in Bangkok to begin the study of the Thai language and to make investigations regarding the field.

In February 1950, C. W. Callaway flew to Chiengmai, Northern Thailand to seek a location for the beginning of the work. In that province he saw Lisu, Miao and Muhso tribespeople. Having read that there were many tribespeople around a lovely little town called Chieng-kam in another province to the east, he desired to investigate. It was evident that here indeed was a wide area with many tribespeople as well as plainspeople needing the Gospel and with denominational work in only a few lowland centers. It seemed God's will for the work to begin in Chiengkam.

On May 11 three ox carts (in front of which walked the three adult missionaries and two little American boys) lumbered slowly into the little community of Chiengkam. Less than a year later (March 1951) Dorothy Uhlig joined the group, who, by this time, if not accepted, were at least tolerated. Later that same year Garland and Dorothy Bare reached Bangkok, arriving in Chiengkam in December Mel and June Byers came in March 1953. Like the Callaways, they had sought entrance to Burma but were denied resident visas. Mel had previously spent about two years in West China and Northern Burma. One year after their arrival in Thailand, Don and Roberta Byers, brother and sister-in-law of Mel Byers, joined them in the work.

The main activity for most of the missionaries in Chiengkam during the early period was the tedious, but very necessary, process of learning the language. Among the languages dealt with were Bangkok Thai, Northern Thai, Chinese and Yao. (Others were added later.) Services were held in the village but a denominational element in the community, steeped in sin to the point of being a definite hindrance to any witness that was borne, made the response slow. However, a few sought for the deeper life and through contact in the medical clinic, which was conducted by Dorothy Uhlig, assisted by Imogene Williams, some came from the ranks of heathenism.

A visit made by Imogene and Mrs. Callaway to the Leper Village at Sope Waan (three miles from Chiengkam) in August 1951 resulted in the biggest evangelistic success of the early days of their work. Seventy of the villagers were baptized during 1953. When the first ones, after patient teaching, showed a desire to be baptized a special prayer meeting was called in their behalf. The next day, instead of the dozen that had been anticipated, thirty-six wended their way to the front of the tiny bamboo building. One by one as conviction came upon them they stated their faith in Christ and were immediately taken to the river for baptism. Again and again the missionaries taught, giving all they had, yet it was not until the Spirit moved in the hearers' hearts that they were even able to believe. It is understandable when you consider the complete difference in all their religious training. They are concerned with merit-making and propitiation of the evil spirits, then the missionary tells them of atonement through the blood of Jesus Christ. It is so diametrically opposed to anything they have ever heard, they simply cannot believe it until the Spirit opens their understanding.

Imogene Williams took a course in Leprology in Chiengmai in 1951 and for a number of years did most of the medical work among the lepers. Others of the missionaries helped in the teaching program. For several years they conducted Bible-Literacy courses for the leper children who were not allowed in regular government schools. Eventually the government did provide medical aid and a special school, thus the missionaries' efforts could be placed in more direct evangelism.

Both Mel and Don Byers were well-fitted physically and spiritually for the rugged mountain evangelism found useful in this field. They made many contacts with the forgotten tribes of northern Thailand, preparing the way for new openings for Gospel preaching. As the opportunity of evangelism in neighboring villages increased there was a real need for wisdom in guiding and instructing them that the work thus established might be permanent.

Prayers followed the missionaries as they left on trip after trip to find the tribes in the mountains and the people on the plains.

Finally, with assurance of the Lord's leading, two outposts were established.

One of the tribal areas visited by Mel Byers and Garland Bare was in Nan Province about fifty miles south and east of Chiengkam. Tribes in this area included T'in, White Miao, Black Miao, Yao, and Khamoo. Interest in this section was so encouraging that early in 1954 the Garland Bare family moved to Pua as a new base for their work. Progress in this area proved to be slow, but a triumphant day came in August 1955 when nine adults in the Khamoo village of Nam Mong were buried with their Lord in baptism. Immediately a wave of persecution began which sorely tried the faith of these new believers. The ringleaders were three men who stood to lose much social prestige if many villagers became Christians. Yaum and Khaek were witch doctors and village elders. Kham Mong was the headman's 25-year old son and the social leader among the young people. To combat the slanderous attacks, a campaign of prayer for the ringleaders was begun, the outcome of which greatly strengthened the Bares' faith in the power of prayer. By the beginning of 1956 a change was noted in the attitude of the persecutors. Eventually all three became Christians and sought to continue study of His Word. The church at Nam Mong was instrumental in beginning new churches in two other villages in 1959. During the following year fifty-eight souls were added to the Lord. One major difficulty was that only four could read.

Along with his other work and language study, Garland Bare revised the Thai Old Testament that it might be more understandable to the tribes who are bi-lingual in the north Thai dialect. For a number of years the Bares were absent from the field while Garland completed medical training, first in the States, then in Thailand. He is the first American to take medical training in Thailand—in the Thai language. He received his degree in January 1969. Following furlough they should be able to resume their work among the villages, but this time he will have a new and effective tool to reach some of the hearts of the people.

For a number of years Imogene Williams and Dorothy Uhlig longed to work among the Miao people in their own villages, but instead they remained at the "home" base to witness to the Miao and other tribespeople who came for medicine and to listen to Gospel recordings in their own language. Occasionally they were able to make trips into their villages along the Laos border. Thai natives regard the mountain people as inferior. They consider them to possess the mind of an animal. Only recently has tribal languages been reduced to writing.

Portions of the New Testament are translated into the Miao language. The mountain people have been exploited and corrupted by opium and are slaves to devil worship. Thus the work was not easy where they attempted to witness to both the Thai and the mountain people at the same time. The love of God is strong enough, however, to eventually remove these barriers and make them brothers in Christ.

Miao hostel children returning from school.

Playing Gospel recordings in native language.

In October 1963 when the Bares left their work at Pua for medical school, Imogene moved to take over the hostel for Miao tribal children who were attending the local Thai school. At that time there were only five children. By the end of 1967 there were forty-one living at the hostel. Three are baptized believers, though others of them believe. Regular Bible classes are held for the children as well as singing each evening. Parents of the children come often to visit and listen to Gospel records and tapes. By the end of 1968 over 2,000 Miao tribal refugees had resettled on the plains near Pua. Weekly visits and caring for their sick is helping to win their friendship and interest in the Gospel. Imogene also worships with the seven Miao Christians at the camp. Though the Lord never permitted Imogene to move to a Miao village He arranged for the village to move to her.

Miao girls in tribal clothes.   *Miao girls in Thai school uniforms.*

Miao children learning to tell time.

The C. W. Callaway family laid the groundwork in the first Yao village in the spring of 1952. They found the Yao to be a peaceful, happy-natured people, quieter than their Miao neighbors. They are seemingly cleaner and more refined in some ways but are still a very uninhibited people. The biggest blight on their lives is their constant fear of demons. Perhaps the greatest obstacle to their becoming Christians was reluctance to give up their very lucrative illicit opium trade.

When the Callaways returned to the States in 1953 for their furlough they enrolled in the Summer Institute of Linguistics. This course is designed especially for missionaries who work with tribes that have no written language. The first Yao primer and dictionary were mimeographed in 1959, and a rough draft of Acts was started late in 1958. A translation of Mark and John, accomplished by those of the former China Inland Mission, was mimeographed into the new Thai-Yao script by the Callaways.

Until December 1960 the Callaways lived in the Yao mountain villages but eventually government orders forced them to leave, due to border warfare (fifteen minutes from their village). They came down to Chiengkam where Dorothy Uhlig and the Byers families still lived. They continued to translate material and were permitted to visit the Yao villages occasionally for teaching and preaching. As trouble persisted in the mountains the Yao tribespeople were moved to the plains in a resettlement area six miles from Chiengkam, thus the Callaways were able to resume a complete teaching program, both Bible and literacy. With opium no longer a product of income, the Yao turned to embroidery work, with the help of the missionaries. Evangelistic efforts are bringing results in this area, among the Yao, Luh and Khamoo. A dozen Chinese were baptized by the fall of 1968 and there were some evidences of life even among the slow-moving Thai population. The Callaways work with six congregations. In 1968 they were able to visit with the eight hundred Yao refugees that have settled at Pua.

The Callaways started plans for a more extensive youth program. This began abruptly one day when four Miao boys came to seek a home. A remodeled granary became that home. Other buildings are being remodeled so that dorm space can be provided for both Yao and Miao children for the new school term in May 1969.

Lisu Christian in Thailand.

Refused again a permit to enter Burma to work among the tribespeople, Dorothy Sterling came to Thailand in August 1959 where, in the northern section, live Lisu and Karen tribespeople. Following a period of language study in Bangkok she settled in Chiengmai to further prepare for tribal work. In Burma the Lisu were eager to learn of Christ and would walk many days' journey to beg someone to come teach them, but in north Thailand the Lisu and Karen were indifferent

205

to the Gospel. In 1962 and 1963 she witnessed to many different people, including the H'tin people along the Laotian border where few had heard the Gospel. However, in 1964 she returned to Chiengmai, the largest city in northern Thailand, to set up a medical clinic through which she is able to witness to the hundreds who come for treatment.

Also in 1959 David and Delores Filbeck arrived in Thailand. Their early efforts were to master the Thai language, then they began a pioneer missionary work among an unevangelized tribe. They analyzed and reduced to writing the Mal tribal language, and made a start in translating Bible stories into that language. In 1963 they were able to help establish the first church among the Mal. Within a year following their return from their first furlough in 1965 the devil won a great victory when all the Mal believers returned to animism. Further efforts to evangelize brought no visible success at that time. Thus in October 1967 the Filbecks moved to Chiengmai to begin Gospel radio programs in Lisu and Miao tribal languages in cooperation with South East Asia Christian Mission. Matwang tribal language programs are now also being prepared. The transistor radio has penetrated even the remotest areas of Asia. Not only do the Filbecks prepare programs but train personnel for radio programs in Bible while still carrying on a ministry of evangelism and teaching among the northern Thai (whom they have found to be very indifferent). They continue to pursue linguistic and anthropological research among the Mal tribe for further re-entry to teach them.

Christian Miao family listen to radio.

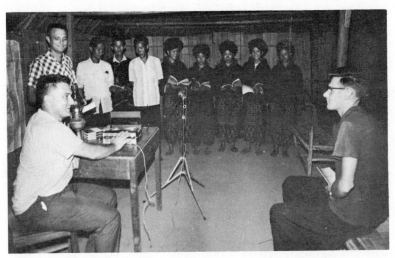

Recording session in Yao village (recording hymns).

The Byers' families returned to the States in 1968 to Stateside ministries, but their work will not be forgotten.

The Harry Schaefer family, missionary veterans of India, entered a new phase of work when they entered Bangkok in 1960 to work among the Indians there. Brother Schaefer accepted a teaching position in an International School, which gave them opportunities to survey the various areas. They witnessed to the 250,000 Indians, the largest untouched national group in the country. An Indian Christian Information Center was opened to concentrate the witnessing. Special classes were held. Radio programs were broadcast four days a week for part of their stay in Thailand. The Schaefers found the high mobility of the Indian population a difficult factor in establishing anything of a permanent nature, thus after four years they returned to the States for further study and are now serving the Indian population in Kenya, Africa.

The challenge of Thailand is a field white unto the harvest and laborers are few. One may enter provinces in the north to begin new work where no other missionaries have been. Thousands of tribal people are not even familiar with the name of Jesus Christ.

There are many people of many tongues, and each must be dealt with in his own tongue to be effective. As one native said when he heard the missionary tell the Gospel story in his own language, "You speak to my heart." Faith cometh by hearing and hearing by the Word of God.

Australia

THE LAND . . . .

The smallest of the continents, Australia lies between the Pacific and Indian Oceans, southeast of Asia. Neighboring areas include New Guinea to the north, New Zealand to the southeast, and Indonesia to the northwest. Owing to its isolation, Australia was not discovered by Europeans until early in the 17th century, and the first British settlement was not made until late in the 18th century.

The continent stretches 1,907 miles from north to south and 2,400 miles from east to west. Its total land area is slightly less than that of the United States (excluding Alaska and Hawaii). No continent has a smoother coastline or is more compact than Australia. One distinguishing feature is the Great Barrier Reef, longest and most spectacular coral reef in the world, which extends for about 1,200 miles off the east coast of the northeast state of Queensland. Less than 7% of the land is above 2,000 feet elevation. The only river that has a year-round flow is the Murray River, which is fed by the Darling and Murrumbidgee rivers, in the south east. The largest lakes have no outlet and are usually dry.

Although there is a wide diversity of climate (due largely to the amount of rainfall), in general Australia is relatively warm and dry, with no extreme cold and little frost. Long hours of sunshine are characteristic. The center of the continent is extremely arid where it may go without rain for several years. About 40% of the country is desert, another 40% is subhumid. On the whole it is a hot rather than cold continent. In most places there is only a small temperature difference between the hottest and the coolest months.

Long famous as a land of sheep, it is still one of the world's leading producers and exporters of wool, along with mutton, beef and wheat. All basic foodstuffs, that are required, are grown here, with large surpluses for export. Wheat is by far the most important crop grown in Australia. Other important grain crops are oats and barley. Nearly all types of fruit are grown. Since World War II considerable progress has been made on irrigation projects that greatly benefit the suppliers of wine, fruits, and dairy products. Most farmers must lease land for their agricultural efforts and good land is scarce.

Australia is also a highly industrialized country. Large deposits of coal and iron have become the basis for an iron and steel industry. Industry, both primary and secondary, is almost entirely privately owned; nearly all utilities are owned by public authorities. Chief needs are petroleum, rubber, and certain chemicals.

The mineral resources of Australia, though not as great as those of the United States or the Soviet Union, are still important. More than sixty varieties of minerals and metals have been commercially produced. The country is self-sufficient in coal, iron ore, and talc, and produces more than it needs of lead, zinc, silver, gold, tungsten, and a titanium ore. Recent discoveries have led to a new mining boom.

The total forest area of the country is small, thus imports of both timber and paper are considerable. Extensive reforestation has been introduced in an effort to help combat soil erosion, but it will be sometime before it will help supply any of their needs for lumber.

. . . . THE PEOPLE

Nearly twelve million people live in Australia. The vast majority of the population is of European, mainly British, origin. The aboriginals, who occupied the land prior to its settlement by the Europeans, were pushed to the north and northwest where they now live on "government reservations". There are about 45,000 full-blooded aborigines and 30,000 half-castes. Once considered an out-cast, the government has now adopted a policy of integration. The aborigines now qualify for social service benefits and are entitled to vote. Their University education is even subsidized. Most of them are nomadic hunters and food gatherers, without settled communities, but a few are employed at cattle stations and some serve as trackers for the police. Their social organization is among the most complex known to anthropologists.

Almost all the European population live in the well-watered narrow fringe of land parallel to the east and southeast coasts, or in a small corner of the southwest. Virtually no one lives in the arid interior.

English is spoken by more than 99% of the population. The characteristic Australian pronunciation of English has developed through a combination of several influences. Many languages or dialects are spoken by the aboriginal tribes, but phonetically they are markedly uniform. They have no written language.

Education for the European people is free, compulsory, and secular, and is provided by the individual states for their own students. Education is compulsory from ages 6 to 14, 15, or 16, depending upon the state. Secondary schools in the cities are divided into boys' and girls' schools, but in the country areas they are coeducational. There are some church-related private schools, mostly Catholic. Special primary and secondary schools have been opened in the areas where the aborigines live.

In times past community leaders have emphasized the virtues and needs of the practical man, so most Australians tend to prefer outdoor living and sports rather than the pursuit of learning and the arts. The most popular sports are horse racing, tennis, Rugby, football (by their own rules), and swimming.

According to the constitution of the country there cannot be a state religion. Neither can the exercise of any religion be prohibited nor a religious test be required as a qualification for public office. Most of the people are Protestant, about three million are members of the Church of England. Roman Catholic, Methodist, Presbyterian, Baptist, Congregational, Lutheran, and Jewish faiths have substantial memberships. The aborigines practice black magic and many rituals, some with religious significance.

. . . . THE MISSIONARY . . . .

The beginning of the Restoration Movement in Australia began in September 1845 when Thomas Magarey, who had been baptized in New Zealand, moved to Adelaide, Australia and commenced meetings there. In 1852 Albert Griffin in Sydney was influenced by Church of Christ publications sent from London, and he began a small group. From this small beginning the movement has grown to 405 churches, with 287 ministers, and 44,000 members. (Government census credits the church with a membership of 102,545.) There are three Bible Colleges (Brisbane, Sydney, and Melbourne) where young men and women are trained for the ministry and missionary service. Approximately one hundred and twenty are presently enrolled in the four-year course. One hundred and twenty missionaries are supported in India, New Guinea, New Hebrides and among the Aborigines in Australia itself. Prior to the establishing of their own Colleges, many ministers were trained in America.

In the early days growth of the movement was greatly assisted by American evangelism, through revival campaigns which lasted up to six weeks. The Sunday evening evangelistic meeting has also provided a means of growth to the work. Following the introduction of T.V. to the country these evangelistic efforts have been less successful than in earlier years. Greater dependence is now placed on visitation programs. To date little use has been made of the T.V. or radio for mass evangelism.

Reggie Thomas, American evangelist, and his team held meetings throughout Australia in the summer of 1967. Don DeWelt, Meredith Williams, and Wilbur Fields, all professors from Ozark Bible College,

Joplin, Missouri, will conduct revival services from June 15 to August 15, in the summer of 1969.

To assist in a more permanent way are three newly-arrived recruits. Darryl and Mrs. Carol Krause, sponsored by his home church in Honolulu, reached Sydney in October 1968. They will be assistants to David Mansell at the Wollongong Church of Christ. Their work will center around the youth activities, Christian education, and assisting in personal evangelism, along with pastoral visitation. When they have had an opportunity to familiarize themselves with the culture and environment of Australia they expect to assume full responsibilities of another congregation.

Delroy Brown, a national from Kingston, Jamaica, reached New South Wales, Australia, in November 1968 to begin his witness for the Lord in that place.

Central America

"The six republics of Central America resemble the links of a chain holding together the nations of the Western Hemisphere."

1 British Honduras
2 Guatemala
3 El Salvador
4 Honduras
5 Nicaragua
6 Costa Rica
7 Panama

216

El Salvador

"Littlest America"

THE LAND . . . .

El Salvador, tiniest of the six Central American republics, is also one of the most prosperous and best developed. Though the smallest, it ranks second in total population, over three million in 1966.

El Salvador consists of a broad upland valley between two not-too-high mountain ranges, plus a narrow coastal plain along the Pacific. Except on the mountain peaks, all the land is habitable and extremely fertile. About 61% of the population is rural; 30% of the land under cultivation.

The chief crop and source of income is coffee, ranking among the world's first five nations in coffee growing. The most unusual product of El Salvador is balsam of Peru. This is a resin extracted from trees that grow nowhere else in the world than the Pacific coast of El Salvador, and is used in making medicines and cosmetics.

The chief local industry is cotton textiles; most cotton is exported, chiefly to Japan. Although the country is one of the most industrialized in Central America, industry provides only about 15% of the gross national product.

The climate is tropical, but temperatures are somewhat cooler in the mountains. Rainfall is heavy throughout the country from May to October, but during the rest of the year dry north winds prevail and there is almost no rain.

Native animals include varieties of monkeys, jaguars, coyotes, tapirs, armadillos and ocelots. Crocodiles and alligators abound, plus both poisonous and non-venomous snakes, which includes the boa constrictor.

El Salvador's best known tourist feature is Izalco, the most active volcano in Central America, often referred to as the lighthouse of the Pacific, because its smoke and flames are a guide to ships.

. . . . THE PEOPLE

El Salvador's population today is almost 5% Indian, and nearly 93% metizo. Less than 2% are white or of European descent. The vast majority of its people have adopted the language and culture of Spain, although the Indian element, Toltec or Aztec, has influenced some of its culture. Because it has no frontage on the Caribbean, and was not exposed to slave trade, there are few negroes. The official language is Spanish; a few Indians speak Nahuatl.

The level of health has steadily improved. To improve this the government has waged war against yellow fever, malaria, and hookworm.

In doing so it supervises water supply and sewage systems and inspects products sold in markets and stores. Principal causes of death are gastroenteritis, influenza, malaria, measles, pneumonia, and bronchitis, caused or complicated by malnutrition, bad sanitation, and poor housing. The Ministry of Public Health and Social Welfare supervises institutions and hospitals for the infirm and aged and child welfare and maternal care services.

In the early 60's more than half of the urban dwellings still had earthen floors and adobe walls, and many had straw roofs. Rural housing conditions were more primitive. In a large percentage of the city homes even, there are no facilities for sanitation.

The rate of illiteracy is about 50%. Primary education is free and compulsory, but truancy is high, particularly in rural areas. A large number of rural families cannot afford to dispense with the labor of their children. The National University, with an approximate enrollment of 3,500, enjoys a good reputation throughout the hemisphere.

The dominant religion, due to the Spanish influence, is Roman Catholicism. Separation of church and state is provided for by the constitution, thus there is complete freedom of worship, theoretically speaking. There are many Protestant missions throughout the country, including Baptist, Lutheran, Mormon and Seventh-Day Adventist.

. . . . THE MISSIONARY . . . .

The Richard Gring family journeyed to the border at Eagle Pass, Texas early in 1963 to work with Harland Cary at Colegio Biblico. Learning the language and gaining some background information of the Spanish-speaking people, the Grings went on to Guatemala in August 1965 where they witnessed until May 1967 when they moved to El Salvador.

The Grings settled in San Salvador and the Lord opened the door for personal work among some of the people. There are opportunities to speak to indigenous groups such as the "Prince of Peace" group. They are also meeting with a college-age group that is directed by Inter-Varsity. Two groups, at Santa Ana and Curgagualo, east of San Salvador, are worshipping regularly. A new work has been begun among the "richer" in the capital city itself. There have been ten baptisms in the work in El Salvador. (The non-instrumental group has around ten groups meeting in El Salvador and more in Guatemala.)

Late in 1967 the Frank Dodd family entered El Salvador to begin a varied ministry of witnessing. One of the first programs was a Saturday children's hour club for English-speaking young people from ages 5-13. On Sunday evening a meeting was held regularly for teen and college age youth. From this group several accepted the Lord in obedience to His Word. Other activities included a women's study group and a night Bible study meeting. Opportunity came for Frank to present a weekly radio broadcast on Sunday night. For awhile Mary Dodd oversaw the correspondence course, "Light of Life", which the station offers. A national Christian girl was trained to take over this work. If the Dodds are able to return to El Salvador they plan to initiate a follow-up program.

Early in 1968 immigration laws were changed and the missionaries were forced to leave by the end of summer. The Grings paid the high cost of the residence papers and have returned to their work; the Dodds are in a States' ministry awaiting the new ruling allowing missionaries to live in the country without paying fees. This is the position that the Catholic priests have already.

Europe

"Land of contrasts"

1	Ireland
2	Scotland
3	England
4	Norway
5	Sweden
6	Finland
7	Denmark
8	Portugal
9	Spain
10	France
11	Belgium
12	Luxembourg
13	Netherlands
14	West Germany
15	East Germany
16	Switzerland
17	Italy
18	Austria
19	Czechoslovakia
20	Poland
21	Hungary
22	Yugoslavia
23	Rumania
24	Bulgaria
25	Albania
26	Greece

Belgium

"Land of the kitchen gardens"

● Antwerp

Genk ●

✩ Brussels

B E L G I U M

THE LAND . . . .

One of the smallest countries in Europe, and one of the most beautiful, Belgium covers an area slightly larger than Maryland, with more than three times as many people. There are more than fifteen times as many people to the square mile in Belgium as there are in the United States, a total of nearly nine and a half million inhabitants.

The greatest length is 120 miles, the greatest breadth, 145 miles. Belgium's coast line is only 42 miles long. Her borders touch three great trading countries, lying as a wedge between France, Germany, and the Netherlands.

Because Belgium is so far north, summer days are long, and warm and pleasant. Winter days are short and gloomy, with clouds and fog, but rather mild. The average rainfall on the coast is 28 inches but is double that in the interior.

Land is Belgium's most important natural resource. All the land that can be farmed (about 55%) is under careful cultivation. They create new land as well, reclaiming large tracts from the sea, called polders. This empoldered land is some of the most fertile in the country. Orchard crops are grown where vegetables do not thrive. Endive, white asparagus, fabulous hothouse grapes as big as plums and brussel sprouts all have international reputation; hence the title "the land of the kitchen gardens". The Belgian cooks are lavish with butter, cream and fat. Theirs is one of the richest diets in the world.

The country has great mineral wealth too; including coal, iron ore, zinc, lead and copper. Accessibility to some raw materials from the once Belgian Congo may be hindered until such time as the economic condition in the free Congo can stabilize itself under new leadership. Because of its economic importance, coal has been called 'black bread of Belgium'. One tenth of the country's man power is employed in its production. Textiles constitute the second most valuable export. Antwerp, one of the world's greatest ports, is a center for diamond cutting.

. . . . THE PEOPLE

'Ruled—but never dominated' is a description often given to the hard-working people of Belgium. Due to years of occupation they have a strong dislike for most forms of authority and an intense love of independence. There is another saying concerning these people, 'of all these, the Belgians are the bravest'. Their recovery from the war years has been called by some, the miracle of Belgium. By 1948 the national budget was balanced.

The population is made up of the Frankish, Dutch-speaking Flemings of the north, and the Celtic, French-speaking Walloons of the south. Thus the two official languages are French and Flemish, the latter being much like the Dutch language.

Most of the people work in large manufacturing industries, only a few, percentage-wise, on the small, extremely fertile, farms. They readily adopt new and more efficient ways of doing things, except for the individual farmers.

Most homes are small but comfortable. Everyday dress is simple. Farmers often wear wooden shoes to keep their feet dry.

Bicycling is a favorite national pastime. Pelote, a combination of tennis and handball, is likewise popular, and played by amateurs and professionals alike. Soccer and canoeing are also popular.

There is little organized sport in the Belgian schools. Education is free and compulsory for eight years beginning at age six. Classes are taught in the language of the region with the other national language taught on the side. They are one of the most literate nations in the world, in fact illiteracy is virtually nonexistent. Government supported high schools and junior colleges are common. The country offers many opportunities for higher learning. The private school system, largely Roman Catholic, enrolls over half of the students.

Most of the people are Catholic; however, there is freedom of religion. Though no census has been taken, it is estimated there are 24,000 Protestants and 35,000 Jews in Belgium. The government supposedly pays part of the income of all "clergymen".

. . . . THE MISSIONARY . . . .

Planned by the mind of God, supported by churches and individuals, convicted and led by the Spirit, another trained and yielded family was born into the service of Christ Jesus in Europe.

This story too had its beginning because of war. Though World War II was over troops were still everywhere in Europe, some going into a zone of occupation, others to ports of embarkation—and home. Here it was that Don Sharp, an American service man assigned to Military Police duty in Lille, France, met Monsieur Don Castelein, the interpreter assigned to their company. For this job he was an excellent choice, speaking not only French, but Flemish (Belgian) and German as well. These two became close friends in these months of duty, but in the early spring of 1946 Don Sharp returned home to the States. An effort to make contact with his friend overseas was unsuccessful. The letter returned "address unknown", so he resigned himself to the fact that they would probably never hear of each other again.

In 1949 the greatest single event occurred in the life of Don Sharp —his acceptance of Jesus Christ as Saviour. Later that year he entered the ministry at Johnson Bible College. No other event occurred dealing specifically with this story until at the end of 1951 when a letter arrived from Lille, France.

In France, Donald Castelein had lost his friend's address. One day in December 1951 his wife asked him to repair a dresser. He had trouble moving one of the drawers, and when it was finally freed he found a small scrap of paper, on it was the lost address.

This was the beginning of an exchange of letters that led to the journey of Don Sharp and Elliott Massey, backed with prayer of students and faculty of Johnson Bible College, to France in March 1952 to make a personal witness to Don Castelein of the saving power of the Gospel. On the day after their arrival both Don Castelein and his wife were immersed into Christ, in a lily pool in the park. The desire of the Casteleins to train for a Christian ministry marked the beginning of the French Christian Mission, and Brother Castelein was flown to this country to enroll in Bible College in the fall of 1952, followed by his family some weeks later. They were tempted in many ways through various people to remain in the States following graduation but the still small voice told them to go into the darkness of countries filled with paganism, idolatry and communism. It was in this hour of decision that a message was received from Dr. Deelstra, a school teacher in Belgium who was leading the only non-Catholic endeavor in East Belgium. By November 1956 the Casteleins were in Genk, Belgium, laboring for Christ. It was not an easy field. Those who would accept Christ must ofttimes give up their earthly family to gain the heavenly.

For a time after their arrival on the field, the Casteleins met with a group in a Protestant school building. There were about fifty-five conversions and baptisms from November 1956 until the end of July 1958. At that time the property was taken over by the Baptists and the church moved its meeting to the Castelein home, where attendance by summer of 1960 was reaching the seventy mark. From mid-1958 to the end of September 1960 there were thirty-one new converts. These were the result of personal evangelism, house to house calling, plus the efforts of Spirit-led church members. Prayers changed the hearts of quite a few who opposed the work, several of whom are numbered among those who have found the Lord. This work continued to flourish and brother Castelein spent himself in his witness. His life was taken very suddenly in May 1965 from a heart attack. Mrs. Castelein remained on the field but felt the need of assistance.

The call was extended to the Milton Duhons to come as evangelists to Genk in September 1965. They were able to continue the program of teaching and calling. Under their guidance the congregation became self-supporting and a sanctuary was completed. During their 1968 furlough the elders assumed preaching responsibilities and continued to do so. In 1969 the Duhons hope to establish a new congregation in Houthalen, a few miles away from Genk.

In July 1969 the Harold Fowlers, who have served previously in Italy, came to Genk to make it a center for a teaching program. Christian Leadership Training Institutes will be held in various centers as the need arises. Others who will assist will be Milton Duhon, Ron Butler in France, and Guy Mayfield, as his schedule allows.

European Christians are to be found scattered all over the continent in groups as small as two or three persons in a town and sometimes twenty-five to thirty, but rarely as many as seventy-five to one hundred in one place. These groups plead for help to augment their Christian witness, but there are not enough foreign evangelists to go around. The answer could lie in European evangelists but here a problem is presented too. Any likely prospect has to work for his living and would find only limited, part-time Bible study possible. Further, there may be ten churches in all of Europe that fully sustain their own preacher; the rest have men who support themselves by regular jobs and preach as a sideline. However, these teaching Institutes will assist in better preparing these to preach His Word. By January 1969 they had completed teaching the first series of lessons to an Italian group in France. A similar session was held in Germany for Americans and Italians. Brother Fowler drives thousands of miles most weeks to visit these scattered Christians, bringing them specially planned lessons, showing them how to be self-sustaining, without American funds, self-governing, and self-propagating.

David and Sharon Stitt arrived in Genk in August 1968 and, with the assistance of the Christians there, were able to find a place to live. While they are engaged in language study they are able to teach the youth at the church (enough of whom know English and can translate for the others who don't). The Stitts have made several survey trips to determine where best to begin a new work in Europe. Many areas in Germany, France, and Switzerland are wanting help in starting Bible study groups and churches from contacts made through the radio program carried on by Ed Fauz in Germany.

Jim and Charlea Cormode plan to go to the field in the summer of 1969 for a year and a half internship. He has had special training in the area of radio broadcasting.

In August 1967 Guy and Thelma Mayfield, who have served in Italy, came to Brussels where brother Mayfield is teaching in a new American high school. On the week-ends they work in both Italian and English-speaking churches. Since Brussels is a center for Congo missionaries to study their French language, they have had at various intervals several representatives in Brussels. In 1967 there were seven. The Mayfields also sponsor a service camp and retreat for military, business men, and missionaries. This is held each year in Switzerland. Much of their work is with Christian service men who are stationed in Europe.

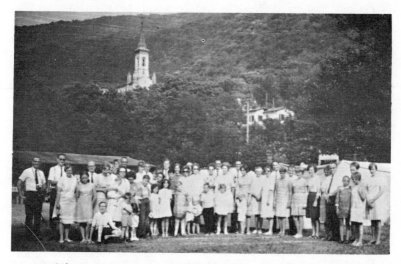

The Lugano Retreat and Christian Service Camp—1968.

England

"Land of the Kings and Queens"

ENGLAND

Liverpool
Manchester
Leeds
London
Southampton
Dover

0   50   100

THE LAND . . . .

England lies in the southeast part of the island of Great Britain, covering three-fifths of the area. It is a small country in size but one of the most important in the world. It covers an area smaller than the state of Alabama, yet its people built the first great industrial civilization. The population now totals over forty-six million.

Low rolling, fertile plains cover most of England. Rugged mountains rise in the north and west parts of the country. The western area is mild and wet in winter and cool and less wet in summer, while the eastern area is cold and dry in winter and spring, and hot and less dry in summer and autumn. The south coast occupies an inter-mediate position—climate-wise.

The amount of sun experienced in various places varies naturally with the seasons, though there is more sunshine recorded for some coastal regions than for inland areas. It is estimated that mists, fogs and clouds obscure the sun for about two-thirds of the time.

The cultivation of wheat finds highly suitable soil in the east, but the climate in many parts makes harvest risky. Oats, more tolerant of rain, are grown in the north and southwest. Barley is grown in many different areas. Fruit orchards of apples, plums, and cherries are important in several of the counties.

The most numerous land birds are probably the chaffinch and the blackbird, the most familiar are the house sparrow, the robin and, to the Londoners, the pigeon. The coast is very rich in the sea birds and waders.

. . . . THE PEOPLE

The English people developed a strong love of freedom early in their history, hence the saying 'an Englishman's home is his castle'. They enjoy the customs and traditions that go with their form of government.

They are usually good-natured, tolerant, and naturally moderate. Their 'aloofness', as it appears to Americans, is their way of regarding the privacy of others because they are a people who live crowded together.

They have a keen sense of humor but do not display it with the use of practical jokes. Recreation is an important part of English life. They believe that boys should learn courage, sportsmanship and quick thinking by playing games. Cricket is the national sport.

All children between the ages of five and fifteen must attend school. Elementary and secondary schools, financed by localities, provide free textbooks and supervise student health. Schools serve free milk and may sometimes provide free lunches. England is a country of one language, but many dialects. Modern movies and radio are having their effect upon the spoken language, making pronunciation more uniform.

The Church of England is the official state church, established by the Parliament. In belief and ritual the Protestant Episcopal Church of the United States is patterned after the Church of England. The Monarch must belong to the Church of England, but every other person in the country is free to worship where and as he pleases. Most of England's people are members of this Church, however, only about one-fifth of the membership is active. There are many Protestant groups (Methodists—over one million, Baptists—335,000, Congregationalists—225,000) while Roman Catholicism numbers nearly as many as, if not more than, the Anglican Church. Islamic mosques have been established in Birmingham, London and Manchester, and there is even a Buddhist temple in London.

. . . . THE MISSIONARY . . . .

It is in Manchester that a new gospel work was started by the Dean Wegwart family. This new field is a direct result of the "search the Scriptures" English broadcast heard over Radio Luxembourg. Their first work was in the follow-up program of the response to the broadcast, which includes correspondence, personal calls and arrangements for meetings of various groups to the end that churches may be established after the New Testament pattern.

In 1961 they moved to the smaller area of Cheshire where they contacted four hundred families and started a Bible study class in their home. In 1964 a door opened in London when a call came from thirty Christians from the West Indies who had immigrated to England since their conversions. Brother Wegart conducted Bible studies for them for several months but his other work, plus the travel distance, prevented a continuation of this work on a permanent basis. According to our last report the Wegwarts are no longer working for the cause of New Testament Christianity, though verification of this has not been received.

France

"Playground of the world"

THE LAND . . . .

France, a republic, is the largest European country west of the Soviet Union. She has been a nation for longer than any other European country. In some respects France is a fortunate country: not over-populated (due to wars and adoption of birth control measures), able to produce almost all the food she needs, and is a lovely placce in which to live.

Once a part of the Roman Empire, France transmitted its Latin heritage to northern Europe, and it has been at the heart of Western cultural life since the High Middle Ages. In the 17th century France became the major power on the continent and even in the 20th century she continues to play a leading role in world affairs.

Within its area of 210,039 square miles it possesses a varied climate and landscape, a rich agriculture, and a thriving industry and technology. Three types of climate may be found within the country: oceanic in the western part (cool summers and ample rainfall); continental, found over much of the eastern and central portion (warmer summers—colder winters); and Mediterranean, widespread throughout the south of France, is one of cool winters, hot summers, and limited rainfall.

The majority of the people are no longer employed on the land, as they were a century ago, but the peasant is still the highly respected backbone of the country. However, France is a major industrial country—ranked as the sixth economic power of the world. It has more iron than any other country in Europe, and is the largest producer of wheat and milk in Europe, outside of the Soviet Union. Three-fourths of the people are classified as urban, with one-sixth of the nation's population living in the Paris region. Unemployment is practically nonexistent. One enterprise gives a paid four-week vacation period to about 80% of its employees.

More tourists go to France than to any other country in the world, and many resident aliens live and work in France, but few Frenchmen ever permanently leave France.

. . . . THE PEOPLE

The present population of nearly fifty million is the result of thousands of years of ethnic mixing, though over 85% are native-born. However, three physical types can be distinguished: the Mediterranean, the Alpine, and the Nordic. The Mediterranean type is short and slightly built, with dark hair and eyes and an oval face. The Alpine type is short and thickset, with intermediate coloring. The Nordic type is tall and muscular, with blond hair, fair skin, and blue or gray eyes. Besides, there are nearly one million foreign-born Italians living in France. Virtually everyone speaks the French language, although a considerable number of people are bilingual, and languages other than French are spoken in remote parts of the country.

Three-fourths of the housing of France is at least forty years old. Though annual construction has been stepped up there is still a housing shortage. The 1966-1970 development plan provides for 500,000 additional housing units, of which 20,000 were to be low-income units.

Education is free, but not a state monopoly for about 14% of the elementary school children attend private schools. School attendance is compulsory from the ages of six to sixteen. Technical schools that prepares a student for a career has replaced secondary education for many young people. Since 1956 the number of students in higher education has tripled.

France has no official state religion, but all religious groups are authorized by law to form associations for worship. The majority of the French people have been "baptized" in the Roman Catholic Church, but only about 10% are active in the church. There are about one million Protestants, mostly Calvinists and Lutherans, perhaps 500,000 Jews, and a large number of immigrants from Algeria who are Muslims.

. . . . THE MISSIONARY . . . .

The first contacts in France were made in the latter part of 1966 by Milton Duhon and Ron Butler. Brother Duhon continued to visit the area as the work in Belgium permitted. The original invitation to work in the area was extended by a young Italian Christian who moved from Italy to northern France where a large labor force of Italians have moved to find employment.

When the Ron Butlers were granted permanent visas in March 1968, it was to this group of people they first witnessed. They are located in Libercourt, fifteen miles south of Lille, or one hundred ten miles north of Paris. Their group has numbered over thirty. Youth programs reach around twenty each week, representing several nationalities. A Bible correspondence course was started late in 1968. Nine initially began the course. This will help fill the need for sound Bible doctrine and can be the means of making contact with new people interested in New Testament Christianity, not only in France itself, but in half of Belgium, a third of Switzerland and in the Congo as well. Leadership Training Classes were begun in January 1969,

240

conducted by Harold Fowler who comes weekly from Belgium. Radio work is planned for the future but a greater command of the language is a necessity first.

The Butlers plan to also work with the French people who, as a whole, have accepted the faith in the god of materialism and deny the existence of any other. They continue to study the French language so that real communication will be possible.

Greece

"The kingdom of Hellas"

THE LAND . . . .

Greece is an independent nation lying at the tip of the Balkan Peninsula in southeastern Europe, including a large number of islands in the Ionian and Aegean Seas, the largest of which is Crete. Three sides of the mainland area are surrounded by water. Easy access to the sea has resulted in a long tradition of maritime activity, and modern Greece is one of the world's great shipping nations.

Greek civilization flourished for hundreds of years before the birth of Christ, yet the Greek nation has existed for little more than a century. Though ruled by others she has had her effect upon the world. The culture of classical Greece has been an important element in the development of Western civilization. Few people have risen to such glorious heights, and few have fallen into such poverty and obscurity, for Greece is one of the poorer countries of Europe. The land is arid and rocky and the people have suffered from periodic wars, plagues, and famines.

The climate of Greece is characterized by summers that are long, hot, and generally dry—and by usually mild and fairly rainy winters. But because much of Greece is mountainous and is irregularly outlined, there is an infinite variety of highly localized climates. The mountains make their own climate which is a wetter and cooler version of the lowlands. Percipitation is heaviest in the north and in the mountains.

Once a well-wooded country, the forests have been cleared and have allowed serious soil erosion, although 21.4% of the total area is still forested. Plato wrote concerning Greece, "it is like the skeleton of a body emaciated by disease, as compared with her original relief. All the rich, soft soil has been worn away, leaving a country of skin and bone".

Much of the wild life has disappeared with the forests. Although deer is almost extinct, rabbits and hares are common. Larger forms of wild life are still to be found in the mountainous regions. Wolves still exist in the high mountains.

Only 40% of the land is cultivable, yet farming supports about half of the population. Approximately 33% of the export earnings is derived from tobacco, which can be grown on unirrigated land unsuitable for other crops. The government seeks in every way by tax exemption, subsidies, etc., to encourage expansion of agricultural production. Leaf tobacco and dried fruits constituted over 52% of total exports in 1964.

Industry, ranking next to agriculture as an income earner, depends on imports for its raw materials, machinery, parts and fuel. In 1964,

245

13% of the labor force was engaged in manufacturing. Yet the present average per capita income was still less than $400 a year.

. . . . THE PEOPLE

The modern Greeks are basically of the same stock as the Greeks of classical antiquity, though influenced by non-Greek peoples who entered the area through the centuries past. At the end of 1964, the population was estimated at 8,560,000, of which 92.8% were Greek. The rate of population increase has been kept low by a relatively high rate of emigration, most of which were young male adults seeking work in more prosperous areas.

Modern Greek is the language of the country and is spoken by 98% of the population. English, learned mostly outside the school system, and French are widely spoken. In 1965, illiteracy was still 17.7%, though education is free and supposedly compulsory for all children between the ages of six to fifteen. State and local governments support the costs of schools and private schools are state regulated.

Almost the entire population adheres, at least nominally, to the Greek Orthodox Church. The constitution establishes Orthodox Christianity as the state religion, but guarantees religious freedom, however, proselytizing by other religious groups among Orthodox Christians is forbidden. Muslims form the largest non-Orthodox religious group and numbered over 100,000 in 1961, the latest year an estimate was given.

. . . . THE MISSIONARY . . . .

A native of Greece, Christos Danikas came to America to study in a Chicago University. During this period of study he was converted to Christ and the plea of New Testament Christianity. He began study in Minnesota Bible College and graduated in 1964. In December that year he went to Greece where he began teaching in homes and in study groups. In 1967 he married his childhood sweetheart. They returned to the States to seek aid for the work in Greece. Due to unexpected political development they were unable to return to their work. The land was under marital law; freedom of press, speech, and assembly was suspended. So while this condition existed in their country they began a study course in Hays, Kansas. Chris will earn his Masters in English literature this year. This will be an asset to their planned work in Greece. By tutoring English, he will be able to penetrate many homes which would otherwise be unapproachable for New Testament evangelism because of the existing strict laws. Secondly, it will help them to become gradually self-supporting which they must eventually do if they want the church in Greece to become completely indigenous.

Taped messages from Christians in Greece in the summer of 1968 indicate that they are remaining loyal to the Lord. They assemble in private homes to study and worship.

During their present stay in the States the Danikas are preparing a Bible study correspondence course which they plan to initiate following their return home. A fellow Greek graduate student at the College was baptized in late summer of 1968. Following two more years of study towards a Ph. D., he will likewise return to Greece.

The State church of Greece was successful in her efforts to have the military leaders add a new article to the proposed Constitution, which states categorically that "any direct or indirect attempts to proselytize members of the State Church are strictly forbidden". This will make New Testament evangelism more difficult but Christos Danikas feels that "no human power can stop the communication of the redemptive message of our Lord, and there will always be open doors to reach and evangelize souls for Christ".

248

Holland

"Land of the wooden shoes"

Amsterdam

The Hague
● Rotterdam

H O L L A N D

0   50

250

THE LAND . . . .

More properly known as the Netherlands, this country is bounded by the North Sea on the west and north, by West Germany on the east and Belgium on the south. (Holland actually applies only to the coastal plains.) The country falls into three natural topographical divisions: the eastern uplands, the western dunes, and the "polders" (land reclaimed from the sea and lakes) which lies between the other two. About two-fifths of Netherlands consists of land below sea level. Since the year 1200 more than 1,800,000 acres have been reclaimed from the sea by the use of dikes. Windmills, once a symbol of the country's landscape, have been replaced by electric power.

The eastern section, once the most backward part of the country, has been transformed into a productive dairy region. The lowlands in the center have become productive farmland. The west is comprised mostly of sandy soil where flower bulbs are grown in great number. The brilliant tulips grown in the Netherlands are noted tourist attractions.

The Netherlands has a maritime climate, one of mild winters and cool summers. Cloudy, windy days prevail in the colder period; the summers are slightly less cloudy although long periods of clear weather are rare. The climate is not the most pleasant, but it is healthy and produces the energy for which the Dutch are known.

About one-third of the total land area is under cultivation. Although primarily an industrial nation, the country depends upon agriculture, not only for home consumption, but, also for foreign income. They export dairy products, especially cheeses, and meats throughout the world. It is the world's largest exporter of eggs. Most farms are small but effectively managed and highly mechanized. Since most of the land is too wet for crops, it is planted in grasses and dairy herds have been developed. Dutch dairy herds are noted for fine breeding qualities.

Since the end of World War II the Netherlands have become a predominately industrial nation. Most all raw materials are imported for the majority of the industries, so that the Dutch add only their skill and labor to complete the product. However, the building-material industry is based on native resources. The textile industry is one of the oldest in the country while shipbuilding is one of the most important. Most Dutch industrial enterprises are small.

. . . . THE PEOPLE

The Netherlands is one of the most densely populated countries in the world. In 1966 their population was over 12,375,000—900 people per square mile. The Dutch are a mixture of an ancient Celtic stock with a later influx of Germanic elements: Frisians, Saxons, and Franks.

In 1899 two-thirds of the population lived in rural districts; by 1964 this percentage had fallen to 20% (due to increased population they shifted to industry).

During World War II more than 25% of Holland's two million dwellings were damaged; nearly 100,000 were completely destroyed. Until 1950 housing shortage was acute. By 1970 the government hopes to end this problem through a controlled construction industry.

Due to a raise in the standards of living, improvements in nutrition, hygiene, housing, working conditions, and the expansion of public health measures, the general health situation in the country is excellent. They enjoy sports immensely. Soccer is a popular game for both spectators and participants alike. Other popular sports are ice skating, swimming, fishing, sailing, and track and field events.

Culturally the Netherlands is considered a rich nation. With its long and great art heritage, it remains particularly interesting in painting and the plastic arts. It has not neglected literature, music, architecture, and other fields. In the sciences they have produced many Nobel Prize winners.

Holland, or Dutch, is the official language as well as the universal language except in the province of Friesland where most of them speak the ancient Frisian language (closely related to Anglo-Saxon). Dutch itself is a West Germanic language. Secondary schools teach English, French and German. The relative freedom permitted Dutch educators is largely responsible for the great variety in types of schools and methods of tuition. Each school management is free as regards the appointment of teachers and in choice of books and other educational aids. Illiteracy is virtually nonexistent in the Netherlands. School attendance between the ages of seven and fifteen is compulsory. After primary school 10% of the children receive secondary and preparatory higher education.

Complete religious freedom is provided for by the constitution. The greater part of the population belongs to Protestant denominations, of which the Dutch Reformed Church is the strongest. However, nearly 40% of the people are Roman Catholic. Lutherans and

252

Baptists each comprise less than 1% of the total population. Other religious faiths are small.

. . . . THE MISSIONARY . . . .

In the summer of 1968 a Dutch Christian Crusade was conducted under the leadership of the Bernard Zylstras of West Burlington, Iowa. Accompanying them were Gary Kins and Leonard Brandson, students of St. Louis Christian College.

The first stop was Maastricht, Limburg. Eleven hundred tracts were distributed and advertising was placed in the paper. Only twelve people responded with any curiosity at all. After home studies were made with the use of film-strips, translated and recorded in Dutch, only one remained interested and, hopefully continues to study.

Ten weeks of survey work were conducted, 12,000 tracts distributed, 10,000 calls made. Out of this effort only about one hundred seemed vaguely interested. After a second and third call this number was reduced to twelve persons. After further study with these only two still continue to study to find the truth. Names of interested persons were given to our brethren there for follow-up work.

On the Lord's Days the survey group made effort to worship with one of the four non-instrumental churches in the Netherlands. These are totally dependent on the American dollar and have a total attendance of about one hundred. They were received with mixed emotions. The American missionaries were reserved. The Dutch were very friendly.

The Dutch people are an austere people. They worship with great reverence and formal dignity. Huge cathedrals invite them in and mammoth organs reverberate the great songs and psalms of the church, leading the people to worship the God of the Reformed. When a mission of our people comes along, they rent a small, totally inadequate, building, take out the beautiful organ music, sing off key, provide them with American accented missionaries, and tell the people, "We have the true Gospel and are the true church'. The Dutch simply laugh us to scorn.

The Dutch people are not nearly as stubborn as they are "tradition-bound". It is impossible to expect to use methods of preaching the Gospel to the Dutch that are used in heathen countries where Christ is not known. It is the belief of brother Zylstra, who is himself a native of Holland, that to restore the Church of Christ Jesus one must begin within the existing religious church of the land. This will require teaching them the way more perfectly, one by one.

Italy

"The Boot"

THE LAND . . . .

Italy is a boot-shaped mountain-ribbed peninsula stretching from the Alps to the Mediterranean, 708 miles. At no place on the peninsula proper are you more than sixty miles from the sea. Italy includes not only the mainland but the larger islands of Sicily and Sardinia, and about seventy smaller islands. This entire territory is only slightly larger than the state of Nevada. It is a crowded country having a population of over 53,000,000.

The geographical position of Italy makes it one of the hottest countries in Europe, however, great differences exist between northern and southern Italy. The great plain of northern Italy is chilled by the cold winds from the Alps. Central Italy has a mild winter, however the central range of the Apennines is the coldest district of Italy. Though snow remains on some of the high mountains in the south, even in the summer, the districts adjoining the sea enjoy a climate similar to that of Greece and the south of Spain. The flat surface of the lowlands and the intense summer heat have made them unhealthful, scourged by malaria.

Over one-third of the land is ruggedly mountainous. Except in the Alps, where large stands of evergreen fir, pine, and larch still survive, little remains of the forests that once covered all Italy, though about 18% is still covered by forests, and only about 20% is plainland. There is really very little level, easily cultivated land. Though rainfall is sufficient, it falls in the winter so irrigation is necessary in most sections. The plains run along the narrow coastal strips and a few river valleys. Yet 43% of the people are engaged in agriculture.

Cereals are Italy's chief crops and wheat is the most important, being the primary foodstuff of the people, used in macaronies and bread. Citrus fruits, grown in the south, are a valuable source of foreign exchange. The other most valuable tree crop is the olive since the oil largely takes the place of other fats in the Italian diet. The vineyards are cultivated everywhere, wine being not a luxury but an essential item in the diet of the people. Sheep are raised on the poor pastureland of the south for meat and milk purposes.

Great industrial towns are mainly in the north. Central Italian towns are smaller but often historically important. In the south are the small agricultural centers except for the port cities such as Naples. Manufacturing is well established as the most important sector of the Italian economy. Industrial production in 1965 was about three and a half times greater than it had been before the war.

Most of the inhabitants of Italy are of pure Italian stock. The more common type familiar to us is the dark-haired, dark-skinned type, rather short of stature and often good-looking. However, invasions from the Alps made the northern people, as a rule, taller and fairer, with greater perseverance and energy. Emotionally, most Italians are impulsive and generous. The love of beauty is inborn. They are kindly, patient and capable of great sacrifice on behalf of family or friends. The cultural tradition of Italy is extremely old and is one of the richest in the world, influencing art, architecture, literature, music, and science.

Italian is a Romance language, based, in its modern form, chiefly on the Tuscan dialect, however, various dialects are spoken in different parts of the country. There are great differences of character, as well as dialects, and customs in the various parts of Italy. In the industrial centers habits and culture are close to that of western European countries but in the south where extreme poverty and centuries of misgovernment have produced a low standard of living it is more like that of North Africa than like North Italy. Many Italians among the poorer classes live the greater part of their lives out of doors. Children play in the streets; women sit at their doors when the day's work is done; men congregate in groups at street corners or in open-air cafes.

Most farm families, who till from seven to twenty acres, live in villages. Everyone must work. The women weave lace, crochet raffia articles and braid straw for hats to add to the income. Even children must work; they watch the hogs or geese, or drive the sheep and goats to the rocky hillside pastures. With the rocks from these pastures their houses (four and five stories high) are built on the winding streets.

The state provides schools for every grade, and most of the universities are state operated. Elementary education is free and compulsory for the ages six to fourteen, but attendance is very irregular. For the great majority of Italian children eight years of elementary school education is the most they can hope to achieve. And even with this there is a high percentage of illiteracy in the south and on the islands where many children may go only three or four months a year and leave school when they are eleven. Organized extra curricular activities play only a small part in the Italian child's school education, but out-of-school sports, especially soccer, played with the local clubs, enjoy wide popularity.

The Communists maintain the most active political youth organizations.

The State religion is Roman Catholicism, and it is taught in the schools. Though 99.6% of the people are Roman Catholic, only about one-third attend Mass regularly. The constitution of the Italian Republic gives comprehensive juridicial assurances to religious minorities. One provision states: "All religious denominations are equally free before the law and are entitled to organize themselves according to their own statutes, in so far as these do not conflict with Italian legal order". Of the other religious groups found within the country, Protestants are the largest body, numbering around 100,000 in the early 1960's. With this apparent freedom of religion comes the use of the radio. Though all radio services belong to the State, only a few are directly controlled by it.

. . . . THE MISSIONARY . . . .

As in the beginning of other missionary activity in Europe, war played its active part in the opening of a mission field in Italy. Brother Guy Mayfield, with a life-time interest in missions, had opportunity to work with the Italian people from 1943-45 while a Chaplain in the Air Force. With the help of some soldiers he organized a school for Italian children. During this period twelve were baptized. Though his group returned to the States he did not forget the Italian people and their need of a Saviour. Preparations were made, and upon his release from service, the Mayfield family sailed back to Italy. Accompanying them was Betheen Grubaugh, a registered nurse. This was July 1947 and the beginning of Mediterranean Christian Mission. They settled in the area of Puglia (the heel of Italy) in the city of Bari. In November of that year Charles and Mary Frances Phipps joined forces with them. The year of 1948 was a busy one for everyone with churches organized in Oria and Latiano, and Bible study classes being held in several other towns, and week-day Bible classes held for the children in Bari. Betheen increased her hours in the medical clinic work (which also included sick calls in the homes), a service through which many contacts were made. As a result of this a number were baptized into Christ.

Bari Bible Institute began its first session on January 3, 1949 and operated as such for three terms. Coming during the second term to assist in the witness was Evelyn Jones, who arrived in November of 1949. The school was closed in June 1951, having trained some forty young people. Though much good was accomplished (five

259

churches started and over one hundred people baptized) it did not seem that the Bible Institute was producing the results in Christian leadership for which it was organized. The missionaries, limited with time and funds, were led to use their efforts in other ways for the spreading of the Gospel there.

In 1951 the Mayfield family went to the United States for furlough. Because of the Korean war, brother Mayfield was recalled to service as a chaplain, in which capacity he served for seventeen months.

In 1953 the Phippses were forced to leave Italy due to malta fever from which Charles could not seem to recover while in the country. They never lost their love and concern for the Italian people. They served at Midwest Christian College until they were able to return to the field.

Early in 1953 the Malcolm Coffeys came to serve with the Mediterranean Christian Mision, to be followed in May by the Charles Troyer family. With the closing of the Institute a different phase of the work began. Services were still conducted in Bari and the other towns, but along with this began more hours of person-to-person teaching, which is effective where folks are fearful to come out to attend a service until they are truly convinced of its value. In such a way a witness was carried to an 80-year old woman who had never been to a non-Catholic service. There was a demand everywhere for the missionaries to call and to teach, and week after week they traveled to meet those many appointments for God. Many of those contacted have taken correspondence courses. Many lasting results of the work of Mediterranean Christian Mission have come from the Italian Christians themselves, who have served faithfully in spite of persecution and hardship.

In October 1953, free again from active duty in the armed forces, brother Mayfield and his family returned to Italy. This time they came to work in Rome. "So, as much as in me is, I am ready to preach the gospel to you also that are at Rome".—Romans 1:15.

The first attempt on the part of the Mayfields to bring the plea of New Testament Christianity to the city of Rome began in 1949 when their family came from Bari for language study. At that time, through a number of contacts, three people for baptized and became members of the church established at Ciampino, a small community just outside Rome's international airport. The Mayfields also conducted a Bible school for U.S. Air Force personnel stationed at the airport, attendance averaging about eighteen. Along with this work the Mayfields began publishing a paper, Appello Christiano, which was used in the follow-up program for the Bible Christian Broadcast from Luxembourg. They are now also publishing The Bible Christian Call.

A niece and children of Vito Gentile, minister at Ciampino.

In 1960-62 the Mayfields worked and evangelized among the Italians in Toronto, Canada. In 1962 they returned to Europe and began teaching in U.S. military schools for dependents. Their evangelistic calling, among the Italians and American and Canadian service men, took them over much of the country. The Mayfields have found the Italians are often more receptive when they are outside their own country. Some are now very active workers in the churches in Italy who were first contacted in other countries. In connection with their long-standing interest in service men, brother Mayfield, in 1968, led in the formation of the Christian Military Fellowship.

Through the grace of God, Charles and Mary Frances Phipps were able to return to their beloved Italy in November 1958. They settled in Perugia, north of Rome, where, in April 1959, they took over the radio program on Luxembourg (formerly produced in Japan). When Mac Coffey became ill near the end of 1959 and was forced to leave Bari for awhile it was decided that the Phipps should return to Bari, where they could continue to produce the radio broadcasts. The program called "Search the Scriptures" is an English-language broadcast that reaches some 2,000,000 listeners in sixteen European countries and the British Isles. The Phipps are kept busy in much of the follow-up program, which includes correspondence courses, teaching letters, plus "teaching" meetings for a week or longer, and classes for women and men .

The Roy Goldsberry family moved to Italy in 1965 from their previous mission work in Africa. After a period of language study they took up residence in Terracina to assist Italian evangelist, Guiseppe Italiano. Their work was largely in visitation evangelism and tract distribution. They also helped in training elders, deacons, and evangelists in the churches. Through recent door-to-door contacts in Bari and Taranto they gained 1,500 Bible correspondence students. In 1969 when the Phipps returned to Italy from furlough they moved from Bari to Terracina to take up labors with the Italiano family while the Goldsberrys moved to another area to work. The Coffeys and Evelyn Jones will continue to labor with the churches in the Bari and Brindisi areas. Guiseppe Italiano, as a boy, studied in the Bari Bible Instiute. He continues his secular education that he might become a teacher in the public schools, which will help him to support his family while he continues to witness and work in the churches in Terracina and Fondi. The Phipps plan a more intensive follow-up program for the radio ministry with the view to establishing Bible study groups in the various cities where listeners have asked for help. At Terracina a concentrated work with the children, through the establishment of a children's Study Center, is being planned.

In August 1954 the Charles Troyer family began a separate, but cooperative, work at Lecce, some seventy-five miles to the south of Bari. The city of Lecce offered the Troyers a great challenge as a new field of service because no non-Catholic work of any kind existed in that city.

After getting settled in their new home, the Troyers had their first service on Sunday evening, September 5th, with eight persons present (besides their own family). That very morning a priest in the nearby Catholic church informed the people at mass that it was forbidden for anyone to go to the Troyer home, threatening excommunication to any who would dare to do so. The first three baptisms were in January 1955. They were three young men who had studied each evening for three weeks prior to their baptism. Two months later, two other young men, brothers of the first three, were baptized into Christ. Much good was accomplished through private study with each person who showed interest in learning more of God's Word.

The Troyer home served as a place of worship in the first years at Lecce. In the fall of 1956 they began printing Bible School literature in the Italian language; during the second term this was done on a weekly basis, meeting the needs of other areas as well as their own. In a few years they were preparing graded lessons for weekly use, VBS, and day camps. They have had such success in reaching young people that they hope to be able to establish a day nursery and "Dopo School" which would offer daily opportunity to provide a Christian environment and Biblical training. (A Dopo School is a place of study where the older young people would come each afternoon to prepare their lessons for the following day. Thirty-minute Bible lessons could be presented to them in the middle of the afternoon.) It is urgent to reach these youth since adults are not receptive to the Gospel. The parents of most of these children are indifferent toward the church and knowledge of God's Word, but they have expressed confidence in the missionary and willingness to permit their children to attend. The attendance at the Lecce church worship numbers about twenty-five.

After a period of language study in the mid-sixties (the usual "first" for all missionaries) the Harold Fowlers settled in a suburb of Albano, twenty kilometers south of Rome. There they helped to establish a church and assisted in various teaching programs: a preacher-training clinic, summer camp, and vacation Bible school. Since their furlough they have moved to Belgium where they continue to witness to Italians who have immigrated for work. Their work revolves much around the training clinics which are being held in various areas of Europe (not in Belgium alone).

Europe is probably one of the hardest fields in the world as you may understand from the words of one of the first converts in Lecce: "In these times it is difficult to be a Christian, especially in Italy, for the way of salvation is made still more difficult by the enemies of Christ, among whom are the priests who have been responsible for sowing in the world the seeds of hypocrisy and deceit." Young men in Italy may lose their jobs with little hope of getting others, as well as be ostracized from their families, if they accept the position of the New Testament church. How thankful we are that there are those who love Christ enough.

Poland

"Not yet forsaken"

POLAND

Gdansk

Warsaw

Lodz

THE LAND . . . .

Located in northeast Europe, Poland is bounded by the Baltic Sea, East Germany on the west, Czechoslovakia on the south and by the U.S.S.R. on the east. The southern part is mountainous while the northern two-thirds is a low-lying plain. It is generally agreed that the name Poland is derived from a word whose original meaning was "plain" or "meadow".

Poland has a continental climate, conditioned especially by westerly winds. Winters are basically cold. Only the southern areas are humid, although northern Poland has wet summers with the most rain falling in July during heavy thunderstorms.

The soils of Poland are extremely variable. The richest soils are found in the south. It is still a well-wooded country, with about 24% of the total area under forest. Timber is second in the list of the nation's natural resources. The government was against private farming, but as of 1965 Poland was the only Soviet-block country in Eastern Europe to hold out against collectivization, but uncertainty as to the future reduced the farmers' incentives to improve their farms. However, through taxation, state set prices, etc. the government effectively controls agriculture. Slightly more than 50% of Poland is arable. Even with a continued increase in production it has been necessary to import large quantities of bread grain and fodder.

Polish industry is highly diversified. Meat, meat products, and eggs are the most important agricultural food exports and accounts for more than half of national income. Industries producing foodstuffs, textiles, fuels and machinery are the major employers. Poland's major economic problem is the provision of expanded nonagricultural employment opportunities for its growing population.

Although Poland has rich coal deposits (world's sixth largest producer), it lacks other important natural resources such as petroleum and iron ore.

. . . . THE PEOPLE

Before World War II Poland had large national minorities amounting to nearly one-third of the entire population, but of the present population of nearly thirty-two million, 98% are ethnically Polish.

Polish, the universal language, is one of the western Slavic languages using the Latin alphabet and the only major Slavic language to preserve the old Slavic nasal vowels. Many Poles speak German,

Russian, and English and understand other Slavic languages in varying degrees.

Complete socialization is the aim of the Polish government, and they are well on their way to obtaining it. Increased medical care for mother and child has lowered infant mortality rate by over 60% just since 1950/51. A working pregnant woman is entitled by law to a 12-week paid maternity leave.

Almost the entire Polish population is literate. Before the war there was free and compulsory education for all between the ages of eight and fifteen. Secondary education consisted of two stages, grammar school for those from twelve to sixteen and lyceums for those sixteen to eighteen. The grammar schools were maintained by the state, cities and private organizations. After World War II the Communist government introduced state control and censorship over all educational institutions and textbooks. Independent schools, managed by individuals, societies or the Catholic Church, were closed down or taken over by the government. Now the education is still free and compulsory to the age of fourteen. Special attention has been paid to the development of vocational and technical schools. The only free private university in the entire Communist world is the Roman Catholic University at Lublin.

Religiously speaking, 94% of the people are Roman Catholic. Nearly two million are members of Protestant groups, largely Lutherans, Calvinists, Methodists, and the Greek Orthodox. Religious freedom is provided for by the constitution, but the United Workers (Communist) Party seeks the eventual establishment of a society without religion.

. . . . THE MISSIONARY . . . .

After centuries of spiritual darkness and soverign rule of the Roman Catholic Church, the light of the Gospel started to shine in Poland in 1921. Hundreds responded to the invitation of Christ, under the leadership of brother Jaroshevich. Thousands of copies of the Bible were in the hands of the people. Polish and Russian Christian magazines were being published. By 1939 there were many churches with a well-trained leadership. One of these young leaders was Paul Bajko.

World War II brought complete destruction to the country, and was a great blow to the church of Christ. Many ministers died or were killed. Paul Bajko was separated from his family and church, and was sent to a slave labor camp in Germany. Only a small part of the Church remained in Poland. Nevertheless the work was renewed by brother Jaroshevich after the war. Following the liberation, Paul Bajko began studying for the ministry. In 1950 the Lord opened the door for him to come to America as an immigrant. After further education he was called to Eastern Christian College as Director of Missions. Through his efforts he has brought about a fellowship between the American and Polish churches that had ceased to exist.

Today twenty ministers are supported by American funds. Used clothing is shipped regularly to needy families. Assistance is given in the remodeling of church buildings. Perhaps of greater value is the money sent for the purchase of Bibles in Poland. Brother Bajko published song books and Life of Christ Visualized booklets. A Polish magazine is published regularly and distributed freely. With his family he has made two personal evangelistic tours in Poland where services were conducted from three to six hours daily.

In 1968 Paul Bajko was refused permission to enter Poland but a tour group to Russia, conducted by Gene Dulin and John Huk (including the Vernon brothers of Christian T.V. Mission) was able to spend some time in Poland encouraging and witnessing to the brethren. To produce more lasting effects will be the efforts of two Polish students, Kostek Jakonicek and George Bajenski, who, having completed their studies in the States, have returned to Poland to preach.

Where the missionary cannot go, where the printed word cannot reach, the radio message usually has an open door. There were no religious programs in Poland—but there was a need. The Cobles, founders of Gospel Broadcasting Mission, saw that need too, and began sponsoring a fifteen-minute broadcast in the Polish language. Not only does it reach Poland, but Czechoslovakia, Russia, France, Germany, and Belgium, as well. Where is it not needed? Due to this broadcast some new churches have been established. Since early 1968 Boleslaw Winnik has been the radio minister. He carries on a mailing service to fill requests for Bibles and religious literature. When in Poland he preached to hundreds, but now through radio and literature he preaches to thousands.

Russia

"Behind the Iron Curtain"

RUSSIA

Tallinn
Leningrad
Riga
Vilna
Minsk
Moscow
Kiev
Khar'kov

THE LAND . . . .

The vast land of the Union Soviet Socialist Republic spreads half way around the world across Europe and Asia. Nearly three times the size of the United States, the Union is the largest single state in the world and covers one-sixth of its dry surface. (Russia is a term still widely used although it applies to a restricted area.)

The greater part of the Soviet Union consists of an immense, flat to gently rolling, plain. It is interrupted only by the low, wooded heights of the Ural Mountains. East of the Yenisey River, however, towering, high mountains and plateaus occupy the central and eastern parts of Siberia. Along the southern border of the Union is another series of high mountains which forms the third natural division. Most of the country has a continental climate with a wide range of summer and winter temperatures and relatively low precipitation. The lowest temperatures of any of the world's inhabited area are found in Siberia.

Agriculture has long been the backbone of the country but only in more recent years has proper machinery been manufactured for their needs. This is due partly to the "Five-Year Plan" which was placed in effect in 1928. Machinery is available through "Machine Tractor Stations". Also in the "Five-Year Plan" collectivization of farm lands became a reality. Each farm consists of several thousand acres. The center of the farm is the village, in which live the men and women who work the land. Each farmer has his own individual garden plot (an acre or less) next to his house and whatever he grows there is his. He is free to sell any excess produce. Actually there is very little good farming land in Russia. Vast areas cannot be sown—in the north because the soil is frozen, in the south there is lack of adequate and reliable rainfall.

The Ukraine produces some crops in enormous quantities. The lower Volga region rivals the Ukraine as a surplus food producer. The Ukraine is also of importance in Soviet mining and industry. The vast steel mills, foundaries, chemical works, machine shops are there—ready for peace or war.

There has been war in its history. Books have been written of Russia's defeats and its victories. By 1948 there were so many disagreements between the Soviet Union and its former allies that people began to speak of a "cold war". International relations have been strained ever since.

. . . . THE PEOPLE

Within this enormous country dwell some 232 million people, the third largest population in the world (after China and India). This includes more than one hundred nationalities, the majority of whom speak a Slavic language, Russian, Ukrainian, or White Russian.

The Russians, who now constitute the majority of the Soviet people, have given the nation its main language, and the political, social, and economic framework for which it is known. With one exception (that of the Jews) ethnic groups recognized as "nationalities", even when territorially dispersed, are granted such privileges as schools, newspapers, publishing houses, and theaters in the national language, plus instruction in their cultural and historic traditions.

In 1957 when the Soviet scientists launched the first earth satellite, the whole world became aware of the fact that the Russians, for the first time in their long history, had ceased to be a backward nation (at least in the field of technology). These advances cost a great price. For many years living standards were among the lowest in Europe. But they have paid a greater price in individual freedom. Russia has never known true freedom of speech, or of the press, or of religion. Police rule, censorship of the press, the radio, the theater, the arts, these are all part of the price paid for the material achievements of the Soviet regime.

In learning, Moscow is the undisputed center of the nation. Moscow University, Russia's oldest, has an enrollment of around 25,000 students. One of the more recent accomplishments has been to practically eliminate illiteracy. Education is free and compulsory after age seven (for eight years). School programs are uniform throughout the USSR. Higher education is technically free. Soviet education, particularly at the higher levels, tends to be more specialized than education in the United States. The publishing of books and magazines is strictly controlled by the government, but the amount in print is impressive.

Various forms of Christianity have existed for many centuries in Russia. The Armenians in the very south are among the oldest Christians in the world. The Russians of Kiev (Capital of Ukrainian Republic in the west) adopted Christianity in its Eastern Greek Orthodox form near the year 1000. The central area was inhabited by Moslems in its early history, although the Islam's commandments are no longer obeyed, and mosques are just as deserted as many of the church buildings. The Moslems remain the second largest religious community. Under the constitution, all citizens enjoy freedom of religion. Most

274

Russians have become atheists. Since the revolution more than two-thirds of the houses of worship have been closed. Church building construction is not planned for in new Soviet cities. Anti-Semitism is legally prohibited in the USSR but the Soviet press has published many attacks against Judaism as a religion and against individual Jews as anti-social elements. Other religious groups include Seventh Day Adventists, Methodists, and the Molokans (a group formed in the 19th century who opposed the sacraments and ritual, and emphasized the authority of the Bible).

The aims of Communism in Russia have been twofold from the very beginning: establish Communism at home and make it strong enough to withstand any foreign attack, on the one hand, bring about the triumph of Communism all over the world, on the other. The first has never completely been achieved—the latter never completely neglected.

. . . . THE MISSIONARY . . . .

In the early 1900's word spread among the New Testament Christians that there were about 10,000 people in Russia of similar faith. Z. T. Sweeney, a faithful Christian and the American Ambassador to Turkey, had opportunity to visit these people, reporting that they were as emphatic and insistent upon New Testament Christianity as the Christians of the United States. It is interesting to note that there was even a Bible College in Russia during this era. It finally had to close its doors due to a lack of financial support. The Communist revolution had its beginnings in the same building that was once used for Bible college classes. The Revolution, of course, resulted in oppression of the church and the western world lost contact with the Russian Christians.

In December of 1961 Gene Dulin of Toronto Christian Mission was holding a meeting in Alberta, Canada when he heard that there was a Russian church in the very city where his work was centered. Upon his return to Toronto he sought out the Russian church. As a result of persecution some members of the early Russian restoration movement had immigrated to Canada. Fifteen such congregations now exist in Canada, four of which are in the province of Ontario. Brother Dulin found that these people held fast to their belief in immersion and in the local autonomy of the church.

As a result of this contact Gene Dulin and John Huk, a Russian minister in Canada, made a tour in 1963 to Russia itself. They visited and strengthened our brethren in Christ behind the "iron curtain" and made contacts which resulted in expansion of this work for Christ. To their surprise they were allowed to preach in the Russian churches— and with a great deal of freedom. They were cautioned, however, not to preach the same message twice. They were also asked to use a variety of Scriptures since the people copy them down and later commit them to memory. They found a great lack of Bibles and religious teaching aids. On their return home, with renewed zeal and determination, they had 10,000 Russian New Testaments printed and ready for delivery in a short time, though these cannot be shipped in through normal procedure.

Correspondence continued and a second tour was made in 1967. During a 27-day period of time they visited eight major cities, preached in nine different churches and held numerous conferences with the leaders of the "Union of Evangelical Christian Baptist Church", as well as many private conversations with Christian ministers and other members of the church. The government has required the Evangelical Christian Church and the Baptist church to unite though they actually work independently of each other. They noticed in this second tour that the youth were becoming increasingly more active in the Russian church, however, the government will not allow young people to be baptized until the age of eighteen (even then permission is often granted rather slowly). In one instance two Christian boys were not allowed to graduate from a Russian University because they would not renounce their faith in Christ. They finally moved to Poland and were allowed to graduate and work there.

According to Russian law churches must be registered with the government; then certain restrictions are placed upon them. Secret police are assigned to attend church services. In view of all this many Russian Christians have decided to follow the example of Peter and John in "obeying God rather than men" (Acts 4). These are more zealous than those who are worshipping according to the laws. Their boldness sometimes mystifies the officials. One man, for instance, was arrested for carrying a Bible on his person. When the police threatened to send him to Siberia he sincerely suggested that if they would give him six months time he could pay his own travel expense there. He was released and sent home—without his Bible. His Word is powerful!

In recent years some progress has been made within the sphere of the registered churches. The wife of a former government official has accepted Christ, and officials have made some concessions to the churches. During 1968 the government granted permission for a correspondence course for one hundred people. At least this is a starting point for needed training for elders and ministers who will faithfully preach the Word. When a third tour was made into Russia in 1968 with thirty-two Christians from various walks of life, they found that twelve new churches have been registered in Russia, one of which is located in metropolitan Moscow.

Another tour is scheduled for the summer of 1969. Meanwhile Russian Bibles are being printed for further distribution. A monthly magazine is also being printed and distributed to Russian Christians throughout the world. The Christians in Russia appear to be morally and spiritually strong in spite of the fact that the government does its best to promote atheism and does exert certain pressures upon them. Some have been imprisoned because of their belief yet they still faithfully follow the way of the Lord.

West Germany

"Land of Hope"

Hamburg

Berlin

WEST GERMANY

Bonn

Frankfurt

Mannheim

Nürnberg

Stuttgart

Stammheim

Augsburg

Munich

THE LAND . . . .

West Germany is situated in central Europe with Denmark on the north, East Germany and Czechoslovakia on the east, Switzerland and Austria on the south, and four nations, Netherlands, Belgium, Luxembourg and France, on the west

This divided country is 186 square miles in area, much larger than East Germany, and has a much greater variety of relief and landforms. Its four major geographical divisions are: (1) in the deep south are the Alps, which contain the highest mountain of Germany, and an area that is largely forested, (2) north of the Bavarian Plateau, which fronts the Alps, is the area called the "scarplands", (3) the three areas in the Central Uplands is made up of an east-west belt of highlands, (4) the north German Plain varies from a width of one hundred miles in the west to two hundred miles near the Polish border. The surface of the Plain varies greatly. Along the border of the Plain, just north of the Central Uplands is one of the most productive farming areas of Germany. In general the soils of West Germany are not particularly fertile or productive.

The climate is moderate, but changes of weather are frequent. The summers are basically warm, the winters cool and rainfall occurs at all seasons.

Fifty-seven percent of West Germany is devoted to agriculture and 28.8% to forestry. Agriculture is the least effective sector of the West Germany economy. The farms are excessively small and severely under capitalized. Land has to be wasted on access roads and units are often too small for the employment of machinery, though some consolidation is being made. Slightly more than 30% of the total land area is covered by forests. West German coal deposits are the most important in Western Europe, and with these deposits is the greatest producer of electric power in Western Europe. Though there are several large oil fields, considerable quantities of oil products, especially fuel oil, is imported.

West German industry is well-developed and highly diversified; including metallurgy, chemistry, textile, automotive, shipbuilding and consumer industries. It is an important trading country, exceeded only by the United States.

. . . . THE PEOPLE

Of the nearly sixty million people of West Germany about 99% are German. The Danes are the sole national minority, although there are nearly a million foreign workers now in the land, mostly Greeks, Turks, Italians, and Spaniards. The Germans, like other Europeans, are of mixed ethnic strains. The Nordic physical types are predominant in the north and the Alpine type predominant in the south.

West Germany is a prosperous middle class society. There are no major poverty areas, and no traditional ruling class. Most working class people have middle-class aspirations and tastes, and the top level have come from middle class families. Those who did not lose their prosperity in the war pay a special tax used to make possible a new economic and social start for the 20% of the population who were "refugees"—a plan called "equalization of burdens". This prevented what could have been a source of political and social unrest.

The German people, of all classes, take a lively interest in sports. Popular sports include soccer, swimming, ice skating, skiing, hiking and mountain climbing. Physical training is required in primary and secondary schools. Education is free between the ages of six and eighteen; illiteracy is negligible. All children attend elementary school eight or nine years and then enter a three-year vocational training course or the secondary school. Besides various types of universities and colleges, there are some thirty centers of adult education which provide residence courses, plus over one thousand schools for higher adult education.

German is the official language, and although there is some differences in dialects, High German is standard. Health standards in West Germany are higher than in most other West European countries; average life expectancy is estimated at 66 years.

Freedom of religion is guaranteed. The number of Protestants and Roman Catholics are nearly equal. Some 30,000 Jews live in Germany, also. Protestants are in the majority in the north while Catholics are dominant in the south. Religious affiliation in West Germany is counted on the basis of a tax, for the support of religious communities, which is withheld along with the income tax. A person must formally renounce his religious membership before a state agency to be free of the tax.

. . . . THE MISSIONARY . . . .

Though Germany is a nation torn in many ways, her greatest tragedy is her division from God. Physically, mentally and spiritually the German people are being turned to false teaching on every hand. Communism has a firm grip on the East; Catholicism has its strongholds extending throughout the South; and internally, Germany is confused by the conflict of denominationalism, modernism, materialism, and rationalism. No wonder that Germany today is offering one of the greatest challenges to the missionaries of the New Testament church.

It was these conditions that Edward Fausz saw while serving with the United States Army as radio operator and interpreter during World War II. His desire to share his new-found freedom in Christ prompted the decision of the Fausz family to re-enter Germany as missionaries.

They were especially equipped for the task. Brother Fausz had been a member of the German Evangelical Reformed Church, the state church of Germany, for 23 years before his acceptance of the New Testament position. As a child he had been brought up to speak the German language, which, he in turn was able to teach his wife. Most important of all, their hearts went out to a nation who had forgotten God. Their plan of action was simple and sincere. On arriving in Germany in February 1956 they located in Frankfurt to begin their personal witness, door to door, and in the public proclamation. The first services were held in their home. Later, by moving to a new location, they were able to rent a meeting-hall for the Lord's Day worship services.

Like the "voice of one crying in the wilderness" the Gospel Broadcasting Mission, through Radio Luxembourg, laid a path for the Fauszs in Europe. With the cooperation of the Fauszs of the West German Christian Mission and the Gospel Broadcasting Mission a broadcast was set up in October 1958. This program, produced and broadcast by the Fausz family, was a German language broadcast entitled "Search the Scriptures". The purpose of the broadcast was four-fold: 1) to establish initial contacts with interested listeners; 2) to follow up these contacts with personal calls and correspondence; 3) to hold preannounced evangelistic meetings in those communities from which they have heard; and 4) to have the interested listeners to serve as a nucleus on which to build a New Testament congregation in their community.

The Lord laid it upon the heart of Ila Belle Henning to return with the Fauszs for their second term of service in July 1961. She was able to use her secretarial abilities for the Lord, not only in the correspondence that accompanied a radio ministry but eventually she learned to operate the printing equipment that had been obtained to supply their teaching needs. (She is now serving in the States.)

The radio ministry continues under the leadership of the Fauszs

283

with marvelous results. Copies of the sermons are mailed each week to those requesting them and a growing list of radio listeners request a quantity of sermons to hand out to friends and relatives. Letters are being received from souls interested in New Testament Christianity from twenty-five different countries on both sides of the Iron Curtain. The broadcast is within complete hearing range of all the German speaking people of Russia, Poland, East Prussia, East Germany, Czechoslovakia, Romania, Bulgaria, Hungary, Yugoslavia—all of which are under Communistic rule. In Western Europe, the broadcast is being heard in Norway, Sweden, Denmark, England, Scotland, Wales, Ireland, West Germany, Belgium, Holland, France, Luxembourg, Austria, Switzerland, Liechtenstein and northern Italy. It is also heard as far south as Algeria in Northern Africa. The German-speaking people of these combined nations represent a total potential audience of one hundred million souls who are being given an opportunity to hear the Gospel of Christ. As a result of this broadcast there are more than twenty Bible study groups in western Europe.

Radio is the only method that can be used in orally proclaiming the Gospel to the people who are enslaved by Communism. A total picture is not available but it is reported that because of the broadcast there are fifty-five congregations in the two countries of Bulgaria and Romania. There is supposedly an equal number in Yugoslavia. There is an undisclosed number of Christians and New Testament churches in East Germany and East Berlin.

Along with the radio broadcast, brother Fausz wrote and translated tracts, Bible study lessons, and periodicals in the German language. It was urgent that someone take over the actual printing of this material. Experienced in off-set printing and challenged by the need, the Sid Allsburys came to Frankfurt, Germany in September 1967. When Sid was a child he wanted to be a missionary to Switzerland. In time that dream was forgotten, yet today they are only five hours from Switzerland. Besides the special teaching aids that are printed, they print approximately 1,000 radio sermons each week, and the Bible Christian Call of Guy Mayfield in Belgium.

Seeing the need of the European people for the true gospel of Christ, Merwyn H. Greene determined to go as a missionary to them after World War II, but on a battlefield in France he gave his life for his country, July 22, 1944. Though he could not carry out his plan, his death brought about a missionary venture that more than fulfilled his dreams of taking Christ to a war-torn world. "He being dead yet speaketh". The Gospel Broadcasting Mission was first conceived by

Mamie and Walter Coble after the death of their nephew, Merwyn Greene. Grieved by his death, the Cobles began searching for a way to help fulfill Merwyn's dream of taking the message of Christ to Europe. They started a memorial fund in honor of their nephew and intended to use this money to help send one or more missionaries to the European field. After the war had ended there were no recruits preparing for this field; and interest in this memorial had all but died out.

In the summer of 1951, a door was opened with an offer to produce a radio program of Gospel preaching over Radio Luxembourg. Believing it was the will of the Lord, the Cobles used the memorial fund to help get this "Search the Scriptures" program on the air. On April 7, 1952, this first broadcast (a 15-minute English program) was beamed to many souls within an 800-mile radius of Luxembourg.

Besides the original English broadcast, which is now produced by the Phipps in Italy (aired over a different station) and the German-language broadcast which began in 1958, there was a need and desire to reach out into all the world. In 1961 two other broadcasts were begun: 1) Polish, via Monte Carlo and 2) English in Nigeria, West Africa. Later ones were begun in Formosa, Puerto Rico (since discontinued), Korea, and the most recent is the Lisu broadcasts over a Manila station.

Due to the ill health of the Cobles others were sought to take over the actual work of Gospel Broadcasting Mission. Cloyd Christman (former missionary to Okinawa) is full-time promotional director. Assisting are the Burdette Wakemans in programming and the Walter Leepers in the publication work.

During World War II, a religious movement started in Germany through the efforts of a former American preacher, W. A. Waltke. It was in the winter of 1939-40 that the first four persons joined themselves together for prayer in the city of Stuttgart. The prayer band grew larger and larger, as it spread to other cities. By 1945 there were fourteen different districts where these prayer bands were meeting, in spite of hardships inflicted upon them by the Nazi regime and the established church. After the close of the war these people came together at Stammheim. This congregation carried on for approximately sixteen years under the leadership of W. A. Waltke. When his health failed the congregation slowly fell apart until new leadership came in the person of Alva Phillips.

The Phillips family arrived in Frankfurt, Germany in 1963. During language study they began preparing Bible school lessons and workbooks and translated them into the German language. Following this period of preparation they received a call from the Black Forest area. In August of 1964 they moved to Stammheim. Bible study groups were begun in 1965. In 1966 the lessons and workbooks were put to use in a Vacation Bible School.

Handcraft project for youth meeting.

When the Phillips returned to Germany in March 1968, following their furlough, they had recruited two new helpers: Cheryl Shaffer (who accompanied them) and Lela McCauley (who followed after June graduation). These girls will be working largely with the young people, implanting Christ and Christian morals in their hearts. Cheryl will also be doing secretarial work. Linda Romesburg was an interne in the summer of 1968. Others have expressed a desire to share in this teaching ministry in the Black Forest.

Isles
of the Sea

Japan

"The land of cherry blossoms"

Worshipping at shrine on New Year's Day.

THE LAND . . . .

This island empire of eastern Asia covers an estimated area of 142,798 square miles, which is slightly less than California, yet it had a population in 1965 of 98,274,961, which is half the population of the entire United States. To say it is a most crowded country would be a vast understatement.

The bulk of the area is included in four main islands: Honshu, Shikoku, Kyushu, and Hokkaido. These islands are mountainous, (the prince of mountains is Fujiyama) high and rugged, and contain many volcanos. Earthquakes are common and tidal waves often destructive. There are no wide plains and few places are distant from the mountains or the sea.

Most of Japan enjoys a mild temperate climate much like that in the area from Maine to Georgia. However, the humidity is very high, a condition which aggravates the discomfort of heat and cold. Snowfall is heavy in the north and the typhoon contributes its share of damage with its winds and accompanying severe rainstorms and resulting floods. But everywhere the weather changes and variations can be, and usually are, rapid and sudden. During January, the coldest month, Tokyo has a mean temperature of thirty-seven degrees and Osaka is about two degrees warmer. Southern Kyushu, which is the warmest part, has a January mean temperature of forty-five degrees. The mean temperature for the hottest month, August, is eighty-one degrees in Osaka, seventy-seven degrees in Tokyo.

Due to the extreme mountainous character of Japan, the abundant precipitation and the fact that no drainage divide is far from the sea, many short, small and torrential rivers have resulted which are subject to violent flooding without warning. But the river system makes it easy to irrigate and provide Japan with what arable land it has, which is only 16% of the area. However, 30% of this arable land is double cropped.

Agriculture is the backbone off Japan's economic life. Foodstuffs take up more than 80% of the cultivated land. The main crop is rice, the staple of the Japanese diet. Rice is grown throughout Japan but in lesser quantities in Hokkaido and northern Honshu where the growing season is short. Livestock, though still of limited importance, has been increasing in significance. Dairy cattle are especially important in Hokkaido, while beef cattle are dominant in central and southern Honshu.

Japan has extensive forests, which occupy an area four times greater than its farmland, so wood is an important item in Japanese economy. This provides not only a source for lumber but for charcoal wood fuel. With the exception of public buildings and homes of the wealthy, most of the buildings of Japan are made of wood. Wooden utensils are used wherever possible as well. The Japanese rely heavily on charcoal rather than coal for fuel.

Japan is one of the poor countries in mineral resources. A wide variety exists but only a few are of sufficient quantity to meet industrial needs. It must import 98% of its petroleum and 95% of its iron ore.

Silk has long been the great textile fiber of Japan but it is far from being cheap. Cotton spinning and weaving has been an industrial main-stay, however industrial composition has switched from light industries, such as cotton textiles, to heavy industries. In the process Japan has become the world's largest ship builder.

The waters surrounding Japan are a rich source of sea food; the domestic source of protein in the Japanese diet. The fishing industry employs close to a million men, for almost the entire coast is dotted with small fishing villages.

Partly because of the land itself, but largely due to the over-populated condition of the islands, Japan is unable to provide food in sufficient quantity to maintain good health for its people.

. . . . THE PEOPLE

The standard of living of the Japanese people is among the highest in the Orient but is still low compared to the United States.

Generally houses were extremely small and flimsy, poorly heated and lacking in modern conveniences and sanitary facilities, a few years ago. They were low, one-story structures, with sliding screens instead of partitions. The floors were covered with straw mats which are invariably clean, for shoes are removed before entering the house. The rural dwellings still have a strong architectural resemblance to Malaysian forms, being raised from the ground on piles and having a thatch roof and relatively open sides.

In contrast, by early 1966, 94% (next in number to U.S.) of the urban households had television sets, 76% washing machines, 62% refrigerators. However, only 12% had cars, 4% pianos, and 2% air conditioners. Even yet only one-quarter of the urban homes have adequate sewage facilities. Many pockets of poverty still remain.

Rice and fish are staple foods, with sea-weed, eggs, beans and sauce, served on lacquer trays while members of the family sit in kneeling positions before the trays.

Though many dress western style for the office, the native dress is the kimono, made of coarse cotton for the poorer class and embroidered silk for the wealthy. The women also wear the obi, a large sash wound around the waist. Youngsters generally wear school uniforms at least through high school.

The people of Japan are predominantly Japanese though there are some Ainu in the north whose genetic strain give more body and facial hair than is characteristic of the true Mongol whose traits include black strait hair, dark brown eyes, tan skin and what we commonly refer to as "slanting eyes". They are all relatively short of stature and are distinctly roundheaded.

They have an optimistic character, are disciplined to self-control, and are admirers of courage. They have an inherent love of nature and of sports. They excel in swimming and are rabid baseball fans, but the traditional sport is sumo (Japanese wrestling). Judo and Karate (Japanese forms of self-defense) have become international sports. The Japanese have a great fondness for children so adoption is widespread. Children are taught early the value of cleanliness. Praise and ridicule are used most extensively in training instead of physical punishment.

The primary social unit of Japanese society is the family which includes the head of the house and his wife, the eldest son (by birth or adoption) and any of his children, and any unmarried children of the master. Sometimes living with them will be a retired grandfather and grandmother. These all live together in a single household. The social position of the master is reflected in the fact that he takes the first bath, receives the first food and is responsible for the income of the family.

In the life cycle there are several things that mark changes in a social status in his family and the community: Birth, Hiaki (introduction of the baby to the deities, etc.), Early training, Marriage, Retirement and Death.

Compulsory and tax-free education begins with elementary school. Nearly all Japanese from the age of six on up are literate to the place they can read the languages' phonetic symbols. The illiteracy rate, compiled last in 1960, among those fifteen years or older, was 2.2, identical with that of the United States. The language used by middle and upper classes is the standard language of Japan; it has five vowels, and three levels of pitch. Japan's system of higher education is patterned like the U.S. four-year college and university. Entrance into upper secondary and higher education is by competitive examinations.

Religion today is primarily Shinto, Buddhism (which entered from

Korea in 552) and Christianity, though Confucianism and Taoism are also represented. Followers of Shinto number over 80,000,000 while Buddhism claims nearly as many, 69,000,000. Up to 75% of the Japanese disclaim any interest in religious matters, yet it is rare for them not to take part in two or more religions at the same time. Japan's defeat in 1945 had a decided effect on religion. State Shinto, with its tax-supported shrines and compulsory attendance at stated ceremonies, was abolished. However, sectarian Shinto enjoys complete freedom as does any other sect or religious group. Roman Catholicism has shown a new vigor and corresponding increase in membership. Shinto (the way of the Gods) has never had an official creed, nor sacred scriptures, nor moral codes or images. Its priests do not preach nor act as spiritual guides, but merely as keepers of the shrine itself. The Shinto know nothing of a heaven or hell, nor the reward or punishment of either in the life hereafter, It is simply a type of ancestor and hero worship.

Before the outbreak of World War II all Protestant churches were forced by law to unite in a single body known as the United Church of Christ. After the war religious freedom was re-established though some 60% remained in the United Church. Total membership in the Christian sects is little more than 1% of the population. Christians in Japan numbered 711,636, with about two-thirds Protestants. Christian organizations support twenty-two universities and a number of major hospitals throughout the nation.

. . . . THE MISSIONARY . . . .

Brother and sister W. D. Cunningham pioneered in "independent" missions in 1901. Following an attack of paralysis, the old Foreign Missionary Society judged brother Cuinningham physically unfit to send out as a missionary. Believing that "God shall supply all your need according to His riches in glory" they set out upon a progressive missionary endeavor, without promise of support either from individuals or organizations. This venture lasted thirty-five years for brother Cunningham and fifty-two years for Mrs. Emily Cunningham, who died in Tokyo on Christmas day 1953.

The Cunninghams started evangelistic work in a little school in the Yotsuya district in Tokyo. It grew until at the beginning of the war there were twelve churches in Tokyo and approximately fifteen in Korea. During the pre-war years the Owen Stills served with Mrs. Cunningham, and again after the war until 1948. Before the war the policy of paying all workers out of Mission funds was followed.

After the years of severe poverty immediately following the Pacific war, the move was made toward a policy of self-support for each local church. Just six months before the death of Mrs. Cunningham the new policy was inaugurated whereby eventually all church buildings and property would be turned over into the hands of the Japanese Christians.

The Harold Sims family came to Tokyo in 1947 through the invitation of Mrs. Cunningham, feeling called of God to witness for Christ in such a field. After the decision was made Harold was told that twenty-two years earlier his father had wanted very much to go to Japan and work with the Cunninghams, and that one reason he was unable to fulfill his desire was because Harold was on the way. From that time he had been hoping and praying that his son would be a missionary to Japan. All glory to God who does mighty things!

In their first term of service, the Sims led in the establishing of four churches, assisted in the work of Evangelism, Vacation Bible School training, and distribution of the printed Word. They found the most advantageous method to be Bible study groups for various ages. Along with this program, brother Sims also taught in the Tokyo Bible Seminary, which he helped to found.

The establishment of the Tokyo Bible Seminary in 1948 marked the beginning of a new phase of evangelism done by the Church of Christ Cunningham Mission. This preacher-training institution was founded on and dedicated to the grand position that the Word of God is the only legitimate and effective instrument for saving the world and for uniting and edifying the church. The Seminary has since closed, prospective preachers now often travel to Osaka for their regular Seminary training. However, many missionaries still conduct training classes for the leaders in their area.

The missionaries here are giving themselves to more pioneer evangelistic work. The Sims assist in a summer camp that was started in 1957. It has been an effective tool of evangelism. They both teach a regular schedule of Bible classes for different age groups every week. This avenue of service has proven most satisfactory. They plan to relocate and work in another area of Tokyo by 1970.

Andrew Patton arrived in Japan in 1948 and, upon the founding of the Bible Seminary, became a teacher in this institution. Realizing his inadequacy for such a task, brother Patton returned to the States in 1951 for two more years of Bible study. During this period of time he met and married Betty Armstrong. Together they came back to Japan in 1953. Brother Patton assumed the main leadership of the

Seminary, becoming its President until it closed. Mrs. Patton served as the secretary-treasurer for the school.

Sakurayama Church group.

The Pattons continue to labor with the Japanese in establishing new churches and strengthening the churches already in existence. Although their primary work is evangelism, they also maintain a Christian dormitory for young students attending various universities in Tokyo. Another phase of youth work is at the YMCA where brother Patton serves as chaplain during Monday evening worship service. Plans are being made to devise a method of home contacts and evangelism through the distribution of printed sermons.

The Stanley Buttray family entered Japan in 1950 to join the work of Tokyo Bible Seminary and to assist in the churches wherever opportunity presented itself. They helped to establish two churches and have taught in others as needed. Besides the regular teaching and preaching, they conduct some Bible classes in English, special classes for women, and witness through evangelism in rural areas.

The Harold Taylors, compelled to leave China in 1949 because of Communist invasion, worked in cooperation with the Cunningham Mission until their furlough in 1953. They came back in 1954 to minister to the Kamiuma church until they left for Korea in November

1956. Much of their Japanese work was with the all-Japanese correspondence course.

Stanley Buttray preaching in rural home.

Pastor Morohashi teaching songs to children in a park.

Much witnessing is done to the young people who seem more receptive to the Word of God than other ages. The biggest enemy for the cause of Christ is indifference. So Japan does not offer the challenge of an "evangelist's paradise" as it was called in post-war days. In the Tokyo area the people are very slow to accept the Gospel, consequently church growth is slow. There are thirteen churches meeting regularly for services in the Tokyo area. An average of approximately 200-250 baptisms are reported each year.

In another section of Tokyo the work of the Mabashi Mission was begun in 1934 by Vivian Lemmon, Grace Farnham, and Ruth Schoonover. Due to family responsibilities, Miss Lemmon returned to the States the following year. Ruth and Grace continued the work in the Mabashi district until Ruth returned to America on the last boat that sailed from Japan before the war began. The Mabashi church did not unite with the Union Church of Japan, as many did, but later it was discontinued since it was meeting in the home of Grace Farnham who was interned in September 1942 by the Japanese.

Miss Farnham was repatriated to America after one year of imprisonment, but she came back to Japan in 1947. The church which had been disbanded for five years was reorganized. For two years it again met in the rented home of Grace Farnham, but in June 1949 property was purchased.

The work here has always been evangelistic. The three Bible schools of earlier years were reopened after the war. Immediately after the war the Japanese seemed eager to attend the church services. They had suffered greatly, and many were reduced to poverty. Now, however, Japan is prosperous and the people apparently feel no need for the church.

The Julius Fleenors came to Tokyo in October 1950 to assist in the Mabashi work. For four years brother Fleenor assisted in the teaching program of Tokyo Bible Seminary. In 1952 the Shimoochiai church of Christ was established, meeting in his home. This was just the beginning of a great evangelistic effort. In August 1967 the Fleenors began their eighteenth year of service as missionaries. By the end of the year God enabled Julius to find two towns of over 20,000 population (without churches) where he is conducting regular Bible classes in the homes of Christian Japanese couples. Two other towns are under survey for possible Bible classes. Through film evangelism, house to house calling, training of Japanese co-workers, and Bible teaching and preaching, the goal is to establish as many churches as possible in places where there is no meeting of active evangelism by any other group.

The Fleenors have also engaged in an intensive camp program. Eight to ten camps a year are held for young people contacted through

Bible classes and churches. Each summer thousands of tracts and Bible portions are given out at the village festival (near the camp) where 50,000 people flock to Karuizawa Village. Many have been baptized in this place through this ministry.

Stephen Fleenor (a son) and his wife, Carol, spent the summer of 1968 in Japan in active evangelism in view of returning as missionaries to Japan when they complete their education in the States.

The Robert Wests reached Japan in February 1953. Because of the shortage of missionaries in Korea, brother West went to teach in the Korean Bible Seminary for five months. Mrs. West remained in Tokyo and taught some in the Tokyo Bible Seminary as well as holding three English Bible classes in her home. They did assume the leadership of the Mabashi church while Miss Farnham was on furlough later that year, remaining there until the fall of 1955.

In 1956 Miss Farnham began helping one of the native ministers to establish a new work in the nearby prefecture of Chiba at Kashima, a town with 40,000 population. The work was located in a new housing area where the people could be more easily reached than the areas where families have lived for centuries. The young families have broken with many old family traditions and were more willing to listen to a new faith. Grace Farnham retired to the States in 1961 and left the work in the hands of Japanese leaders.

John Kachelmyer was reared in the Roman Catholic Church. It was not until 1954 (when he was in the Air Force) that he read the Bible for the first time in his life. Upon hearing the true gospel preached for the first time he accepted Christ as Saviour. When he completed his service duties he prepared for missionary service, returning to Japan in 1961 as a high school teacher at the Christian Academy (a school for the children of missionaries).

During his furlough year John met and married Deana Horne. In 1965 they returned to Japan. Leaving the Christian Academy, the Kachelmyers founded a Christian Home for Boys for the purpose of providing an education for underprivileged boys under Christian influence. In Japan, education is compulsory and free only through ninth grade. Although high schools are operated by the prefectural governments, they are not free. Thus, for orphaned or fatherless boys there is usually little opportunity to attend. In 1966 they became especially concerned for the problem of mixed-blood children (half American-half Japanese) whose fathers are unknown. The greater percentage of these are now in their teen age years. Because they are severly discriminated against, few of them are able to get an education. Some of these have already found a home with the Kachelmyers. Plans are being made for a home for handicapped children, with the possibility of a sheltered workshop.

The Robert Warrick family came to Japan in the middle of 1965 to settle in the Tokyo area. Following language study, their preaching and teaching centered in an area called Hoya. When the school year began in 1968 they moved to the Christian Academy as dorm parents, but were able to continue their witness at Hoya. They are also advisors (with Kachelmyers) in plans for the handicapped children's work. Practically nothing was done in this field before World War II. A young Japanese Christian is in Loma Linda University in California, preparing to be a physical therapy instructor. An elder in a church about two hours north of Tokyo has given property for a center for handicapped people. These plans are going ahead under the leadership of the Japanese Christians themselves. The Warricks also work in the Karuizawa camp activities. A language school is maintained at the camp year-round, designed especially for the missionaries. Brother Warrick designed and built the electronic equipment (except tape recorders) for the language lab.

Isao Nara, former pole vault champion studying physical therapy in Loma Linda.

Hoya elder who will work with center for handicapped children.

The Dale Wilkinson family will be making their home in Karuizawa for two years while they will be in language study. They plan to later move into Tokyo to begin evangelistic work.

Exie Fultz has served many countries in the cause of Christ through the years in connection with radio work. In early years the work was called Christian Radio Mission, and was produced first from Japan, then in Korea, but broadcast on Radio Luxembourg. She labored long hours on the follow-up program which included correspondence courses. Since 1958 this phase of the work has been carried on in Europe, handled by the missionaries on the field.

For a time Exie continued to prepare and produce radio programs, but more and more she became involved in inner-city evangelism, the challenge to which she had been exposed in Kobe in her early days in Japan. In 1967 she moved to a new area of Tokyo. Her apartment is located on a line between a shopping-entertainment area and a wealthy residential area. Two services are held on Sunday; a Thursday class is conducted for college age students. Outside of her area, Exie teaches five classes of English Conversation at a girl's high school. Two early evenings a week she teaches English Bible in an export company.

Because the Japanese have demonstrated that they are leaders in the Orient in an industrial, educational, and military way, it caused Claude Likins to believe that if they could be converted to Christ they would be spiritual leaders as well, so that not only the Japanese would be won, but also the other peoples of the Orient.

Thus the Lord opened the way for brother Likins and his family to come to Japan in July 1956, after spending the preceding two years in "missionary evangelism". (This was a program of evangelistic efforts with emphasis on missions, which not only was a means of saving souls but acquainted the U.S. Christians with the missionary movement.)

Upon arrival in Japan the Likins immediately entered into a full-time study of the Japanese language, but using the Bible as a textbook they were able to witness for Christ through three English classes. In January 1967, with the major portion of their language study out of the way, they began work with the Kamiuma church in Tokyo, which was established by the Harold Taylors before they went to Korea. By mid-year 1960 the Kamiuma church was under capable Japanese leadership.

In their second term of service in 1962, the Likins family moved to Kobe, where they assumed leadership of Nippon Christian Broadcasting Association which was formed in 1959. This Association produces Gospel broadcasts for airing on commercial stations throughout Japan. Bible correspondence courses are offered in connection with the broadcasts. Contacts are directed to local churches for further teaching and fellowship. Japanese co-workers oversee the work now and the Likins family moved to Akashi at the beginning of their third term. This is about an hour's commuting distance from their former home in Kobe. Only Bible classes and Sunday School are conducted here at the present time.

The work of the Osaka Christian Mission was started by brother and sister M. B. Madden and family in the early 1920's. The Maddens first came to Japan back in 1895. Becoming disappointed with their relationship with the Missionary Society, brother Madden began supporting his family by teaching English in the Osaka Higher Commercial College. This proved unsatisfactory since there was not enough time for propagating the Gospel. So in 1928, he appealed to Christian brethren for support and assistance in the fulfilling of his witness. In those years they were assisted from time to time by their daughter, Grace Madden (Bradley), as well as various periods of efforts by the Bates, Cecil Harding, Pauline Starn, and Ray Sawyer.

The Madden's work, located in the heart of Osaka, was evangelistic in nature. The purpose of the work was to make disciples, baptize and build up a church. In order to have a closer contact with the people the Maddens opened a kindergarten for children (the first of its kind in Osaka) and an English night school for adults. This direct approach resulted in a number of converts, one of which has served Christ in the Osaka area for many, many years.

At the invitation of brother Madden, the Harold Coles came to Osaka in 1937, at which time the Bible Seminary program began. Such a program was hampered by the Japanese adult attitude toward anything other than their own militaristic ideas. However, the seed was planted and the idea brought forth its fruit. The Coles were convinced of the practicability of a Bible training program for Japanese Christian leaders and devoted their efforts to that end.

The Maddens retired from the field in 1949 but brother Madden continued his faithful efforts on behalf of Japan until his death in July 1956. The body was weaker than the spirit but he never ceased to talk about and pray for the work in Japan. The Madden daughter continued to assist in the work until shortly before the war. Though all American personnel were forced to come home at the time of

302

World War II, brother Sugano (the early convert) remained a faithful leader though faced with opposition and persecution.

Harold Cole returned to the field in March 1947, just ten years after his first entrance to the work, to find brother Sugano and a few other Christians ready to begin again. Five recruit families were ready to come at this time but they faced major problems. First, Osaka was a shambles from bombing and the few Christians left were scattered. A two-fold building program was begun. The spiritual building-up of what was left of the church was first, then a building program to house the church and American personnel followed (the latter to meet the Army of Occupation requirements). Largely due to the efforts of brother Madden in the States, funds were provided and the job accomplished.

The Cole family was able to rejoin Harold in the fall of 1947, The following year the Paul Neilsens, who had been in Tokyo for about a year before the Pearl Harbor incident, were allowed to enter Japan. In 1949 the George Beckmans, newly married, came to join the work, followed in 1950 by the Martin Clarks. Ray Mings, a former classmate of the Clarks and Beckmans, entered Japan early in 1951 along with Howard Davis (who had served in Japan in the armed forces). Within a few months of their arrival the Davises went to the Nagoya area to establish a work for Christ there. Also in 1951, Jane Kinnett, forced to leave China, came to Japan. Lucille Sherman (1952) and Betty Whittington (1953) also joined the Osaka workers.

Brother Cole was occupied with the rebuilding program in those first years after the war, but not to the neglect of the chief objective. He gathered a few interested students around him and began a Bible-training program immediately. Brother Martin Clark took over active leadership of the school on his arrival. With the Seminary the center of the sphere of evangelism, new churches were established and the gospel proclaimed in other areas. By 1954 there were thirteen con-gregations meeting regularly, and several other Bible schools being held. Though brother Clark devoted most of his time to supervising, counselling, and teaching in the Osaka Bible Seminary, he found time to teach some English Bible classes, work with Christian Radio Mission (located here at the time), as well as assist in evangelistic efforts in the area, and summer camps.

Osaka Bible Seminary is a completely college-level school. Its achievements are the results of the combined efforts of a wonderful team. The main building was completed early in 1961, called "Madden

303

Memorial", remembering the one, who by the grace of God, had labored so long to make this a reality. A second multi-purpose building was dedicated in July 1968. Through efforts of Akira Oda, professor at Osaka Bible Seminary, the first Greek-Japanese Lexicon was compiled and printed in 1964. Brother Oda, as well as other Japanese teachers, have studied abroad to return to teach and train their own people. Living costs in Japan have rocketed to unbelievable heights. This rise, beginning in 1955, has increased 165% compared to 115% in the United States. The Japanese showed their concern by sharing in the cost of the school. In 1955 no Japanese support was given to the school. In 1968 there were at least eight congregations who budgeted a regular amount to the school.

Osaka Bible Seminary librarian with VBS students.

Osaka Bible Seminary 1968 graduate, Keika Takeyasu.

There are thirty-seven preachers serving with our various missionaries in Japan. Twenty-five of these are graduates of, or received their Bible training in, Osaka Bible Seminary. Twenty of the twenty-three Bachelor of Theology graduates are active in the ministry.

The main emphasis of the work of the George Beckman family has been with Osaka Bible Seminary. Brother Beckman is head of the New Testament department of the Seminary, designing courses that meet the needs of the Japanese who do not have a long Christian background. Mrs. Beckman also teaches in the Seminary. During their first term they began a church at Kyoto where they lived. At present they live at Koyoen, midway between Osaka and Kobe, and commute to the Seminary in about an hour's time. Brother Beckman preaches once a month at the Koyoen and Kyoto churches. Mrs. Beckman teaches in the Bible school and has a weekly Bible study class for women. With Japanese assistance she is helping to prepare materials for use in teaching.

The Ray Mings also teach in the Seminary. Even though this is a vital part of the work they feel that evangelism must not be neglected. He preaches once a month in each of the three churches with which they have close association. They are especially closely connected with the Nakaburi church that meets in their home. He also continues with Bible classes outside those taught at the Seminary. In cooperation with other missionaries and Japanese Christians, the Mings have labored in summer camps and several series of Vacation Bible Schools.

It is a blessing to the Mings (and to the work) to have their sons, Lonnie and Donnie (and their families) serving with them in Japan. Like their father, Lonnie and Donnie both teach in Osaka Bible Seminary and are busily engaged outside the classroom in evangelism. The Lonnie Mings family returned for their second term in July 1967—the Donnie Mings, August 1968.

In her brief time on the field, Jane Kinnett assisted in teaching in Osaka Bible Seminary. Most of her work in Japan, however, was with the young women's groups, teachers' training class and services at one of the Japanese churches. Now Mrs. John Hill, she labors with her husband in a work in Korea.

Miss Lucille Sherman came as a blessing, not only to the work in general (for she assisted in the work of the churches) but to the parents in particular, since she set up the Osaka Christian Day School. Though open to everyone, it was especially designed to train the children of missionaries. Children on the mission field are a great blessing, first to the parents, then next to the people among whom they live. The children witness to their Japanese playmates, often bringing their friends to church. The missionary children of Osaka Christian Day School conducted street meetings, singing and speaking in Japanese. When home on furlough and teaching in the Christian grade school in Akron, Ohio, Miss Sherman died unexpectedly in March 1960.

For awhile Betty Whittington assisted in the Seminary office, training Japanese help. She also assisted in the preparing of radio scripts, summer camps, as well as teaching Bible classes in English. With the help of a young Seminary woman, she conducted evening services for the Inano church until her return from the field.

Bill Turner had his first experience in Japan from 1950 to 1952, when he served with the U.S. Army during the Korean conflict. He was so impressed by the need of the Gospel in this land that he decided he would return to help spread God's Word if he survived the war. Following his discharge from the Army, he enrolled in Atlanta Christian College. In 1955 he met Betty Yarbrough, then on furlough from mission work in the Philippines. Betty returned to her field in 1956, and Bill graduated from College in 1958. He then went to Platte Valley Bible College for medical missionary training. They were married on March 25, 1962. Together they returned to Cebu City and worked for three years in Cebu Bible Seminary. In 1965 Bill was once more challenged regarding the need for workers in Japan. Feeling that their phase of the work could be carried on by trained Filipino workers, the Turners went to Japan in September 1965, planning to help out in Osaka Bible Seminary for a year. By the time they went to the States for furlough in June 1966, however, they had made a decision to continue in the work in Japan. After further education and special training the Turners arrived back in Japan in March 1968 to take up their work in connection with Osaka Bible Seminary.

Bill immediately enrolled in Japanese language school and plans to study for two years. He gives voice lessons on Monday evenings in the Seminary and will gradually take on some of the business responsibilities of the school. After language school, he will also be teaching Missions classes.

Betty has begun her duties as head of the English department. She teaches English classes intensively in the Seminary, and she also has an English Bible class for young women in her home on Thursday evenings. One of Betty's chief interests is in the preparation of literature for publication—particularly material to help present the work in Japan to friends in America.

The Turners are operating a bookstore in connection with the Seminary. A 1968 graduate of the Seminary is helping them in this project.

Brother Harold Cole has taught many hours in the Seminary, which he helped to establish, but he also has devoted much of his effort to the work of evangelism, especially in the Kobe-Osaka area. In the fall of 1959 the Coles resigned from Osaka Christian Mission after twenty-three years of association. This was done to enable the Coles to set-up a printing ministry apart from the Seminary program.

Most of the religious literature in Japan is "Calvinistic and faith only", thus there is a definite need of printed material that will stress "following the Scriptures". The first objective is to make available for all missionaries, tracts, Bible school helps, correspondence courses, VBS materials, etc. This printing ministry continues as funds permit.

Harold and Leone Cole have entered a new phase in the Lord's work in Ono City, a rural area of several villages in Hyogo Prefecture. They are erecting the first unit of a Christian Center. It will provide a place to hold worship services, Sunday school, intensified week-day children's meetings, Bible classes, Christian library and reading room (an outlet for printed materials already prepared), a place for blind Christians to have services and recreation, and housing for a Japanese minister. This Center is located in a residential district of about sixty households, between the Technical and Public High Schools.

New Japanese minister and wife at Ono.

Bible classes are held in two Junior High Schools and at Ono High. Other classes for the same age groups and for adults are conducted in the Cole's home. Two special classes were added in 1968 by request. One is a cooking class for American cooking instruction; forty-five minutes is devoted to Bible study and hymn learning. The other class is in English for adults at the local civic center.

The Nakamuras, a Japanese couple from Osaka, started preaching and teaching the Gospel in 1955 in an area where the message of God had not been proclaimed before. By 1957 they had established three preaching points in the prefecture of Okayama. This work is nearer the island of Shikoko than the work of Osaka, but through the use of bicycles they were able to go out faithfully to serve. Later they moved to this prefecture where they served until 1966. They hope to return to rural evangelism in the future. To assist and encourage them the Robert Wests moved to Hayashino in the Okayama area. Bob and Audrey served in various ways in several places in Japan, first in Toyko with the Bible Seminary, Bob in Korea, then at Osaka Bible Seminary. Even while assisting in the Okayama work they returned to Osaka to teach in the Seminary for several weeks of intensive training each year.

Audrey West now lives in the Emi area of Okayama-ken and continues her faithful witness through teaching and personal witness. The great need is for more teachers and leaders. There is a desire for more training for the Japanese Christians.

Tanabe is a "city" in the country, one hundred miles south of Osaka. It is an old Samurai city, steeped in ancient traditions. The church in Tanabe was begun in the spring of 1948 when Miss Ruth Schoonover (who had formerly been in Tokyo) and brother Kawamura came here, just six months before Miss Schoonover passed away. None of our missionaries had ever worked in Wakayama province before. After Miss Schoonover's death, brother Kawamura continued to preach. When Miss Vivian Lemmon (an earlier co-worker of Miss Schoonover) arrived in 1952 she found a church of about sixty members (now self-supporting). This church was the center of all the work. Besides the regular work, teachers were trained and inspired to evangelize their own people, which they have done in strenuous programs of evangelism in other villages near Tanabe.

Through English Bible classes and personal work, Vivian Lemmon is able to direct people to the Lord. Many would never seek the church otherwise. Resistance to the Gospel seems to be growing in Japan. The Department of Education plans to teach Japanese mythology and the status of the Emperor in the grammar schools, beginning in 1971. When New Testaments were given to students in three Junior High Schools in Tanabe, some parents and the Education Department of Wakayama-ken objected and made the students return them. However, for those whose parents do not object, they may receive their free New Testaments at the library. Miss Lemmon and her co-workers will continue to bear witness to the Gospel at every opportunity.

The call of the villages, known as Tohoku Rural Evangelism, is one of the newer works of rural evangelism begun in September 1955 in Sendai, 219 miles north of Tokyo. Some evangelistic work was done here over sixty years ago by brother M. B. Madden. Because Sendai is the chief of cities north of Tokyo on Honshu, and the center of education, commerce and industry in northern Honshu, it is an ideal location for a center or home base from which to do rural evangelistic work.

The Paul Nielsens served their first full term on the field with Osaka Christian Mission. Upon returning in 1954 they spent one year in language study in Tokyo. In the fall of 1955, however, they came to Sendai with the Takafuji family. Services were begun in the Takafuji home in November of that year with six being present. Fifteen months of labor finally produced the first fruits of the work. During the summer of 1956 the men spent much time in the village areas getting acquainted with leaders and holding evangelistic services. The village people do not know what they seek nor where to find it. They think Christianity belongs to the people of the city. There are hundreds of farm and fishing villages where the Gospel has never been preached regularly—some where it has never been preached at all.

The Katsuo Motoki family, natives of Tokyo, began working in rural evangelism around Sendai in 1963. In 1966 the Nielsens returned to the States on a sick leave. They served the Lord in Colorado and Oklahoma until their planned return to Sendai in 1969.

The Milton Jones family have resigned their ministry in Florida to press forward with plans to serve the Lord in Sendai, Japan. After initial orientation in Japanese language and culture, they plan to work with the Nielsens. They are working toward an August 1969 departure date.

Feeling they could not serve the Lord in any lesser capacity the Howard Davises came to Japan in 1950 to take up their witness for Christ. Within a few months they had located at Nagoya although brother Davis continued to teach an occasional course of intensive study at Osaka Bible Seminary where they served on arrival.

Christianity was new to the people of Nagoya and at first it was generally only accepted by the young people. However, by 1953 the Davises had the opportunity and responsibility of ministering to the needs of four churches, three children's Bible schools, prayer meetings,

Bible study, and a Bible school teacher's training course, as well as studying the language several hours a day.

Associated with the Howard Davis family in the work of Nagoya Christian Mission were the Bob Chambers who came to Japan in April 1952. Seven months after their arrival they were able to begin services in the village of Mukojima on the outskirts of Nagoya, while still conducting an American service in their home for military friends.

In the summer of 1952 the annual Nagoya Christian Service Camp was established. The total visible results of the first four years of camp were: over ninety in attendance with twenty-two baptisms. Not all the converts remained faithful, some turned back to the old national religion since it did not require complete submission as does Christianity.

Like brother Davis, Bob Chambers also assisted in the teaching program of Osaka Bible Seminary, both being thoroughly convinced of the fact that native preachers must be trained to reach their own people. It was hoped that some type of concentrated training could be offered in Nagoya to young people in preparing them to teach in the Bible schools, to participate in evangelistic work and even to preach. Thus it was that a Christian Leader's Institute was started.

Another project of 1956 was to begin holding several tent meetings, both where work had been started and also in new districts. In the late summer the first such meeting was held in Nagashima, located on a little island fifteen miles west of Nagoya. Attendance ran up over three hundred on several nights of the meeting. This town had never had a preaching mission before. Over 95% of the people had never heard the Gospel story before at all. From this beginning the preaching of the Gospel was continued every Lord's day in Nagashima and the church established. In the damaging typhoon of 1959 the building at Nagashima was completely destroyed as the whole island was engulfed. Other mission and church buildings were damaged but no Christians were lost. Through their witnessing in time of stress, the Lord's work gained a stronger foothold in Central Japan.

A program of rural evangelism was planned for the fall of 1957. Calls to present the Gospel came from Kanie, Yatome, and in Taushima (a city of 100,000 where services began in 1959); thus the work began to expand and the Davises changed the designation of their work to Central Japan Mission. The Chambers continued in the work of Nagoya Christian Mission until they left the field in late summer 1959. The Howard Davises returned to the States at a later date, assuming teaching responsibilities at Midwest Christian College in Oklahoma City, Oklahoma.

310

Don Burney often visited Tokyo while in the Navy during the Korean war. He saw the work of the missionaries and the greater need for others to come to help win the lost millions to Christ. This is what brought him back with his family in 1955.

The Burneys chose wisely the island of Shikoku (smallest of the four main islands of Japan) as their field of labor. No church of Christ missionaries were working there. However, they spent the first year in Tokyo assisting with the work there, as they learned the language and customs, as a basis of contact with a new people. In October 1956 they moved to Kobe to strengthen the work of the church there during the absence of Exie Fultz who was on furlough. This move made it possible to make weekend trips to the island of Shikoku to make contacts, arrangements for housing, etc. before they actually moved to their new work in September of 1957.

The Burneys have lived in Kochi ever since. Most of the time they have worked alone, the burden of preaching and teaching falling upon Don. When the need for teaching materials arose they obtained a printing press and began publishing their own materials. Only in recent months has help arrived in the persons of two young Japanese couples and a young woman from Hokkaido. This will make it possible for the Burneys to expand their witness on their return from furlough in 1969.

During the war Mark Maxey was a chaplain in Japan. In his heart was borne the desire to serve Christ here. In August of 1948, though still in the army, the Maxey family began to make definite plans to return to Japan.

Desiring to do a pioneer work where our people had not gone, the Maxeys chose the island of Kyushu and named their proposed work the Kyushu Christian Mission. Learning that Chaplain Paul Cook had baptized a number of converts in the Kanoya area, they decided to begin with this nucleus. Kanoya is a remote 1,000 miles from Tokyo, an arduous journey by train, ferry boat, and bus. They came to Kanoya in October of 1950 and have since engaged in rural evangelism, using Kanoya as the center. In the first five year period they were able to establish eight churches, with additional preaching points, the first ones at a large leper colony a few miles away and the town orphanage. This was the pioneering period.

Mrs. Isabel Dittemore, sister to Mark Maxey, came to Japan in December 1951 after ten years with the Lisu in West China. Following five months teaching in Osaka Bible Seminary she moved to Kagoshima City across the bay from Kanoya. Her mother joined her for two years to help in local church activities and with Isabel's daughter's education. During Isabel's three years on the field six churches were established. More than two hundred baptisms were reported. A Japanese evangelist came to oversee the work. Following a furlough, Isabel moved to Kobe to supervise a radio ministry for the Japanese. She is presently in Taiwan (Formosa).

In the Maxey's second term a Christian Center was built, featuring a Christian library, bookstore, and a place for short-term Bible training institutes. In this period young Japanese ministers began to assist with the work. This made it possible for the Maxeys in their third term to hold numerous classes and meetings in outlying areas. Their theme for the present (fourth) term of service is called "outreach". Because many of the young people from their area have now returned from Seminary training to witness, they are able to reach out even farther with the Gospel. Entry into new towns and villages at the southern tip of the island is expected. A Christian Center is planned for Kagoshima (where Isabel worked) through which they may reach university students. They will continue with leadership training classes in cooperation with the present preachers in the area.

Of the remaining open fields, Japan, with her near ninety-five million people, presented to the Hammonds the greatest challenge of the unreached. With their challenge ever before them, Al and Eleanor

Church service on Tanegashima Island.

312

Hammond came to Japan in May 1954. They first assisted in the Satsuma work for three months before entering Kobe Language School for a year. During the absence of the Mark Maxeys they moved to Kanoya and carried on the work very effectively there. In June of 1957 they moved to the island of Tanegashima for a work of true pioneer evangelism. This island is just south of the Kyushu mainland, making the Hammonds the southernmost missionaries in Japan. They were about one hundred fifty miles from Kanoya—five hours by boat from the coast.

Work had been started on Tanegashima about three years earlier through previous efforts of Mark Maxey. By developing this faithful group (the Nishinoomoto church) and by taking advantage of the opportunities, there could be left a lasting witness on the island. A Christian kindergarten was established offering an indirect method of evangelism. A capable evangelist took over the leadership of the Tanegashima work so that when the Hammonds returned to Japan after furlough in 1958 they went to suburban Tokyo. However, they continued a financial and supervisory relationship with the island work for ten years. The work now is entirely self-supporting, due largely to the economic success of the growing kindergarten.

Kindergarten at Tanegashima.

In Tokyo, brother Hammond continued his own schooling in a Japanese University where he emphasized work among the students, conducting Bible classes, rallies, and camp programs. A church was established to meet the needs of their area.

313

Home Bible study (cottage meeting).

Motosu Christian Camp.

The year 1961 was the beginning of Far East Christian Missionary, a missionary open forum quarterly magazine. The response was immediate and far reaching. Missionaries from all over the world began to share in it. Because of the demand from non-Asian fields, a new name is designed for future issues, though the format will be basically the same.

The Paul Pratts were burdened for the unreached rural people of Kyushu when hearing about the Maxey's work. Their decision to serve in Japan came after much prayer and consideration. They left the States in the summer of 1958 in time to enroll in the language school in Kobe that fall. During this necessary schooling they witnessed through English Bible classes and assisted Mrs. Dittemore in the preparation of the weekly radio broadcasts.

In July 1960 the Pratt family moved into the Kagoshima prefecture to Kajiki, a city of 15,000. There was a congregation here already as a result of Mrs. Dittemore's work. They also helped to continue the radio ministry and produced a 38-lesson Bible correspondence course as a follow-up. Japanese ministers came to work in the area, making it possible for the Pratts to move to Tokyo where their children could attend high school. In the absence of other missionaries they served in two churches, but since 1966 they have lived and worked in Isehara, a city of 30,000 population just thirty miles southwest of Tokyo. Much of their work is with students of the elementary through college levels. However, special efforts are made to reach the families in the community. In addition to the Isehara work, the Pratts have assisted the Fleenors in their leadership training school and continue to maintain the correspondence course to persons in all parts of Japan. Since many Japanese shy away from mass evangelistic efforts, "home" meetings seem to be a key to new beginnings for the Gospel.

Except for a short period when the Christian Radio Mission broadcast was heard in Hokkaido, the New Testament church had been unknown on this northernmost of the main islands of Japan.

Because heavy snow fall makes travel almost impossible in many months of the year, the Wesley Walkers chose Sapporo, a city of 400,000, for the center of their work when they arrived on the field in April 1955.

Theirs is primarily a work of evangelism. Though progress has been slow at times, a few hundred Japanese have been baptized into Christ. This has resulted in a strong church in one of the suburbs of Sapporo City and in several preaching points.

In the fall of 1956 Wesley and Margaret were joined in the work by his parents, Walter and Olive Walker. Early in 1958, Walker became a victim of the Asian flu and entered his reward in glory. At present Olive is in the States.

Each summer the Christian Service Camp presents opportunities of fellowship, training, and evangelism. For the past few years the camp has averaged well over one hundred participants each year.

With the Moiwa church assuming most of its own responsibility, leadership, and financing, the Walkers began seeking new areas in which to preach. Early in 1966 an opportunity to buy a fine bus was presented. The bus is now a mobile chapel used in taking the gospel to the many towns and villages in this part of Hokkaido. Being fully equipped for sound, tape recorder, mikes, speakers, etc., it is also ideal for use in street meetings or as an aid in promoting larger evangelistic meetings. In areas where no meeting place it available, it serves as a chapel for worship services, Bible classes, and Sunday schools. Since it is a bus, it also serves the secondary purpose of transportation for church activities, camps, etc. It may be a new concept in preaching in Japan, but it is accomplishing the main purpose of bringing the Gospel to those who have never heard.

Another phase of the work is the Moiwa Christian Day School. This school was started by Olive Walker in 1957 and continues with over a hundred students enrolled and many more on the waiting list. The school meets in its own building which was completely paid for by the Japanese Christians. Not only are the children receiving good Bible training but the school has been the means of reaching many of the parents with the Gospel.

The Ernest Fabers arrived in Japan in September 1954 and enrolled immediately in Tokyo Japanese Language School. After a survey trip to Hokkaido in 1956 they decided to begin a work in eastern Hokkaido in Obihiro, the center of a large agricultural area. By the end of that first summer they had started a Sunday school and English Bible classes in their home. The church continued to meet there until their own building was completed in 1958. There have been over sixty-three baptisms since the beginning of this work. Three of their youth have entered the field of Christian service. A summer camp program was started in 1958 in conjunction with the work directed by the Walkers around Sapporo. In September 1966 the church at Obihiro called a Japanese leader to be its minister, enabling the Fabers to seek other areas of service. They selected Tomakonnai, an industrial city of 85,000 population. This witness began in the fall of 1968.

The door of Hokkaido is open. There is here an opportunity for the New Testament church to preach Christ without first having to undo the harm done by false teachers. From Tanegashima to Hokkaido the missionaries have a great fellowship in a common goal of witnessing for Christ to the lost souls of Japan.

316

Mark Maxey has summed up Japan's needs in the following statements. "It is a nation of non-religion, a spiritual desert whose people are now drifting, seeking some goal in life. Japan's great thirst for education, pleasure, travel, pacifism, socialism, and materialism has not satisfied the fundamental human longing to 'seek God . . . and find Him'. In 100 years of history, Christianity has impregnated Japan with noble ideals and institutions but individual converts number less than 1% of the population. Japan needs Christ *now!*"

Philippines

"Land of tropical beauty"

Aparri

Vigan

LUZON

Manila

0 20 40 60 80 100

SAMAR

MASBATE

PANAY

CEBU LEYTE

Cebu

SURIGAO

PALAWN

NEGROS

PHILIPPINES

MINDANAO

Davao

Zamboanga   Cotabato

319

THE LAND . . . .

Formerly a possession of the United States, this group of islands, which lies just north of the equator in the Pacific and South China Sea waters, became an independent republic on July 4th, 1946.

The Philippine Islands extend from sixty-five miles south of Formosa to thirty miles east of Borneo. There are over 7,000 islands and islets though the total land area is about the same as Italy. There are eleven major islands; only 462 islands are of one square mile or more in area.

The islands are mountainous in nature, the peaks being volcanic in origin. Yet there is less volcanic activity in the whole group than in a single Hawaiian island. While there are many small streams which become mountain torrents in the rainy season, there are only a few large rivers that are used for navigable purposes, These magnificent mountain ranges, rich with vegeation, are separated by great fertile plains.

There has been a rapid increase in population almost wholly due to the development of the agricultural, pastoral and forest products of the country. In 1965 the population was 32,345,000. As a people, the Filipinos generally have settled chiefly in the areas along the sea coast rather than in the fertile valleys of the interior, yet even the rugged mountains are inhabited.

The climate is tropical but on the whole not unhealthful. It may be divided into the following seasons: the rainy season (June to November); the cool, dry season (December through February); and the hot, dry season (March to May). At Manila the highest recorded temperature was a little over 100 degrees, the lowest a little under 60. This gives a little idea of the temperature on all the islands at or near sea level. At high altitudes the temperature is much lower. Tropical typhoons or violent windstorms are common in the Philippines, and often cause great property damage and loss of life, striking most often at the section north of Manila.

Nearly 60% of the total land area is covered by forest areas which have been preserved to represent a great wealth to the Republic. The islands of Luzon, Mindanao, and Negros are the most important for lumbering. The coconut palms grow everywhere.

Excellent fishing grounds are scattered throughout the islands though the fishing industry has never been developed on a scientific scale. But to the Filipino families, fish are an important item for their diet. Pearl diving and coral gathering are other important industries of the coastal waters. Reptiles range from tiny lizards, that slither over every wall and ceiling, to the great crocodiles that lurk in jungle swamps and rivers. Cobras and tiny green pit vipers are the only poisonous snakes. Small pythons are often kept as pets in native houses to catch rats and mice.

The most important domesticated animal is the water buffalo, called carabao. It plows the land, hauls the cart to market, supplies milk for the family and finally is killed for meat, having served its purpose well.

Primarily an agricultural country, two-thirds of the population were engaged in farming, however, now less than 60% are thus employed. The people are good farmers despite crude methods and primitive implements. Most farms are small; almost half are no larger than five acres. Notable exceptions to this are estates founded by grant during the Spanish regime and holding of corporations. Irrigation is becoming more widely applied, especially in the rice fields which is the most extensively cultivated crop in the country. Corn is now the basic food for about 25% of the population. Double and triple cropping are practiced in some areas in Mindanao. Everywhere the government has encouraged the farmer to adopt new crops.

Philippine industry was devoted almost entirely to agriculture until the beginning of the 20th century. Since that time the mineral wealth in gold and base metals has made rapid progress. The destruction of all mechanical equipment during the war has made rehabilitation slow and costly. The first producing oil well was drilled on the island of Cebu in 1961, to give industry a boost.

Manila, traditional capital, (Quezon, a suburb, is the official capital) is the largest city and the business and financial center of the country. Cebu, second largest city, is the oldest European settlement in the Philippines. As an export center it is only outranked by Manila. Iloilo, one of the prosperous small cities on the islands, is the chief port for the sugar industry. It is located on the island of Panay. Davao City, chief port of Mindanao, is the center for the rich agricultural province of Davao. This area is also the producing region for Manila hemp. The city of Zamboanga on the southwestern tip of the island of Mindanao has the largest land area of any city in the world. It is equal to about the size of Rhode Island but its population is less than that of Cebu City.

.... THE PEOPLE

Three general racial types inhabit the Philippines: the Pygmy, Indonesian and Malayan.

The average height of the Pygmy is just under five feet. Their small size, black skin and fuzzy hair make them entirely different from the other island people. The purest type of Pygmy lives in wandering bands in deep forests. Their houses are a temporary structure of fallen leaves and branches. Practicing no agriculture, they live wholly by hunting, trapping, and gathering of wild forest products. Their principal, and often only, weapon is the bow and arrow. The other class of Pygmy comprises those who have been more or less influenced by the more cultured Filipinos. In some places they build houses of good quality. Nearly all of them hunt in the forest in the dry season for products to use for barter and trade purposes. Many go into the towns to work for a season but they eventually return to the forest.

The Indonesians, settling principally on the islands of Luzon and Mindanao, are a pagan tribal people though less primitive than the Pygmies. Most of these tribes are extremely picturesque. They attract interest because of their customs and dress, their head-hunting, war-like practices and unusual methods of farming. Head-hunting was fairly well suppressed under American occupation though it may still be practiced occasionally. In appearance these tribal people have brown skin and straight black hair. By nature they are loyal and intelligent.

The major portion of the people of the Philippines consist of Malayans who, on the basis of their religious beliefs, are divided into three groups: Pagans, Mohammedans, and Christians (applying in the broad sense of the term). Those of the Mohammedan religion are concentrated wholly in Mindanao and the Sulu Archipelago. Christian Filipinos of Malay extraction constitute over 93% of the total population. They are the dominant people of the islands from whose midst comes most of the agricultural and industrial laborers, the business and professional men, the education and the social and political leaders. The most prominent and progressive of this group are the Tagalogs who live in the central Luzon plain near Manila. Warm brown skin, straight black hair, flattened noses and light, graceful figures are typical characteristics of this group of Filipinos. They are likewise carefree and lovers of music. Thin, cotton garments clothe these Filipinos. Men and boys wear light trousers and a jacket or shirt. A large peaked palm-leaf hat shields them from the sun. Women and girls love bright prints and often wear a wrapped skirt with a blouse of a different color. Though this is common apparel for the rural areas, American styles are worn in the cities.

The presence of Chinese and Spanish blood is quite apparent among the leading people of every Christian area. The infusion of foreign blood has strengthened the Filipinos as a race. A health program and lifting of the standard of living above that of any other Oriental people has made them a heavier and sturdier race.

English and Tagalog, the national official language, are spoken by equal number of people. Less than ½ million speak Spanish, over 100,000 speak Chinese, 27,450 speak Japanese and the multitudes speak over eighty different dialects. The many dialects are related, however, and are enough alike so that a person who knows one of them can learn to understand others without much trouble. Because of the number of dialects and the absence of a common language, the English language was used as the basis of education under the United States rule. So, today English is spoken by some in all parts of the country.

Schooled in the belief that education is indispensable to successful self-government, the American people made education the keystone of American government in the Philippines. The system of public education is free, secular and coeducational. It includes four years of primary and two years of intermediate education; four years of secondary education, a two-year program for training elementary school teachers along with technical education of various types.

Filipino children are apt students but facilities are inadequate, teachers often unqualified, so that one out of eight of primary age, one out of four of intermediate age and three out of five of secondary age were, a few years ago, not enrolled in schools. That condition along with an illiteracy rate of 50% was present shortly after the war (1948). However, this situation has improved over the years and in the last census (1966) 72% were classified as literate, though the drop-out rate in public elementary school is high.

According to the latest religious census about 82.9% of the people are Roman Catholic in belief. Approximately 7.6% are adherents of the Filipino Church (independent) which was established by a former Roman Catholic priest who kept most of the Catholic beliefs and forms of worship. They likewise adhere to modern science which they hold to be superior to Biblical tradition; that is, denying the possibilities of miracles. The Protestants represent only 2.8% of the people, which is only a little more than half of the number of pagans. Tribal religion is based upon the belief in and propitation of numerous classes of greater and minor gods. Among some of the Mindanao tribes human sacrifices occurred as late as the early years of the 20th century.

Figures alone cannot tell the full story of the destruction by the war. The liberation of the Philippines cost hundreds of thousands of lives, much suffering, and property damage amounting to billions of dollars. Almost every city in the Islands was left in ruins.

It was to this land of ruin that missionaries came; not to rebuild a nation but to rebuild lives for God.

. . . . THE MISSIONARY . . . .

The Philippine Islands first received the restoration message in 1901 when Chaplain Williams was discharged from the Army to serve, with his wife, as a missionary on Luzon. Mr. and Mrs. W. H. Hanna soon joined the Williams. When these families moved to another field of labor, the Kershners reopened this one. The Leslie Wolfes arrived in Manila in 1907.

In the early days of the work, all of the missionaries worked together under the old Foreign Missionary Society, but after the organization of the United Christian Missionary Society and the introduction of comity agreements and modernism, the Wolfes found it impossible to continue with them.

Early in 1926, the Wolfe's connection was broken with the U.C.M.S. Later in the year, thirty Tagalog (native) churches also broke from the Society. The Manila Bible Seminary opened the same year and began training workers. Mr. and Mrs. Ben Allison (neé Edith Wolfe) came to assist in this faith work in 1933 (which they continued for seventeen years).

In 1939 Misses Edith Shimmel and Ethel Jones came from Japan to work in the Philippines for awhile before returning for furlough. They remained there until after the war.

J. Willis Hale and his wife came to Manila in 1940. They were interned, with the Wolfes, by the Japanese in the Los Banos internment camp at the beginning of the war, being freed by the U.S. Army in February 1945. Shortly after his liberation, brother Wolfe died but Mrs. Wolfe remained on the field. In 1946 Miss Ruth Smith came to the field to work with Mrs. Carrie Wolfe.

In 1947 the Robert Hanson, Charles W. Selby, and Robert Schondelmayer families came to work in the Philippines. The Schondelmayers went to Cotabato for a period of nearly three years, and the Selbys began the work at Aparri.

In 1951 the Barton McElroy family came and in 1952 the Norval Campbell family arrived, the latter going on up to assist in the Aparri work on northern Luzon.

At first the work on the Philippines was primarily with lowland people, those living in the valleys and along the coasts, on the island of

Luzon among the Tagalog and Ilocano people. The work was not specifically limited to these areas alone but because of language difficulties, transportation and finances, these fields were the logical places of service.

One of the major phases of the work was, and is, the Manila Bible Seminary. Brother Juan Baronia was its president until his death when he was followed in office by another fine Filipino Christian man. By 1955 ninety students were enrolled in the training program of the Seminary. Because of its growth a new site was selected in Quezon City, not far from the new capital buildings of the Philippines. A building program was soon started. The main building was completed and dedicated in July 1963. The Barton McElroys and the Willis Hales teach, along with Filipino teachers, in the Seminary program.

Ronald Hoffman came to Manila in 1962 where he married Jeannie McElroy. After serving a year with the work in Aparri, the Hoffmans came to work with her parents, the Barton McElroys. Brother Hoffman teaches in the Seminary program while Jeannie conducts a Christian kindergarten. Fifty-seven were enrolled in the kindergarten in 1968.

Manila Bible Seminary graduated six young people in March 1968. Their freshman class was the largest one in the history of the school. Graduates serve in many places. One of these is Emiterio Reyes, Jr., who came to New York in 1967 to work with "Go Ye" Chapel Mission among the thousands of Filipino people living there.

The work in Manila is carried on in English and Tagalog (Filipino national language). Seminary-trained evangelists also work with the Ilocanos, Zambals, Negritos, Mangyans, Bicolonaos, Visayans, Manobos, and others. Workers supported by the Philippine Mission Churches of Christ serve in at least seventeen provinces. The located evangelists carry on their work much like the located preachers in the States. In the older and well-established churches, the Mission has only a brotherly interest, for the Churches have been set up according to the New Testament pattern and are self-governing and independent. However, the missionaries often assist them by conducting institutes, evangelistic meetings, and other special services. In more recent years an annual youth seminar on the Seminary campus (during vacation time) has been added.

Brother McElroy is in charge of the evangelistic effort that is carried on by the native evangelists who go from place to place holding meetings, strengthening the faith of scattered brethren, and in general leading out in the spread of the Gospel. From April 1956 through March 1957, there were 2,099 conversions reported and twenty-one new churches established in their work. From April 1958 to March 1959 there were 1,780 conversions reported, and twenty-three new churches established. In mid-July 1963, it was reported that thirty-six new congregations had been established in the preceding eighteen months. This gives you an idea of the outreach and effectiveness of their evangelistic efforts. The Cotabato (Christian) High School established in the Manila area advanced to a full four-year school in 1958. The McElroys will be greatly missed when they return to the States in the fall of 1969.

Miss Ruth Smith, who labored with Mrs. Wolfe for ten years in the Manila area, renewed the efforts of the work in Mindanao when, with two native workers, she came to Davao City in March 1956. This island is the "frontier" of the Philippines with settlers moving in from all over the Islands.

In the summer of 1956, Davao Bible Seminary was organized with sixteen full-time students. By the end of the first full year of labor five new churches had been established and seventy-six had been baptized. The Seminary met in overcrowded buildings until in December 1959 they were able to take possession of the Pilgrim Holiness School campus and buildings in Catalunan Pequeno, Davao City. Student enrollment at that time was twenty-seven.

In the year from May 1959 to June 1960, five churches were established and one closed church revived, bringing the total number of churches to twenty-nine. The total number of converts in the first four years was 267.

Miss Bertha Filer reached Davao City in May 1960. Not only was she a faculty member and librarian for the Seminary but she engaged in Christian education in the Bible schools of the churches in their area.

Filipino teachers and helpers have engaged in translation work for their use in the Seminary as well as tracts for distribution in the field. A hymn book was translated into the Cebuano dialect, a major dialect of the Visayan language group.

Opportunities are unlimited for the work of Davao Bible Seminary and its witness throughout Mindanao.

The work in northern Luzon began with the coming of missionaries, Williams and Hanna, from the Manila area in the early 1900's. Their work began in the Ilocos provinces over on the West coast but it gradually spread over to Aparri and the entire Cagayan Valley. In 1926 the comity agreement, entered into by the United Christian Missionary Society with several denominational groups, gave all of the Cagayan Valley and part of Ilocos Sur to the Methodists. The

Aparri chapel building was also sold to the Methodists, although it had been built for the most part by the Aparri brethren themselves. The printing presses and one of the hospitals were sold; later another hospital was gone and the training school closed. The churches were advised to join with the Methodist Church.

The Japanese occupation during World War II, with its attendant terrorism and disease, destroyed much of the work and scattered many of the churches that had been able to survive the evils of the comity agreement.

When the Charles Selby family arrived in the area in 1947 they found the brethren greatly demoralized and the work almost at a standstill. The only trained native leadership was furnished by Mr. and Mrs. Faustina Peneyra who had labored here for some thirty years.

It was apparent that a trained Filipino ministry was essential if the work was to move forward in the Islands as it should. During the first three years on the field, the Selbys were able to lay the groundwork for the establishment of the Aparri Bible Seminary. On their return from furlough in 1952, this was accomplished. In March 1953 Norval and Mrs. Dondena Campbell arrived on the field and immediately began their work with the Seminary until 1957.

Average enrollment in the Seminary has been around fifty each year. Sixty young people have graduated, completing four and five year courses. At least thirty-five girls have received two and three year teaching certificates. Student preachers are active on the week-ends throughout the Cagayan Valley. Each summer the girls conduct Vacation Bible Schools for one to two thousand students.

Some of the preachers in northern Luzon.

In 1947 there were but two preachers and about ten churches in the Cagayan Valley. As a result of the training program of the Aparri Bible Seminary there are now forty preachers and more than sixty churches in this area. These new churches of the last twenty years have been established by Filipino preachers. They have also been responsible for baptizing around three thousand converts. (Number of converts now average about 250 yearly). The native ministers also lead in the camp program, rallies and conventions. There is a great desire among the churches and preachers to bring about self-supporting, self-extending churches as soon as possible.

Aparri Christian Youth Camp.

Another extensive phase of the work is the Aparri Bible Seminary Press, which is used in the publication of monthly papers in the Ilocano dialect, and in tracts, both in English and Ilocano.

In July 1967 two Christian high schools were opened in the province of Isabella. All teaching staff and facilities must meet government requirements. These schools present tremendous evangelistic opportunities, which was the primary reason for their establishment. In the Southern Isabella Academy not one of the 88 Freshmen who enrolled that first year were Christian. Bible classes are taught every day by qualified Seminary graduates. As these young people are won to Christ it will be a means by which the Gospel can enter many new homes and new villages. It could possibly triple the evangelistic work in the Cagayan Valley. More than four hundred students are presently enrolled. By the time the full four years are in operation, the schools should be self-supporting from tuition and limited agricultural projects. Farm projects would make it possible for some of the poorer students to earn their way through high school.

Isabella camp baptism.

Sid and Marg (Mrs. Selby's sister) Boudreaux came to Aparri in September of 1964 to especially help in the high school work. Sid developed the farm program. Mrs. Boudreaux taught in the Seminary program. After four years on the field they returned to the States to take classes at Ozark Bible College in Joplin, Missouri.

Northern Luzon is a vast field in itself, to say nothing of the many small islands further to the north. Much of northern Luzon remains yet untouched with New Testament Christianity. Only as these trained Filipino evangelists go forth with the Gospel message can they ever hope to reach these lost souls for Christ.

As in most mission fields the evangelistic work is greatly limited because of a lack of well-trained native evangelists. Aparri Bible Seminary is doing its best to fill this need but there are many young people west of Aparri who are hindered from taking Seminary training because of the long trip they must take over the rugged mountains and rivers, and the expense involved, which few could afford.

The need, desire, and opportunity for a Seminary in northwestern Luzon Island was an open door and a challenge for a new work for the Norval Campbells. On their return from their furlough in 1958 the Campbells went to a tiny village two miles east of Vigan, the provincial capital of Ilocos Sur on the west coast, two hundred and fifty miles north of Manila. Two native evangelists had been working part time in the area but this was not nearly enough. Already at this time there were nineteen congregations and preaching points and constantly more opportunities were presented than were able to be filled. Hence a real need for a training school!

A temporary building was put up in time to enroll students in Philippine Bible Seminary in July 1958. Twenty-four full-time students finished that school year. One goal for the future was to make the school self-supporting through various projects. A poultry house was built, a flock started, and a garden planted the first year. The buildings have been built largely through the efforts of students and faculty.

Faculty of Philippine Bible Seminary with camp students (1968).

During the sixth year of the Philipine Bible Seminary the Campbells recognized that the Filipino faculty members of the school were capable of continuing the work without their presence on the field. Thus the entire responsibility for the progress of the work was placed

331

in the hands of the nationals. The Campbells agreed to raise $3,000 a year in the States to help underwrite the training program. The remainder of the funds came from Filipino brethren. Not only have they carried on the work that had been begun, but they also have uncovered latent resources within themselves and instituted new programs. The two levels of instruction, preparatory and college, continue with some vocational courses being added. A Christian Service Camp has been instituted and successfully carried on. A wider program of evangelism is conducted during the dry-season each year. They are often well received even in villages that are predominately pagan. New areas have been evangelized resulting in the formation of new congregations. A printing ministry has been started, which produces a monthly publication, tracts and other items. After a five year's absence, the Campbells plan a summer trip back to this field in the summer of 1969.

In the southern Philippines, Cebu Christian Mission is centered at Cebu City on the island of Cebu. When the war prevented the Ray Carlsons from carrying out their plans to go to the Tibetan border in 1941, they began to evangelize in Cebu, with the Vernon Newland family who had been unable to remain in Tibet. Here the two families were interned by the Japanese for three years. Following their release, the Carlsons labored for a year in that area that resulted in 108 additions to the Church. Due to a physical condition that resulted from neglect and deprivation in prison camp, American army doctors ordered the Carlsons back to America.

In 1947 they returned to the field to start Cebu Bible Seminary. There were seventeen full-time students that first year—and an equal number of part-time evening students. Along with the teaching program in the Seminary, evangelism was conducted in Santander, Balamban, and on Negros Island (west of Cebu).

In 1952 Betty Yarbrough arrived to teach in the Seminary. The Elston Knights followed in 1953. Under his leadership the first unit of the Seminary building was completed. When the Carlsons had to leave the field in 1954 due to the fatal illness of his mother, Elston Knight continued with the Seminary teaching and the radio program that Ray Carlson had begun in earlier years. With an old mission trailer converted into a "mobile chapel", evangelism was carried to all areas of Cebu Province. Due to the ill health of Mrs. Knight, they were forced to leave the field in 1956.

The work continued under native leadership until Miss Yarbrough returned from furlough in the fall of 1956. A month later, Guen Griffith flew to the Philippines to join the Cebu Christian Mission.

332

She came to teach methods of children's work in the Seminary, handle the Seminary library, the Cebu Bible Bookstore, literature distribution and direct children's Bible classes and vacation Bible schools, which she did until 1958. She suffered from what later was studied as a case history of a very rare disease. She was violently allergic to many Philippine plants. She left for Hawaii where she thought her health might improve. Even there her condition became worse. She was transferred to a hospital in California where she finally passed away in 1963.

In January 1957 the John Hasty family entered into the teaching program of Cebu Bible Seminary and assumed the leadership of this phase of the work. However, the tragic death of Mrs. Hasty in June 1957 made it necessary for brother Hasty to return to the States with his two small daughters. This was a great loss to the work. Because the two single girls felt they could not handle the Seminary alone, the school was closed for one year. Instead they taught vacation Bible school classes and did effective calling in the city.

In response to the urgent appeal from the Cebu area, the Ray Carlsons returned in February 1958. They were able to reopen the Seminary for classes in July of that year, and engaged in evangelistic efforts on seven other nearby islands.

Vacation Bible School on Negros Island.

The Don Davis family arrived in Cebu in March 1961 having served one term in India but not allowed to re-enter) to work in the Seminary program. In 1965 they left Cebu to pursue some graduate

333

studies. Miss Yarbrough returned to Cebu in 1962 as Mrs. Bill Turner. She and her husband taught in the Seminary until they left for service in Japan in 1965.

The newest missionaries to the field in some respects are not new at all. Mark Carlson grew up in Cebu, a son of the Ray Carlsons. He has the great advantage of fluency in the language even after an absence of seven years. He has accepted the task of visiting the churches in the Visayas and Mindanao and of planning evangelism to strengthen the nearly sixty churches looking for leadership and help. These churches are scattered throughout the following provinces: Cebu, Negros Oriental, Negros Occidental, Leyte, Samar, Panay, Mindanao, Surigao, Masbate, and Palawn. Several dialects are spoken but there is good understanding between the groups. An estimated 5,000 Christians are living for the Lord in this area. Mark's wife, Susan (who is new on the field) is teaching English in the Seminary. There are twenty students enrolled this year. In Mark's evangelistic travels he hopes to interest young people in the study program of Cebu Bible Seminary.

Cebu City church of Christ.

The growing and expanding work leads those who serve to hope for new missionaries to join them in the work of saving souls in this vast area of the Philippine Islands. Seldom will one find a place so ready for the Gospel. The Filipino has so recently liberated himself from several sorts of political, social, and economic bondages that he is very ready to listen to the New Testament message of spiritual liberty and religious freedom.

Evangelist Joe Garman preaching in memorial grandstand in Manila. Seventeen hundred assembled for opening night.

If we are going to reach the countries of southeast Asia with the Gospel it may well have to be done through Asians. In all of southeast Asia, the place with the most potential is in the Philippines where we have existing 442 churches with approximately 60,000 individual Filipino members. There are five Bible Colleges and Seminaries in the Philippines to train future leaders to do the task. Three accredited high schools have been established. Much credit must be given to the dedicated Filipinos who faithfully witness to their own people.

Ryukyu Islands

"Loo Choo Islands"

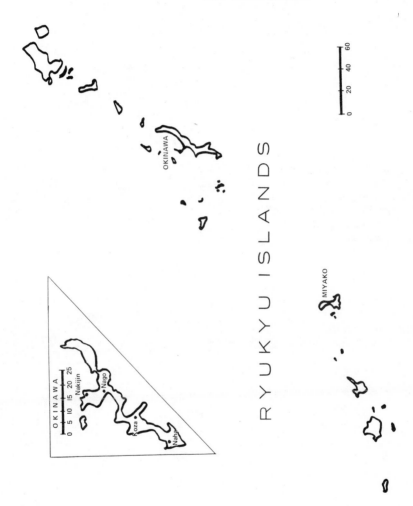

THE LAND . . . .

The Ryukyu archipelago consists of four major island groups, some 150 in number (islets and reefs included). They extend in an almost uninterrupted chain southward from the Japanese Island of Kyushu nearly to Formosa. They came under American control since the war with Japan when they were placed under the United Nations' trustship. The Amami Islands, northern-most group, were returned to Japanese administration in 1953.

The soil of the Ryukyus is fertile, composed chiefly of coral reefs. Here and there are small deposits of coal, copper and phosphate.

The total land area amounts to 844,341 acres, of which 88% is accounted for by nine islands. Miyako Island is the largest of the Sanishimo Group, sixth in area of all the islands and third in population, with over 60,000 people. Okinawa, seventy miles long, with an average width of seven miles, is by far the largest and the most densely populated island in the group. Of the total population of 1,122,000, 82%, at least. live on the island of Okinawa. The northern three-fourths of the island has a rugged terrain; the southern area is relatively low and flat. On the rolling open hills are numerous small farms where rice, sugar, wheat, sago and potatoes are cultivated as well as bananas and pineapples. Pigs are raised in large numbers in the agricultural areas. Fine lacquer ware is also manufactured and fisheries are important. Indigo, textiles and panama hats are other industrial products. The main exports include sugar products, light manufactures, such as cigarettes and clothing, and canned pineapple.

The climate is hot and humid, and during the stormy season typhoons often hit the island. Rain fall is heavy especially in August.

Okinawa was not only the last major ground battle of the war, but the costliest single engagement in the Pacific. Reclamation began following the end of the war. The primary mission of the United States was prevention of disease and unrest in a land that had been devastated. As this mission was accomplished, economic recovery to pre-war level was added to the mission. A workable, democratic government was also set up.

. . . . THE PEOPLE

The natives of Okinawa are short people but slightly larger than the Japanese, and retain many of the early Chinese traits, They are a quiet and peace-loving people. They are closely affiliated racially with the Japanese, having the same straight black hair and facial characteristics, however, they are neither Japanese nor Chinese.

They all speak and write Japanese (though there is a Ryukyu language which bears a close resemblance to Japanese) since they were under Japan's educational system half a century ago. Under the Japanese rule in earlier years they were treated cruelly and kept in the greatest poverty. Although dependent upon U.S. military expenditures, the majority of the islanders desire reunion with Japan. Many inhabitants migrate to Japan in search of better job opportunities. There is a modified resemblance to the Japanese in clothes, dwellings, and customs.

In November, 1946, some 166,000 of the Okinawan children were back in newly built schools to receive training that would help to prepare a nation for better living. That preparation continues through the years to make it so.

. . . . THE MISSIONARY . . . .

The concentration of missionary efforts on the small island of Okinawa was wholly justified since it was rated one of the most densely populated areas in the world. What was once one of the most bitterly contested battlefields of the war in the Pacific is now one of the greatest outposts for Christ and His Kingdom in a war against Satan.

While a Chaplain in the Army serving in Nago in 1945 with the 87th Field Hospital, Harlan Woodruff was greatly impressed with the need of these people for the Gospel message. With 25% of the population killed and 90% of their homes destroyed, the people presented a pitable picture. It was then that brother Woodruff made the decision to return as a missionary. This he did in September 1948, his wife joining him in February of the following year.

From the beginning their work has been of an evangelistic nature. Bible classes were organized in as many villages as possible. Okinawans were trained to assist in the Bible teaching. Okinawa Bible Seminary became a major project. By 1960 twenty-nine workers had completed the two-year course that was offered. These graduates, with the students in school, were conducting weekly Bible classes in eighty-five villages. For as soon as native workers are sufficiently trained they assist in the evangelistic efforts. Those who are out of school are assisted financially by the mission to enable them to place their full-time efforts into this work. Several have been trained in the States to become faculty members at the Seminary and to assume more active leadership of other phases of the work. To these native people has been entrusted the leadership of the 3-week camp program, radio broadcasts, vacation Bible schools, and a Christian monthly newspaper.

Over three thousand copies of the newspaper were distributed to the villages where classes were held. Tract evangelism also became a part of their evangelistic approach. Written replies to the radio and newspaper contacts indicated the value of further emphasis of this form of ministry.

The Seminary was closed in 1963 for a period of time. The following year the Woodruffs moved from their northern location of Nago to the capital city of Naha, the largest on the island. In 1966 they began a new approach to the work in Naha. It includes pre-scheduled home evangelistic meetings. This permits Christian families to invite their non-Christian friends for an evening of religious discussion. There was a total of 79 baptisms reported that year. In Naha a church was established, now known as Okinawa Church of Christ. American military men and their families worship in the same facilities at present (at a different hour).

Church of Christ at Naha.

Plans were made to reopen the Seminary program. A gradual decrease in the number of full-time workers in the past few years convinced them that the need was there for the two-year school to give Bible knowledge to leaders who could work in the villages while

341

studying in the school. Graduates can further their studies at Osaka Bible Seminary in Japan without loss of credits. The reopening became a reality in April 1967. Eventually plans call for a four-year Seminary course, and later an accredited Junior College.

For some time the need was felt to offer the regular seminary courses to a larger group of the Christian people. This was begun when night classes were offered at the Makiya Church. All who wished could take the course; those who took the regular tests and completed the required outside assignments received four hours of regular credit which would be accepted by Osaka Bible Seminary should they wish to attend that school in the future. This project has great potential for the training of solid and loyal leaders for the future of the Church. Similar classes will be opened in other areas as soon as a need arises.

Full-time workers associated with Woodruffs in 1967.

In September 1950 the Mel Huckins arrived in Okinawa. For the first two and a half years they located with the Woodruffs at Nago. During this time they worked out from Nago, traveling many miles weekly to distant points, opening doors for the Gospel in new villages, on the war-torn island of Ie Shima and eventually in the new and unevangelized area of Nakijin.

Early in 1952 the Huckins were led to choose the Nakijin area at the end of the Motobu Peninsula as the center of their future work. They moved into their promised land in 1953, having already begun Bible classes for the youth and adults alike the year before. With the help and effort of native Christian workers, the Bible school which met in their home grew to over two hundred, and another hundred were attending classes in the near-by village of Gushiken. One hundred and fifty people crowded into their home for a mid-week service and sixty young people attended the Friday night Bible study. In June 1953, five of these young people, the first fruits of Nakijin, were born again and the church was established. Before the year was over the number of Christians had increased to seventeen and before their return for furlough in 1954 God reaped the harvest for which they had worked and prayed when twenty-six young people and adults made the confession and were baptized.

In September 1953 a Christian kindergarten was begun and taught by one of the native workers. With this effort her witness reached into the homes of many families who might not have heard of Christ otherwise. By August 1956 there were one hundred students enrolled, taught by two teachers.

By August 1956, through their program of village evangelism, the Huckins had seen 164 persons saved by the power of God in seventeen villages, ten of which had never heard the Gospel before their coming.

In 1960 the Huckins moved to Kobe, Japan for language study, leaving the work at Nakijin under the capable leadership of a national leader, brother Nashiro. Following this period of language study they returned for a period of inter-island evangelism until Mel's severe head pains (suffered over a prolonged period) forced them to leave the field in 1963. Their efforts had extended for 350 miles from northernmost Okinawa to the last island of Yonaguni (only forty miles from Formosa). Besides assisting fellow missionaries and Okinawan leaders in previously established work in twenty-one villages, they opened new work in twenty-five villages. They helped to survey the island of Miyako in preparation for the coming of the Rickerson family. In some areas the converts number in the hundreds, in others, very few. However, no labor for the Lord is in vain.

In January 1592 Carl and Grace Fish set their feet upon the shores of Okinawa and their hearts and hands to the winning of souls to Christ. With their coming it was possible for the missionaries to enter new areas in the program of village evangelism. The Fishes centered their work from the Nago area until the Woodruffs returned from furlough early in 1954.

Many calls came requesting Bible teaching. The village of Tsuha with 1,500 population, heard the Gospel message for the first time in January 1954 when the urgent and repeated request of two fine young men was answered and the Fishes took them the Gospel. This was only one of many villages who wanted and needed the Gospel.

Late in 1954 the Fish family moved to a new location in the Koza area in southern Okinawa where a new field was opened for New Testament Christianity. With three native Christian workers they began setting up new Bible classes. With this, of course, came the task of translating and printing lessons and sermons, and other materials needed each week. Brother Fish, with the assistance of Mel Huckins, organized the first summer camps which proved very effective for the entire Okinawan work.

On the whole the Okinawans have been quite responsive to the Gospel. Work in the south was hampered somewhat by the presence of scores of thousands of American military personnel whose moral influence was detrimental to the spread of the Gospel message.

The Cloyd Christman family arrived on the island in September 1953 where they immediately began teaching (via interpreter) in the villages. During the Huckins' furlough in 1955 their work was guided in the early months by the Christmans until they went to Japan for several months of necessary language study.

In March 1956 the Christmans came back to Okinawa to assist in the Koza work during the furlough period of the Fish family. After having given invaluable aid when needed most they returned to a ministry in the States in mid-1957. The Carl Fishes, due to the illness of Mrs. Fish, returned to a State-side ministry. They are presently serving in Indonesia.

In 1956 the Gerald Downey family, challenged by the fact that more than 500,000 of the natives had never heard of God or Jesus Christ, prepared themselves in language study in Japan to serve in Okinawa. This they did until they returned to the States in May 1960 where they are now ministering.

Elsewhere in the Ryukyu Islands missionary activity is being carried on in the Miyako Gunto. This is a group of six islands in the Ryukyu chain whose total population was over eighty thousand. Sixty thousand of these were on Miyako Shima which is located 178 miles southwest of Naha, Okinawa, and only 350 miles from the China mainland.

In Japan a Mr. Kuninaka became a Christian under the teaching of Miss Vivian Lemmon. In 1945 he moved to Miyako to become principal of the Girls' High School. In addition to his teaching, he began preaching and that year established a church along the New Testament pattern as he understood it with his limited knowledge of the Bible. He remained faithful in this ministry until his death three years later.

It was to help fill the great need for leadership that brought the Don Rickersons to Miyako in 1953. They were assisted by Mrs. Kuninaka, the wife of the man who began the work, who returned to Miyako in November that year. She served as a Bible woman, Mrs. Rickerson's interpreter, and language instructor for both the Rickersons.

The first congregation to be established on the island was at Hirara City. New work was established in 1953 in Chiyoda, Nobaru, and Takachika; all services being in the Japanese language. A Bible class for elderly people was held in a home in Hadato in the Miyako dialect.

In 1954 the Rickersons began vacation Bible schools in some of the villages after which they continued weekly Bible classes. During the summer of 1956 they held schools in six villages with 1,653 children enrolled. At Hisamatsu village, two miles from Hirara City, two hundred children attended the weekly classes. Five miles away, at Shimoji Town, 302 children were enrolled in the second year of vacation Bible school. Five miles away in another direction, 383 children enrolled in the first VBS ever held in the village. Regular weekly classes were begun with the opening of school that fall. It was apparent that the response of the children was excellent. During the summer of 1960, 2,235 children was the average attendance of the ten-day vacation Bible schools held in eight villages.

In 1951 they extended their witness in a greater way at the jail, TB hospital, and to the lepers. A church was established for the lepers with over a hundred converts. They continued their other evangelistic work, not only among the Okinawans but at the American air base as well. In 1966 they returned to the States for furlough. Due to poor health they retired from their work in the Ryukyu Islands.

This work was not left entirely without supervision for the Claire Boultons (daughter and son-in-law of the Rickersons) had entered the labor among the islands in 1957. In April of 1959 they entered the Kobe school of the Japanese language. Upon the completion of this course in 1961 they returned to the work in Miyako in establishing indigenous churches as well as further witnessing on the larger island of Okinawa. In 1967 they founded the Okinawa Christian Institute Junior College. They had 62 students in three departments.

345

Though the Word is being spread throughout the islands, the southernmost islands of over 100,000 population remain mostly un-evangelized.

Taiwan
"Land of Nationalist China"

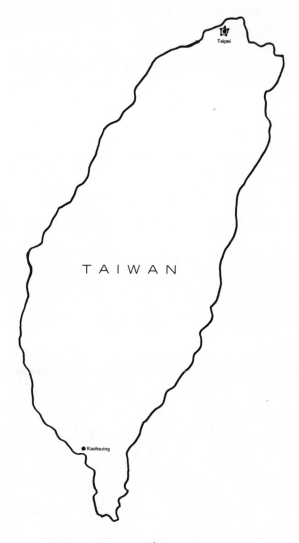

THE LAND . . . .

Taiwan (often called Formosa), the seat of the nationalist government of the Republic of China, is separated from the China mainland only one hundred miles by the Formosa Strait. The province of Taiwan is made of seventy-nine islands of which Taiwan Island is the single largest island, 240 miles long and up to 90 miles wide.

Taiwan is one link in a chain of mountainous islands that extend out from the Pacific coast of the continent of Asia. About two-thirds of the island is composed of rugged foothill ranges of massive mountain chains. In the west is a series of coastal plains which provide the major agricultural lands and are traversed by a system of irrigation and drainage canals. The only navigable river is the Tanshui which flows past Taipei, the capital, in the north.

Taiwan enjoys an oceanic, subtropical, monsoon climate. The warm and humid summer lasts from May until September with a July temperature of 85 degrees. The mild winters last from December to February with a January temperature of 60 degrees. Only the extreme southwest has a distinct dry season. Typhoons may occur between June and October.

The fertility of the soil is variable throughout the island, and arable land is limited (only 24%). Efforts have been made to raise agricultural yields, some double cropping efforts have been extended. Taiwan's rice yield is one of the highest in the world. In the south, bananas have become a major agricultural export item. Sugar has been the chief item for foreign exchange. The country has also become a major exporter for canned, dehydrated, and frozen vegetables—many of which are Chinese food specialties.

Forest resources are vital to the economic well-being of the island. The only significant mining operation is the production of bituminous coal. Other minerals produced are small amounts of sulphur, pyrite, gold, silver, copper, manganese, mercury, petroleum, and natural gas. The western third of the island has adequate amounts of sand, gravel, and limestone for building purposes. On the west coast itself is produced over 200,000 tons of salt annually (by sea water evaporation).

There has also been considerable industrial growth. Conditions are favorable for this development. There are two major harbors which are connected by extensive rail and highways to all parts of the island. Another contributing factor is the abundance of cheap hydroelectric power. The fertilizer and textile industries have both grown rapidly in recent years. In spite of increased industrialization, partly due to a high population density and the prevalent under-employment (for land is scarce and labor abundant), wage levels are low. This is reflected by the pattern of household expenditure, in which food comprises about 60% of the income.

. . . . THE PEOPLE

Taiwan's civilian population at the end of 1964 was estimated at 12,257,000, nearly all of whom were of Chinese ethnic origin. Inclusion of military forces would raise it another 600,000.

The aboriginal inhabitants, probably of Malay origin, were displaced from western lowland areas and pushed into the more mountainous regions where they are today. Though they numer only 2% of the total population, they maintain a distinct cultural identity. They generally have short stature, light brown skin, and straight black hair. They speak dialects of the Malay-Polynesian family and have no written scripts.

The Chinese inhabitants of Taiwan can be divided into two major groups. The term "Taiwanese" is often used when referring to those Chinese who are natives of the island as distinct from those who migrated from the mainland after the end of World War II. The native-born Taiwanese, numbering ten million, speak a dialect of Chinese resembling that spoken in Fukien Province on the mainland. The intellectuals of this group still frequently speak Japanese. The remaining number of "mainland" Chinese are primarily military personnel and government servants, most of whom left China after the consolidation of Communist power in 1949. Since 1945 educational authorities have made definite effort to make the use of the Chinese national language (derived from the Peking dialect) an universal practice.

Education on all levels has made important advances since 1950. Over 80% of the population over six years of age can read and write. Primary education is compulsory and free for children from ages six to twelve. There are three types of secondary schools: academic middle schools, vocational schools, and normal schools. The government educational authorities strive continuously to impart the basic elements of Chinese culture to all school-age children. An educational radio network has been established, and plans are being made to organize an island-wide educational television network.

With a population that has tripled in a little over fifty years, population densities are extremely high. Over 90% of the people live in the lowland areas on the west coast. Housing remains inadequate throughout Taiwan, although the National Housing Commission (assisted by U.S. knowledge and finances) was created to ease the situation.

The main diet of the people is rice and vegetables. The protein intake is poor in quality. Drinking water is piped into only 30% of urban houses and less than 15% of the rural dwellings. Many others obtain water from wells, often polluted; the rest get their water from irrigation ditches. It is no wonder that there are many prevalent diseases. Since World War II the most common and menacing have been tuberculosis, pneumonia, malaria, trachoma, leprosy, parasitic diseases, and diarrhea.

The Taiwan folk religion is a tolerant mixture of ancestor-worship, animism, Buddhism, and Taoism. While the younger generation may be skeptical of the common religious practices, the older and less educated are still deeply influenced by them. The Dutch were the first to bring any form of Christianity to Taiwan. A great persecution took place in 1662 but Christianity made a new beginning in 1860 when a missionary from Scotland came to the island. Since the end of World War II many denominational groups have become established on the Island. There are approximately two hundred local churches representing a 300,000 membership. The Catholic Church has grown rapidly during recent years. Almost 80% of their priests and nuns are refugees from the mainland. There are also some 40,000 Muslims.

. . . . THE MISSIONARY . . . .

New Testament independent mission work had its beginning in Taiwan in 1960, when Isabel Dittemore began a radio correspondence ministry in Taipei. Mrs. Dittemore escaped the persecution by the Communists during the revolution on the mainland and for a period of years served with her brother, Mark Maxey, in the islands of Japan. It was with great joy that she came to Taiwan to labor among the Chinese people, whom she dearly loved (twenty-three years from her first witness to them).

Since founding the work there, she has led many souls to Christ and has established a self-propagating and self-governing church in Taipei. Her radio work began in the Chinese language and she makes use of the Christians she has won to the Lord in producing and recording the broadcasts. She has also been instrumental in getting such books as "Acts Made Actual" and "The Church in the Bible" published in the Chinese language. She also has translated much other materials to be used in teaching in the homes. Radio broadcasts for the Okin-

351

awans were started in 1965. In 1966 broadcasts were also started in English. Isabel's correspondence courses in Japanese are used in Hawaii (as well as Japan), and the English course is used in Hong Kong by the Bill Reeses.

Mrs. Lillian Martin, a young Negro missionary nurse and teacher from Hawaii, came to Taipei in 1965 and is assisting in the work on the Island. She is especially interested in work with children in orphanages and schools. She plans to build an orphanage for children of all races, but especially for those whose mixed blood gives them no status as citizens, nor birth certificates, no chance for an education, and only ill treatment at home or on the streets. In 1968, Mrs. Martin moved to Kaohsuing to begin her orphanage.

Alan and Janet Bemo attempted to enter Borneo for an internship in the Sarawak Province but were refused permission since they did not possess educator's visas. Instead they turned their attention to Taiwan and spent one year of internship there before coming back to the States and Ozark Bible College to complete his final year of training. Following graduation Alan and Janet (Isabel Dittemore's daughter) returned to Taiwan to serve the Lord. They live in the city of Taipei where his main work is with University students. This work includes teaching conversational English in the University, witnessing in student gathering places and conducting Bible study sessions in their home. His labor in this area is proving effective, resulting in the conversion of several college students and some younger students.

Our most recent missionaries to go to join the Bemos is the Ted Skiles family. They arrived on the field very early in 1969. They, too, plan to assist in the witness to the University students as they continue in their language study.

Miss Carol Sue Rhodes, a recent graduate of Platte Valley Bible College, will be spending the summer on the field assisting in vacation Bible schools and the summer camp program.

Following the summer training at Wycliffe Bible Translators, Sam and Virginia Hazelwood plan to leave for Taiwan. They expect to be working in the villages in the mountainous central highlands among the Hakkas. Their desire is to be able eventually to give the Bible to the Hakkas in their native tongue.

Chuck and Molly Johnston were College friends of the Bemos and were directly influenced by the experiences Alan and Janet had during their internship on Taiwan. Thus challenged, they too are making plans to sail for the work in Taiwan, in February 1970.

West Indies

Bahamas

"Gateway to the New World"

THE LAND . . . .

This is the gateway by which Columbus entered the New World. The Bahamas are composed of three thousand islands and reefs, mostly reefs which were formed by rocks and wind blown coral sands. Only twenty of the islands are inhabited, the most important of which is New Providence Island (Size—69 square miles, pop. 65,000—½ of the total). The capital, Nassau, being a noted tourist center, is connected to the rest of the world by air transport as well as by steamer and freighter. The islands extend from about fifty miles east of Palm Beach, Florida for some seven hundred and sixty miles toward Haiti.

The economy of the Bahamas is primarily dependent on tourist industry (U.S. dollars are in wide circulation) for imports regularly exceed the colony's exports. Tropical fruits are cultivated for local consumption, while limited quantities of tomatoes, salt, crawfish, fruits and shellwork are exported. Many items are made of sisal and coconut straw for sale to the tourists.

Most of the islands are barren except for grass, palms, and bushes though some have stands of small pines. Andros and Abaco Islands are forested with mahogany, lignum vitae and ironwood trees but due to lack of labor and good roads nothing much is done about this commercially. Agriculture is difficult due to the rocky nature of the islands. Lacking in streams, the water supply must be derived from wells. In some cases it is even necessary to use processed sea water.

Though hurricanes occur from July to October and the rainy months are from May to October, the climate is agreeable. The mean temperature of the hottest months (June to September) is 88 degrees, of the coldest (January to March) 60 degrees. Due to the porosity of the rock many figures are formed in it by the weather.

. . . . THE PEOPLE

Negroes, descendants of former slaves, form the majority of the population; the white people are mainly descendants of emigrants from the New England states.

English is the common language of the islands. The government supports free elementary schools and five secondary schools; it even gives financial assistance to denominational schools. The Wesleyans and Roman Catholics have colleges at Nassau, and the latter has another institution for higher learning on Harbour Island.

. . . . THE MISSIONARY . . . .

The work in the Bahamas began in rather an unique way. Back in 1951 native workers laboring for a canning company in Fairmont, Minnesota became acquainted with the Church of Christ. On their return to their own homes they wrote several letters to various ministers. As correspondence continued with brother Hubert Prather the Bahamians' interest grew until they requested that he come to the islands to teach. With the support of faithful friends he was enabled to spend six weeks on the field in 1952, teaching and preaching.

Within six months time of this first evangelistic effort, the Floyd Hughes family were on the field at Nassau (New Providence Island) to follow up the work, establishing the Bahamas Christian Mission. In 1953 street evangelism became a definite part of the weekly schedule, proving helpful in the particular areas visited. Several ministers from the States assisted in evangelistic meetings at Grant's Town (where the first work began) and in the Coconut Grove area, where regular services were begun in April of 1953. Vacation Bible schools, with good attendance and attention, were held in both places. Many rejoiced to hear the Word, but the love for sectarian customs and traditions was often stronger than the love for the plain truth.

The Burl Shoemake family arrived on the island in April 1954 to supervise the work at Coconut Grove, while brother Hughes labored at the Grant's Town church. A year after the Shoemakes came to the field, brother and sister Aubrey Payne arrived to help in the establishment of a Bible training program. They saw this become a reality in the fall of 1955 with thirty enrolled (seventeen, average attendance) before they were called back to the States due to serious illness in their families. Later the Shoemakes also returned to the States.

Mary Shimek, student of Boise Bible College, having had many years of teaching experience in her home church, labored in the summer of 1956 with the Hughes.

By the close of 1956 seventy-five had responded to the Gospel, but less than half were "pressing on to the high calling of Christ Jesus". They desired to know the Lord, for indeed the spirit is willing, but how weak the flesh!

On October 17, 1957, brother Hughes passed away from this life and was laid to rest in the land where he had faithfully served. Mrs. Hughes continued her weekly Bible classes in the two established churches, and remained on the field until 1962. The Aubrey Paynes arrived back on the field in November 1958 to continue forward in the work for a period, but they too returned to the States in 1962. They assisted in evangelistic efforts in more recent years.

January 1962 was a big month in Nassau. The Edward Spencer family arrived from Oregon and the James Redmon family from Georgia came to join them. Services during the year were increased from nine to fifteen.

Survey trips were made in the outer islands with Andros Island picked as the next point of expansion. These trips emphasized the need of a boat since this was the only means of transportation to the other islands. (Air service is extended to some now.) A boat was purchased in 1964 that the outer island work might advance in a greater way. The greatest opportunity for expansion is the open door to the out islands.

During 1964 they began a ministry to the Haitian people who had come to the Bahamas to work. A series of correspondence Bible studies was begun with 1,000 enrolled by the end of that year. In the face of rejoicing the government doubled the postage rate.

The Hubert Prathers arrived in 1966 to strengthen the forces of the missionaries. In the fall the three families were able to begin the Leadership Training Institute of the Bahamas. Eight students enrolled though only four completed the first term's work. The number of classes and services conducted regularly every week increased to twenty-seven. There were preaching points in three settlements and the island of Andros, plus two farm labor camps. However, most of the Haitians from the labor camps were forced to leave the islands due to government restrictions. Contact with them has been nearly impossible since most cannot read or write and Haiti is at war with itself. However, in May 1968 James Redmon was able to make a trip to Haiti. The Haitian Christian who accompanied him was separated from him at immigration and immediately imprisoned. Arriving at a time of political turmoil James Redmon was not permitted to keep his scheduled appointments but hopefully was able to strengthen those who desire to serve Christ even in perilous circumstances. Work with other Haitians has been carried on in Grand Bahama Island, ministered to by their own native people.

The young Haitian, David, who was imprisoned on his arrival with brother Redmon, was tortured and finally released after sixteen days of imprisonment. However, he was not permitted to return to the Bahamas at that time. After eleven months of living in fear for his life he was finally permitted (after payments to officials) to leave Haiti in the spring of 1969.

When the Spencer family returns from furlough in 1969 they will be settling on Andros Island, our first permanent American missionaries to live there. A Bahamian, Edwin Forbes, has served there for some time.

Because of the nearness of the Islands, plus the fact that the Bahamians understand English, each summer several Bible College students journey to the Islands to assist in VBS and evangelistic services in the various churches.

Barbados
'The Bearded"

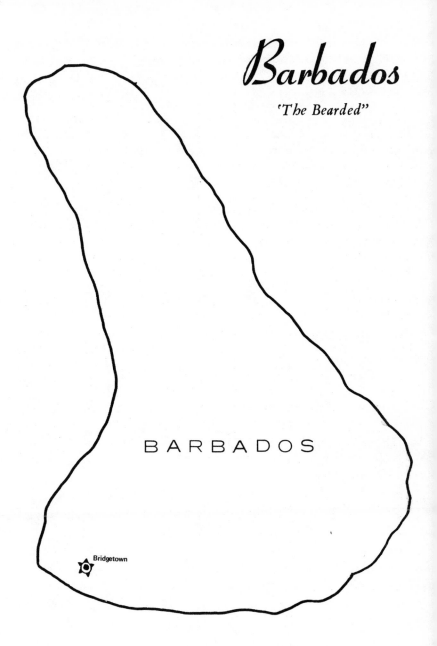

BARBADOS

Bridgetown

THE LAND . . . .

Being under three hundred years of unbroken British rule the island has been often called Little England, however, it received its independence in 1966. The island received its true name which means The Bearded from the beard-like clumps of vines hanging from the numerous wild fig trees.

Barbados, triangular in shape, 21 miles long and 14 miles wide across the widest part, is the easternmost island of the West Indies. It is one of the most densely populated islands of the world, having over 250,000 persons living on its 166 square miles. It is actually no larger than an average U.S. county. Bridgetown, the capital, is the only port of entry. That, plus one other town, supplies the urban community for the entire island.

The soil is fertile, having been built up of coral. Of 106,000 acres, 65% of it is arable, 46,000 acres of it raising sugar. In fact two-thirds of the people are employed in the sugar industry; sugar cane being the chief crop. Leading industries manufacture sugar, rum and molasses. Some 2,000 men are employed in commercial fishing. At one time the island was forested with mahogany but most of the trees have been cut down. A dairy was established in 1965, and the milk industry is now expanding.

The temperature rarely rises above 86 degrees or falls below 65 degrees. The island is free from malaria. Leprosy, once widely spread among the colored population, has since become rare. The island lies on the southern border of the West Indies hurricane zone.

. . . . THE PEOPLE

Indians and Negroes outnumber white persons fifteen to one. Percentage wise they are: African descent 77.27%, mixed descent 27.35%, European descent 4%. Of the total, three-fifths are women.

The public elementary schools are entirely maintained by the government which also makes grants toward the cost of operating the secondary schools, however education is not compulsory. There are likewise private schools for boys and girls. Technical and vocational training is offered. In 1963 a constituent arts and sciences college of the University of the West Indies was opened in Barbados. Illiterates comprised only 1.3% of the population in 1964.

In 1965, government health facilities included general, mental, leper, and maternity hospitals and three public health centers in which were public wards for free medical treatment.

The Church of England is the established religion, however, it is losing its hold upon the people. There are 132 different religious groups registered with the government but the majority of these are one group affairs. However, the Pilgrim Holiness, Nazarene, and Church of God are well established while Roman Catholicism is advancing since they have several schools and a college. Methodists and Moravians predominate the religious scence.

. . . . THE MISSIONARY . . . .

Since the message and influence of New Testament Christianity had never extended into the Caribbean area past Jamaica and the Bahama Islands, many were concerned about sending a missionary to the lower Caribbeans.

Concerned enough to go were the Vernon Osbornes who left in July 1953 for the island of Barbados. This particular location was selected because it is the center of culture, commerce and education for most of the islands in the area.

After the early months of survey, personal work, and tract distribution, a few Christians were found upholding the essentials of the Apostles' teaching. The late Charles C. Leacock, a native minister, had led this small group for many years without joining any denominational mission. Within a short time the Osbornes were invited to come to teach this group, which is now known as the Oistin Church of Christ. The nearest New Testament church was 1,000 miles away. That gives you a clear picture of the scope of their work.

Due to the need of special surgery the Osbornes had to return to the States in 1954 but were able to come back to their work in 1956, bringing with them Bill Gage and his family. Brother Gage began an evangelistic effort in the fall of that year in the Silver Sands area. Though there were only eight baptized believers at the end of 1956, as many as seventy-five to three hundred came to hear God's Word.

In November 1956, the first Bible School was held at Spooner's Hill. Facilities here were very meager compared with that of the Nazarenes and Seventh Day Adventists. This is the area where the Gages were living at that time. However, they moved to Silver Sands to remain a year in order to do a more effective job of establishing the church there. To assist in this teaching program a paper was printed and distributed to eight hundred homes bi-monthly. Being British, the natives speak English, though it is a dialect all their own.

Even this eliminates the long period ordinarily required for language study. A weekly radio broadcast was also begun.

Though the Christians appeared to be well indoctrinated they lacked the ability to train and support native ministers to spread the work. For the hope of the future years a week-day class for children was conducted by Mrs. Osborne. The Osbornes were forced to leave the field again in May 1958, due to ill health.

The plan to set up a preacher-training program to reach the masses and provide them with their own leadership, to assist in an extensive program of evangelism of Barbados and the neighboring islands, was begun. With revised immigration regulations among the British possessions in the West Indies, a preacher-training school here in this strategic location could be an endless source of a ministry to all the islands of this Caribbean area.

The school enrolled six students for its first session in August 1956. In the early months of 1957 those enrolled in the Bible-training course engaged themselves in a program of evangelism in the rural and neglected areas of the island. This was the first real means of practical experience for these young preachers, and a truly indigenous evangelistic effort. There was a need to set up a manual training shop in which to train the preacher students in trades so that they would be able to partially support themselves while in the ministry. The native people are so poor that to pay someone else a living wage is almost impossible. The best way to keep the work indigenous is never begin to do anything for the people that they can do for themselves.

During their Florida ministry the Lewis Smiths were able to meet and witness to immigrant cane field laborers from Barbados. In 1958 the Smith family accepted the challenge to serve Christ in Barbados, but due to lack of financial support they were able to serve only nine months in the islands.

Like the Smiths, the Bill Scott family had long been interested in the work of Barbados Mission Churches of Christ. With the expansion of the work they felt the personal need to go ·and assist the other faithful workers in their witness for Christ.

In May 1958, under the heading of Lower Caribbean Christian Mission, the Scotts arrived on the island. A study class, started a short time after their arrival resulted in the Church Village congregation at St. Philip. The Rock Hall congregation was a Pentecostal group but it took a New Testament stand—so the simple Gospel message continued to be presented and requests came for more teaching. By the end of 1959 there were six meeting places of Christians only, and the number of active members was over 250.

During the Gage's furlough the Scotts were helping in twenty-seven services a week, as well as continuing the training program and weekly radio (rediffusion) program. With the summer workers of 1960 they conducted nine revivals with thirty additions. These summer workers included Tracy Wilhoit and Dave Berthold of Lincoln Bible Institute, Orvel Griffith of Minnesota Bible College, and the Bruce Ammermans of Ozark Bible College.

The Gage family arrived back on the field in time to assist in the VBS program. Five such schools were conducted with between 450 to 500 children enrolled. Building programs began among several of the churches. The Enterprise church met in a tent for two years but started a block building in 1960. The Gages returned to the States in 1963.

Tracy Wilhoit (following his internship) returned with his wife for a period of labor in open-air evangelism. Two new churches were started through his efforts.

Betty Enabnit came in 1961 and has worked for a period of years, interrupted by the illness of a sister and later her mother. She assisted in various avenues of the witness, but one new venture was the classes she held each week at some Industrial schools. In the summer months of 1966 several young people (18 boys—9 girls) made their confession but permission to be baptized would not be given by the school authorities.

For youth not thus restricted, a camp program was begun on the island in 1961. Since that time at least twenty-two campers have left the island. Their influence may be felt throughout the world.

The Rupert Bishops, natives of Barbados, came to the States to study for the ministry, returning to the field in 1965. Mrs. Rupert is the daughter of Charles Leacock who was a major influence of the first work in Barbados. Accompanying them to the field were Larry and Kathy Calhoun who came to survey during the Scott's furlough. The Scotts are back on the field now and with the Bishops continue forward with work of the existing six churches with a full program of youth activities and evangelistic endeavors. There were 56 baptisms reported among the churches in 1968.

The work in Guyana (formerly British Guiana) was begun by a native evangelist, George Cleare, who became acquainted with the New Testament church when in the States. Leaving the Anglican church he returned to his people to preach the Gospel in 1959.

In 1963 William Scott, from Barbados, began to lend encouragement and evangelistic help to the Christians in Guyana. The church moves ahead now under the leadership of David London. Their VBS program in 1965 reached over one hundred children.

Jamaica

"Isle of Springs"

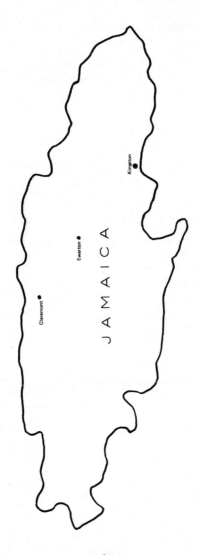

THE LAND . . . .

The largest former colony of the British West Indies, an island paradise of tropical vegetation, Jamaica became independent in 1962. Jamaica, the largest island of the colony, is 145 miles long with a maximum breadth of 45 miles. The commanding feature on the eastern side is the Blue Mountain Range; highest peak, 7,388 feet. The central and western area is an elevated plateau of deep-white limestone. More perfectly here than anywhere else is shown the extraordinary results of exposure of the limestone rock to tropical rainfall. Many basins and valleys have been carved into the plain, whose numerous streams flow underground to the sea. The lower slopes are covered with luxuriant vegetation such as pimento groves and brilliant flowering shrubs—begonias, orchids, cacti and ferns. The higher levels have dense forests of mahogany, fustic, and logwood, all of which form an important export. There are no royal palms but all-spice trees are found here and found no where else in the Antillean region.

The island lies within a zone of frequent earthquakes and hurricanes which are occasionally destructive. The coastal area is warm and humid, tempered by sea breezes, with a mean temperature of seventy-eight degrees. The uplands are delightfully mild and equable. Except near morasses and lagoons, the island is very healthy. Insects abound, especially the mosquito and sand fly. Yellow fever, once prevalent, is extinct. Strict enforcement of local sanitary and quarantine regulations brings the death rate down much lower here than the other islands of the Antilles.

Sugarcane is a major economic crop but bananas have more recently become the chief crop, providing sixty percent of the exports and twenty percent of the world's supply. Coffee, cocoa, coconuts, citrus fruits and tomatoes are cultivated on an extensive scale for the export market. Agriculture is the staple industry. Stock raising is carried on to a considerable extent.

Jamaica is the world's leading producer of bauxite and has the world's largest reserves. Good quality marble is found in the Blue Mountains, and prospecting for copper, iron ore, and oil is carried on.

. . . . THE PEOPLE

The estimated population of Jamaica at the end of 1965 was 1,811,000. The Chinese settlement of over six thousand are the shopkeepers; the halfcasts are largely employed in the trades and professions. The Negroes, who form the majority of the population

(90%), are generally indolent. The quantity of mango and its abundant use in the diet discourages industry among them.

Housing is forever a problem. While middle and upper-income housing is comparable to that in North America, facilities for low-income groups are poor by any standard.

Education on the island is free in elementary schools, but compulsory attendance is limited to areas where it can be conveniently enforced. Secondary schools have offered government scholarships to twenty percent of its enrollment. Jamaica is likewise the site of the University College of the West Indies. English is the predominent language of the people.

Religiously speaking there are reported to be over 350,000 Anglicans, around 93,000 Presbyterians, and 70,000 Roman Catholics. Status of the remainder of the population is not reported, though there is a small Jewish community. There is freedom and equality of religion on the island.

Grand Cayman Island, attached to Jamaica for administrative purposes, is only seventeen miles long, and four to seven miles broad. Its estimated population of 7,000 is about half British-white and half Negro. It is located 185 miles west. of Jamaica and 475 miles south of Miami, Florida. The conditions of the island are much like that of the island of Jamaica itself.

. . . . THE MISSIONARY . . . .

The movement to evangelize Jamaica with New Testament Christianity began as early as 1858 when brother and sister Beardslee were sent out to the island by the American Christian Missionary Society. One hundred and seventy-two were reported to have been immersed in that first four-year period.

In 1876 a family was sent by the Christian Women's Board of Missions. Not too much of the work is known during this period, though the number of Christians was reported to be nearly 6,000. After 1900, the spirit of restoration began to fade and with the entrance of the United Christian Missionary Society the work began to die out. In 1925 the Disciples in Jamaica reported 2,776 Christians, 39 organized churches, and 109 baptized for that year. Perhaps one reason for the decline is that this group, no longer with a distinctive witness for the New Testament Church, freely cooperated with denominational movements, including supporting community churches.

Brother Neil MacLeod was the connecting link between this

phase of the work and the resoration movement that exists in Jamaica today. Sent by the CFBM, he stayed in the home of a family which had a young son whose name was C. Vincent Hall. This boy learned much about the restoration of New Testament Christianity, but as he grew older he was influenced first by the Congregationalists, then baptized by the Baptists. Later he fell into disfavor with Congregational leaders for his scriptural preaching. Coming to the United States for medical aid he again came in touch with the church of Christ and apparently became fired with the vision of undenominational Christianity. Returning to Jamaica in 1935 with this new plea for Christian unity, he stirred the central part of the island to a mighty revival with many hundreds of converts. He was particularly successful because he was a respected Jamaican with influential connections. Besides that, he was a powerful speaker and a student of psychology. It appeared for a time that a restoration movement had seized Jamaica.

Brother Hall felt the need of American material and spiritual assistance and in answer to this call the Luke Elliotts came to his assistance in 1939. Their special purpose was to train a native leadership. Because of the war the Elliotts returned to the States and did not come again to Jamaica until 1944. Later these two separated and the Elliotts bought property at Ewarton, a poor community in central Jamaica, where they set up a Bible Seminary. The Richard Elliotts, Donald Hurleys, Lonnie Devers, and James Hergets each served a number of months between this period and 1950 when the Elliotts resigned their ministry on Jamaica island.

In January 1951, the Donald Freams came to Jamaica, followed by the Woodrow Phillips in the spring. These families picked up the work left by the Elliotts, evangelizing the area and continuing classes at Jamaica Bible Seminary. They moved a little later to Kingston, which is the largest city on the island. The James Hergets returned to this work again in 1952.

By 1953, forty-five congregations were reported with an additional thirty mission-preaching points, with a membership of approximately 3,000 persons. About this time property was purchased in Kingston and the first seminary building was completed. Of the thirty-one students who passed through the doors of the Seminary seeking spiritual knowledge only two are now preaching for the independent work of the churches of Christ.

Early in 1954 the Grayson Ensigns arrived in Jamaica. Twice before they had considered coming to the field, but they had continued teaching at Cincinnati Bible Seminary. This time the way opened and they engaged themselves immediately in the teaching program of the Seminary in Jamaica. However their influence and labor did not stop here. In the first sixteen months on the field they were used of God in starting three new churches; one on Grand Cayman Island and two in Kingston. The Phillips and the Freams also encouraged the Grand Cayman work by their teaching visits to the island. For two succeeding summers, Bob Allen, a student from Ozark Bible College, worked for short periods when on his way to and from Jamaica. In April 1957 he was united in marriage to Carolyn Bodden, a Bible school teacher of the church in George Town, Grand Cayman. In February 1956, Paul Smith spent three weeks on Grand Cayman, teaching and preaching, and discussing the possibilities of moving here to assist in the work. This he was challenged to do, and with his family moved in December of that year.

The whole purpose of the Grand Cayman work, as it is in Jamaica, is to establish churches after the New Testament pattern so that everyone on the island may have an opportunity to hear the true gsopel. To assist in this witness a weekly sermon was published in the "Caymen News" (a publication widely circulated throughout the island). While the Smiths were in the States on furlough in 1960, Harvey Bacus, who served in a summer teaching program in 1957, came to supervise the work.

When the James Hergets returned to the field they helped to establish three other congregations on the island of Jamaica, but much of their energies was directed to the establishment of Jamaica Christian Boys' Home. This was accomplished in 1954. By September 1956 this family had grown to nine children. This Home, established to build Christian character in the lives of needy Jamaican boys, and to demonstrate to the world that God hears and answers prayers, soon became a testimony to its purposes.

Mr. and Mrs. Harold Hill joined the work of the Home in May 1956. They soon became involved in the necessary building of a Christian Day School. Education is a scarce commodity in Jamaica and many parents are able and willing to pay for the education of their children in a well-organized school, especially one with a Christian influence. This school is known as the Jamaica Christian Prep School, and was housed in the building used for the Seminary which closed in 1959. A new building program has enlarged the capacity of the school. A kindergarten has been added. Facilities now will care for two hundred fifty children, and thus broaden the outreach of Christian influence. The Hills also print and mail a monthly paper "The Jamaica Christian".

Another new event for 1956 was a summer camp program which resulted in ten baptisms. Expansion in all of this work is partially dependent upon the addition of new evangelists. A great loss to the Jamaica work was the Phillips' leaving in the year of 1956 due to a tropical illness that did not permit their continued living in the islands.

George Westefeldt came to hold the fort for the Freams during their furlough in 1957. He immediately began teaching in the Seminary, ministering to the Constant Springs church, sharing in the general evangelistic efforts, and keeping up the very necessary office work. On the return of the Freams in July they conducted the second Christian Service Camp which resulted in twenty baptisms during Junior week. The camp program is now under the Hill's direction. Last year 219 campers benefitted from the camp program.

To help fill the great need for evangelists on the field, the Fred Hintz family was invited to share in the work of Jamaica Christian Mission. Brother Hintz visited the Jamaican work for two weeks in November 1956, where he preached, prayed, and worked among the Jamaican people. Later he and his wife came to work there. His main program was one of evangelism. Because there were approximately forty churches already on the island at that time it was of paramount importance that there be men who could preach the Word. Men's Institutes, teaching sessions in the churches, and constant visitation aided this program.

To bring indigenous churches into being it was realized that more effort must be concerted in the important towns and cities. With this in mind the Hintz family moved to central Jamaica to start a new work in Mandeville in May 1959. Fred later went into secular work and is no longer active in the church. Mrs. Hintz continues to labor with the Hills in their ministry.

Also in May 1959, the Donald Fream family left the island and are now laboring in a teaching ministry at Ozark Bible College. Later in 1959 the Grayson Ensign family returned to the States.

In 1958 Guy Whitley, a recent graduate of Roanoke Bible College, found his place of service on the island of Jamaica. For a number of years he was closely associated with the Hergets in the work of the Jamaica Christian Boy's Home. Their work expanded in 1962 to include a needy medical clinic where many came for treatment. Spiritual guidance was offered along with physical assistance.

It was in 1966 that brother Whitley began preaching in a central city of Claremont (near to St. Ann's Bay). He moved to this location in 1968 though still associated with the Hergets in their program

375

of work. His major work is in direct evangelism in the homes of the people, though responses are relatively slow.

Harvey Bacus was one of several summer internes in 1957. By 1962 he and his family returned to Jamaica. They have evangelized throughout Jamaica and the nearby island of Grand Cayman. Their ministry at the Penwood Church has brought many to Christ and more than tripled Bible school and church attendance.

The Earl Hobsons came to Kingston in 1967 not as missionaries in the ordinary sense but as Christian laymen who could support themselves as school teachers. Feeling that their place of service in the States could and would be filled by someone else if they left, they sought another area in which to serve the Lord. God opened the door in Jamaica when an opportunity came for brother Hobson to teach in a government school, called the Priory. They assist in the ministry of the Memorial Chapel in Kingston—in preaching, teaching Sunday School classes, helping with preacher-training classes on Monday nights, etc. Some assistance is given to the rural churches when possible, in revivals and vacation Bible schools. Their two-year term will be up in August of 1969 and a decision for future service will have to be made.

Because of the ease with which a person can get to Jamaica, it is possible for summer internes from the Bible Colleges to serve here as many have done and are doing. In the summer of 1969 Vincent Graham, a native Jamaican, is home again, conducting revival meetings throughout the Island. He is enrolled in Ozark Bible College for completion of his education.

There is a real need for veteran preachers and evangelists to come serve for brief periods of teaching and evangelizing. At one time there were more New Testament churches and preaching stations than at the present. Jamaica has often been beset with problems within the churches. In the past two seminaries have been built but neither of them exist now.

Another situation is that Jamaica is on the move—from the farm to the city. Most of our existing churches are in rural areas and we have neglected to start work in the cities.

The Disciples of Christ and our non-instrumental brethren are both quite well established in Jamaica also. There is a close association with our Canadian brethren who labor here among whom are the Carlton Mullings and Heather Matheson McLaughlin.

The future of the Jamaican work holds promises and problems. Materialism, sin, paganism, and crime are on the increase. Denominationalism has been entrenched on the island for three hundred years. It is over-populated with American cultists. In spite of the obstacles, powerful prayer and hard work can spread the Gospel to the glory of God.

Puerto Rico

"Land of transformation"

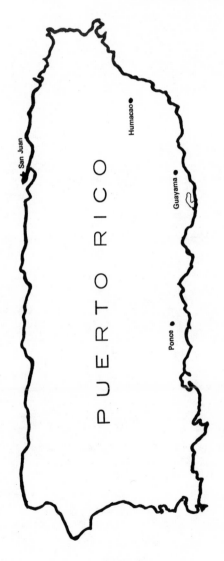

THE LAND . . . .

Puerto Rico, the smallest of the Greater Antilles, lies in the Caribbean Sea about 1,000 miles southeast of Miami, Florida. It has the unique status of a commonwealth in association with the United States, whose inhabitants possess the right and obligations of the U.S. citizen, except the right to vote in national elections and the obligations to pay federal taxes. The island is shaped like a rectangle, with a maximum length from east to west of 111 miles and a maximum width, north to south, of 39 miles. The island was discovered by Christopher Columbus in 1493 and called San Juan Bautista (St. John the Baptist). The present name, meaning "rich port", referring to the large protected harbor on the north, was added soon after the first Spanish settlement was made in 1506.

Hills and mountains with very steep slopes cover three-fourths of the island, with a narrow coastal plain and some inland valleys providing the only low-lying terrain. Though the rivers are non-navigable, except for very small boats, they do provide hydroelectric power and water supply.

An agreeable climate is one of the island's most attractive characteristics. The mildly tropical climate is moderated by the surrounding sea and seasonal variations are slight. Only five or six days a year are entirely without sunshine and rains are typically brief. Puerto Rico is in a hurricane region and has suffered in some destructive ones through its history.

During the early years when the island was largely a military establishment, the meager economy consisted of little more than subsistence cattle raising and farming. In the twentieth century the economy has been developed rapidly (largely due to U.S. aid and investment). The most remarkable development has occurred since 1940 through the sugar industry, which is still its most important crop.

Economic improvements are visible everywhere in various forms: new housing, public buildings and service facilities; new roads and communications, and in quality and quantity of food and clothing used by the population. Nevertheless, the standard of living for many is still very low. Progress in the mechanization and diversification of agriculture is lacking in some areas and industrialization is just beginning. The major portion of the island's exports come to the United States, which, besides sugar, includes lingerie, parts of electrical machines, textile goods, plastic products, leather goods, medicines, glass products, paper goods, rum, and carpets. By 1962 imports included

180,000 television sets that had been brought in since television service was inaugurated in 1954.

. . . . THE PEOPLE

The population of Puerto Rico, numbering 2,633,000 in 1965, are predominantly of Spanish and African origin. Most of the settlers came from Spain and through the ensuing years of disease and hardship, the original inhabitants (Carib-Indians) were wiped out. The importation of Negro slaves was authorized in 1510 and slaves were not abolished until 1873.

More than 700,000 Puerto Ricans live on the mainland, mostly in New York. This extensive migration is a reflection of the economic distress that has caused them to seek employment in alien areas. This migration has helped to better the local economy somewhat.

At the end of the 19th century Puerto Rican society consisted of the two-class traditional colonial structure, a system that was fixed and no one moved beyond the barriers. However, modern society is different. Universal education and the rapid development in the economy have created much wider opportunities, so that now people are divided into social and economic classes by differences in education and income. Through a survey, 7% considered themselves in the upper class, 60% in the middle class, and 33% the lower class.

Back in 1900 school attendance and literacy were meager but in spite of a continuing shortage of teachers and classrooms by 1962, in those ten years of age or older, literacy was 89%. Spanish is the official language, but many of the people speak English, which is taught from the first grade on in the schools. Higher education may be obtained in one of the four Universities and Colleges. In 1964, there was an enrollment of 23,000 in the University of Puerto Rico.

Due to the Spanish background of the people it is only natural that the religion of the people is predominantly Catholic. About 85% of the population regards itself as Catholic, although a much smaller number regularly attends services. About 10% are classified as Protestant, and some groups apparently have a wide following. Many believe and practice spiritualism.

. . . . THE MISSIONARY . . . .

After training preachers and teachers on the Mexican border for several years, the Gordon Thompsons felt a definite need to take the Gospel to the Spanish-speaking people of the islands of Puerto Rico.

They arrived in this field of service in September 1954, in the city of San Juan. They started services immediately in their home with wooden crates and planks serving as benches; another crate was the pulpit. Friends in the States eventually supplied them with more adequate equipment.

Glenore Chestnut joined the work during the Thompson's first year. A real reaping of souls began the second year with sixteen making their confession in one night. Parents bitterly opposed some of these decisions thus only about half of the converts were baptized. After doing must for the work by way of teaching, making teaching charts, etc., Glenora completed her period of service and returned to the States.

Several indicated a desire to preach so an evening training program was started and continued for some time. Preaching in other areas was also a part of the witness at that time.

The Christian Day School at Caparra Terrace was started in 1958. With the beginning of the Day School came the dream and prayers for a complete elementary-high school and a preaching-training program. In May 1961 the School was temporarily closed so that Gordon would have more time to build up other phases of the work and to enable Mrs. Thompson to fulfill the ever growing need of translating tracts and other teaching needs in the international language of Esperanto. The school was able to reopen again with various teachers assisting: Lynda Davis, Letha Solliday, Miss Magoon, Judy Buzieck, Raymond and Therma Bond. By 1965 they had ninety pupils in kindergarten through fifth grade. Another hundred students were turned away for lack of facilities and teachers. In 1966 brother Thompson's health was overtaxed and help was desperately needed. The closing of the school once more left the island in serious need with an important arm of evangelism cut off. Private schools in Puerto Rico are popular. Parents are eager for their children to learn English well, and classes in the Caparra Terrace school were in English.

During a period of recuperation and recruitment the Thompsons returned to San Juan with new teachers to reopen the school in 1968. Fern Wort, Katherine Rhodes and Jane Cameron (all Ozark Bible College graduates) were joined by Joyce Munn, Eleanor Schonfeld and Wanda Leighty. This made up the teaching staff with Jane assuming most of the office work. Only seventy enrolled with the reopening of school that year but the number is sure to increase in 1969 sessions. With this qualified staff the Thompsons could spend more time with the work of the church. Here too the young women were of great assistance. They all teach in vacation Bible schools.

Fern and Joyce began a junior age Saturday afternoon class. They are "earning" their own Bibles through memorization. Jane and Wanda are especially working with the high school youth. These young people are active in the church program. Often when any of the groups "perform" their parents come to services for the first time.

The newest recruit is Karen Mutsch who will be arriving in July 1969 to teach art classes and assist with other duties. Others are needed that classes may be divided properly for more effective teaching.

Larry Green has labored in the area of evangelism the past two years.

North America

CANADA

UNITED STATES OF AMERICA

MEXICO

Canada

"Land of Change"

THE LAND . . . .

The largest country in the Western Hemisphere and third largest in the world, Canada lies immediately north of our United States of America. It includes many of the small islands to the east, Nova Scotia, Newfoundland, and Labrador, and is divided into ten Provinces and the Yukon and Northwest Territories.

Three principal types of vegetation occur: the mosses and lichens of the Arctic and high mountains; trees and bushes of the humid temperate climates; and grasses, though present everywhere, dominate the semi-arid prairies.

The Canadian climate is dominated by the northernly position of the country, its massive size and simple structure. It is a cool country with short summers and long, cold winters. The Northwest and Yukon Territories have an arctic climate with an average January temperature of twenty degrees below zero. Hudson Bay is frozen about nine months out of the year. Most of the maritime provinces have a fairly warm climate, heavy rainfalls, thick fogs, cool but sunny summers. Cyclonic storms produce most of the precipiation which causes the fertile soil to be the greatest natural resource. The prairie provinces have a dry climate with cold clear winters. Along the Pacific coast the climate, mildest in the Dominion, is warm and rainy. Flowers bloom the year around in British Columbia and the south part of the Yukon Territory.

About as many people live in Illinois as in the whole of Canada. Most of those twenty million live within a hundred miles of the U.S. border.

Ottawa is the chief center for lumber milling. Mining is the chief industry in Ontario next to agricuture. Almost the entire world supply of nickel comes from this province.

Manitoba, in the southern part, is one of the chief wheat-growing districts of Canada, and the predominating interest of the province naturally is agriculture. However, mining is becoming a very important industry.

Essentially an agricultural country, with twice as much wheat being produced here as in Manitoba, Saskatchewan is about equally divided into prairie and wooded sections.

The prairie land of Alberta is semi-arid, suitable for grazing but it must be irrigated to be used profitably for agricultural purposes. In the north, mineral resources of great value are only partially developed. Petroleum development has continued since 1947, making Edmonton the "oil capital" of Canada. In 1964, 67% of the total production was found in Alberta.

British Columbia largely occupies a mountainous region, the Rocky Mountain Range to the east, and smaller and lower ranges to the west. The rivers and lakes of this province occur in deep valleys between the ranges. The interior plateau forms a good ranching country and in the valleys, with irrigation, fruit farms are successful. Mining is second of this areas major industries. There are less people living here per square mile than in any other province.

Newfoundland is the youngest and most eastern province. Labrador is a rugged area covered with lakes. Chief resources other than minerals, which are largely undeveloped, are fish, furs, forests, and water power. The island itself is in general a plateau of rolling relief, and important in transatlantic air communication being the closest point to Europe. Most of the population live close to the sea and 99.3% of them speak English.

Nova Scotia consists of a peninsula about two hundred and fifty miles long and one hundred miles wide at its greatest breadth. Parallel to the length of the Atlantic seaboard run ranges of low hills; the south is wild and rocky. Villages and towns are usually situated on the coast at the heads of numerous bays while agricultural activity is confined to the river valleys. The north shore shelters celebrated orchards. The chief region of mining and industrial development is in the northeast portion.

Between two sections of hills lies a triangular low-lying plain of New Brunswick. It is a country of fine rivers. Lumbering is the principal industry; dense forests, largely of spruce, cover most of the province. Important deposits of base metals like lead and zinc have been discovered in this province.

Prince Edward Island, the smallest province of the Dominion, is one hundred forty-five miles long and at the extreme breadth, only thirty miles. The island is fertile everywhere and for the most part is cleared for cultivation.

Quebec, the oldest and largest province, formerly a French colony, is still largely occupied by French-speaking people. The chief agricultural district lies in the valley of the St. Lawrence River. Next to agriculture the chief industries are lumbering and mining.

The province of Ontario is the most populous and wealthy. The peninsula is favored with excellent climate and soil. Its southern portion is the principal fruit growing district in Canada. Here are peaches, grapes, strawberries and apples.

The mountain system of the Territory of Yukon is a series of parallel ranges and the Rockies. This area is the most remote and least populated. Only 8,000 people inhabit the entire territory. Industrially speaking there are important lead and silver deposits in this area.

The Northwest Territory is not as remote as it once was since air transportation has been made to all parts. The valley of the Mackenzie River produces vegetables and some cereals in its long days of a short summer. The fur trade, still a considerable industry, is carried on over the entire area of the Subarctic forest. Population is increasing with the growth of the mining industry. Though still in its infancy, it produces gold, radium-bearing pitchblends, silver, native copper and petroleum. And it is one of the greatest sources of uranium.

. . . . THE PEOPLE

Canada is a country of comparatively large families. Overwhelmingly white in race, some 82% of the population is native-born of British and French origin. The largest foreign-born element is from the British Isles, while others are France, approximately 30%, Germany and Holland 5%, Ukraine and Poland 4%. Asiatics, especially Chinese and Japanese number near 74,000 while the Negro population is nearly 25,000. The Indian and Eskimo population is near 125,000.

Certain important characteristics are common to all Canadian Indians. The skin is dark brown (not red or yellow as sometimes described), the black hair is smooth and the cheekbones prominent. The face is broad and the nose well-developed. The Indians differ much in culture, physical characteristics and language, but the importance they place on religious beliefs and practices is the same everywhere. They are universally influenced by the belief that supernatural beings are close at hand ready to assist or to harm. In many areas they believe in a personal guardian spirit.

The Eskimos who inhabit the shores of the Arctic from Siberia to Greenland present an appearance very different from that of the Indian. Their hair is equally as straight but the skin lacks the warm brown color of their southern neighbors. The nose is narrow and conspicuously set in a broad face with prominent cheekbones. The eyes are black, hands and feet smaller than the Indian, and the stature is usually less.

There are two official languages in Canada—French and English. In 1961, 67% spoke only English; 19% spoken only French; and only 12% spoke both languages. One per cent spoke neither French nor

English, and 13% had a mother tongue other than these two. Ninety seven per cent of the adults are literate. Education is primarily a provincial responsibility. Native Indians are wards of the federal government, and attendance is compulsory until sixteen years of age at schools provided. The average youth attends school ten years but only about three per cent of the young people complete college of which number there are twice as many boys as girls.

Religiously speaking 46% are Roman Catholics, 20% are of The United Church of Canada which is a union of most of the Presbyterians, Methodists and Congregationalists, 15% are of The Church of England, 7% Presbyterian, 4% Baptist, 3% Lutheran, and the remainder varies.

. . . . THE MISSIONARY . . . .

It has been said that the last cenutry belonged to the United States, but that the next century belongs to Canada. This could very well be, as recent beginnings of development of Canada's great natural resources and the rapid increase in her population seem to indicate.

The bright future of Canada, coupled with our failure to evangelize this great area in the past, makes it one of the most important mission fields in the world today from the standpoint of New Testament Christianity. Truly it is one of the great frontiers of the New Testament church.

Most of the churches of Christ are located in the province of Alberta which, in area, is larger than the combined states of Ohio, Indiana, Illinois, Kentucky and Missouri. In the province of Alberta there is just one congregation for each 70,000 people while in the five states named there is approximately one New Testament church for each 7,000 people. This will give you an idea of the scarcity of New Testament churches even in an area where most of the work is concentrated. In the Yukon and Northwest Territories there are no New Testament congregations to our knowledge, though there are some towns with the population of more than four to five thousand.

In a way it is rather remarkable that U. S. Christians have never received the vision of the tremendous possibilities for evangelizing Canada with the true Gospel of Christ. For the most part the congregations have been started within the last two decades. This new movement may be largely due to the efforts of Alberta Bible College, now in its 38th year of pioneer preacher-training. Alberta Bible College began in the midst of the "great depression" in July 1932. The elders of the church in Lethbridge gave their minister,

Charles Phillips, permission to found a college and to devote the necessary time to teaching. That first year seven students (one full-time) and the Principal assembled behind a curtain in an unfinished church basement. The college was a child of faith and of vision and need in a pioneer West where no other institution existed to serve the Restoration cause. The founder was a man of great faith and strong conviction. Despite hardship, it was not long before the college began to grow and gain strength.

In 1937 it was decided to move the college from Lethbridge to Calgary, a fast growing city more central to the Province. A. G. Spaeth, an elder of the Vulcan church, purchased an unused public school building which served the college's needs until they moved into the new and more spacious building in the fall of 1962.

During those years the college felt its growing pains. Because of failing health, Dr. Phillips was forced to relinquish active work in the college. The principalship was placed in the hands of J. Merlin Hill and M. L. Breakenridge. In 1962 the Constitution was changed dividing the responsibility of principalship into two offices. Dr. E. G. Hansell served as President until his death in December 1965. Dr. Robert E. Gonyea served as Dean until his resignation in May 1967. Boyd L. Lammiman became President in September 1967.

The ministries of more than half the churches of Christ in Canada are served by graduates of Alberta Bible College. Several serve churches in the States. Others labor on various mission fields. Many serve Christ in numerous non-professional avenues. The number of graduates totaled eighty-four in 1968.

Frank and Mrs. Marie Rempel were instrumental in organizing a church in Grande Prairie late in 1945, when a few families of Christians gathered together to observe the Lord's supper and to worship in spirit and in truth. First services were held in a church building (though incomplete) in October 1946. In 1948 the Rempels responded to the call of the mission field in India. In their place came the Howard Rashes to continue on with the work. (The Rempels returned to Grande Prairie from India in 1969.) During the Rashes' ministry eleven persons were immersed into Christ and Bible school increased from four to seven classes. Having established the work on a firm foundation, the Rashes left the work in 1955 to witness in Taber, assisting Jim Phillips who ministered to the church at Lethbridge. In 1957 the Howard Rash family moved on to Weyburn and, with the help of a 50-year old congregation in Yellow Grass, Saskatchewan who gives 40% of its offerings to missions, began setting up a permanent work for Christ there.

Challenged by the lack of New Testament churches in Canada, through the personal witness of C. H. Phillips, the Robert Sanders of Oregon accepted the call of the Grande Prairie work, beginning their witness there in July 1955. The church grew under their leadership through preaching and personal evangelism. They made great progress especially with the youth work. The church became self-supporting in 1960 when the Sanders left the field for further education. During their five year ministry, seventy were added to the church. Dick Scruggs accepted the call of the Grande Prairie church, challenged by the many opportunities in the area to reach out for Christ. In 1957 one could go 300 miles to the east, 1,600 miles to the north, 800 miles to the west, and 600 miles to the south to find the nearest churches of like precious faith. Surely there was, and is, a need for more workers and leaders to come to labor in this vast section of Canada.

The Gilbert Cays began their work with the King Edward Park church in Edmonton in May 1946, with a nucleus of eight Christians. Though over one hundred persons have identified with the church, active membership was never over fifty at one time during their ministry which closed in September 1955. They also assisted in the establishment of the Whyte Avenue church to which the Owen Wilmots ministered for two years. Both families are now serving in the States.

The decision of the Joe Kaisers to make western Canada their field of missionary endeavor came in March 1953 after they had heard of the great needs of the area from the Elmer Walters who had visited the field as summer workers in 1952. Through the invitation of Gilbert Cays, they came late in 1953 to assist in the work of the King Edward Park church in Edmonton. This church called its first full-salaried minister (Jim Phillips) in 1962.

Late in 1954 the Kaisers received a "Macedonian call" to lead in the establishment of the new Rosscarrock congregation in west Calgary. The Kaisers held their first service there in March 1955. Progress was not as rapid in this area as it has been in some others, due to entrenched denominationalism (formal church type) and indifference. They found they got the greatest response when approaching the parents through the children, so much effort was placed in the children's work. Miss Gayleen Murray, graduate of Alberta Bible College, joined the Kaisers in the fall of 1956 to direct the youth work, week-day religious education program, visitation, and to take over secretarial duties. In 1962 the Kaisers moved to Missoula, Montana to begin a new church there.

Upon coming to Vulcan, Alberta in 1947, the Jim Chapmans were instrumental in starting a number of churches in Alberta Province. The Vulcan church itself reached an average attendance of 135 by 1956. It is self-supporting and the largest in this section of Alberta. Here, too, it was found that the work with the children was most effective. Jim Chapman's sister, Anne, spent three summers, 1948, 49, 50) assisting in this phase of the work. During those summer months Anne saw a door opening up where she could witness the whole year around. Giving up her excellent teaching profession, she migrated to Canada for the express purpose of helping to reach souls for Christ—a school teacher for God. She established a full-time Christian kindergarten, week-day Bible classes and special evening classes. Her activities were not limited to the Vulcan area alone, for she traveled to assist in summer camps, vacation Bible schools, and evangelistic meetings. She was well prepared to teach in the Christian day school in Hawaii when that decision was made in 1956.

Working in the area of Saskatchewan in 1957 were two faithful families who were rtained at Alberta Bible College. The Ralph Whitrows lived and labored in Big River. Over one hundred miles west, the Harry Mathesons centered their activities in the Morin Creek community about twenty miles from Meadow Lake. Under great handicap these missionaries did a very commendable work among a people to whom the plea of New Testament Christianity was virtually unknown. The Roman Catholic church has a strong hold on the Wood Cree Indians of this area, and the United Church of Canada has infiltrated its doctrine in this section as well.

Both of these missionary families had to do some secular work to sustain them, thus were not able to devote themselves wholly to the church activities. Even with this limitation they were able to lay a solid foundation for the ongoing of the Kingdom. Here in this section, as in many of the other areas, the work among the children was most beneficial. If you could view the children you would know that the labors of the missionaries are not in vain.

Through the faithful efforts of the H. L. Richardsons, the churches of Christ have been represented in a labor of love and hope among some of the Indians (such as the Ojibways, Sioux, Saulteaus, and Crees) in the provinces of Manitoba and Ontario. They found in Indian hearts a hunger for simple New Testament teaching. By mid-'55, one hundred twenty Indians and associates had responded to the Gospel and been baptized. Much of their effective work has been among the Indians in Manitoulin. When in Manitoba, they ministered to many of the different reservations. They endeavored to go where the people were—using open air services, or indoor services in the homes. It was from Aylmer that they did their printing work and shipping of relief goods to the various sections. Many of the families had meager supplies. Children were sometimes without stockings, shoes, or warm clothing. So it was that a great testimony of the love of God was given in the supplying of some of these needs. Other faithful workers, like E. A. Gray, Little Current, C. A. Carter and Ronald Dakin, Portage la Prairie, Mrs. Blake Fleet, E. A. Prince, and others, assisted in the witness for Christ in these regions. Mrs. Richardson passed from this life of ministering in November 1959. Brother Richardson remained at his post to serve as long as possible.

"If God opens the door, don't hesitate to enter" is a favorite motto of the Gene Dulin family. Submission to this principle led them to Toronto in 1957 to begin what is known as Toronto Christian Mission. Their work was to lead in the establishment of new congregations, the first of which was Westway Christian Church. Other persons, such as Robert Secrist, Richard La Gros, and John Vallance, assisted in other new congregations in the area (five in Ontario). Doors opened to assist at least ten older congregations in desperate need of encouragement.

Youth, needing Christian training, prompted development of a camp program. Toronto Christian Seminary was opened in 1959 with eighteen students enrolled. Gene Stalker, Flora Mason, Mary Ann Brown, and the Richard Wrights have served at various intervals with the Seminary and church leadership.

Toronto's international complexion brought the Dulins in contact with Christians from Russia. More doors opened! Opportunities came to preach in numerous European countries. (These are reported in countries where they traveled.) The 1969 missionary tour group left Toronto in June for Paris, Budapest, Moscow, Volgograd, Kiev, Warsaw, Berlin, and Zurich.

A great need was soon realized for printed material, not only for use in Canada, but overseas as well. With the situation in the Congo unstable as it was, the Clifford Schaub family brought his printing experience to Toronto Christian Mission. Their week-end ministry with the Grand Valley church soon challenged them to move onto the field, which they did in the summer of 1968. From this area they will handle the management of the camp, Ontario Christian Assembly.

To fill the need of the printing ministry, Bill and Zee Schoeller arrived in Toronto in July 1968. Their first work was the completion of the Rawang Reader and Hymnal for use in Burma. The early

1969 project is the Russian New Testament. This edition will include the entire New Testament, Psalms, all Bible study outlines (of the first edition), plus several more pages of doctrinal and sermon outlines.

John Huk, a native-born Russian, directs the Russian work for the Mission. He does all the translation of material and typesetting for the Russian printing. Mary Ann Brown continues to work with the mission. She sets the type for all the English publications (besides her teaching work in the churches). Sharon Shaffer came to the mission in January 1968 to work in the office, associated with the expanding printing ministry (besides her youth work in the churches). In May 1968 Delores Scarbrough joined the mission staff, preparing all publication for mailing and assisting in the new church work.

In December of 1968 Dewey Thackston (minister of Niagara Falls church since 1965) moved to Toronto to participate in the Russian department of the mission, and to assist in the many other phases of the work. He has been studying the Russian language and has a working knowledge of it that will benefit him in this ministry.

Clyde George, Youth Minister of the First Christian Church, Dewey, Oklahoma, recognized the need for a challenging youth program in Ontario. He accepted the call to move to this Province and give leadership in developing extensive activities for young people to challenge them for Christ.

Throughout the history of Toronto Christian Mission special attention has been given to reaching youth. Not only is the future of the church dependent on reaching young people for Christ, but the present church needs desperately the vitality of youth with the enthusiasm and vision which come from young and dedicated Christians. As the work has progressed, a very small youth rally developed into a monthly rally with young people attending from several churches, even though distance has been a great problem. Since nearly 400 miles separate two of the several participating churches, some congregations get to attend infrequently.

Brother George will serve as Dean of the camp week for delinquent and underprivileged boys in August 1969. This will allow him to become acquainted with the boys and some of their problems. He will then carry out an extensive follow-up program with these boys and their families, fully expecting to reach not only the boys, but the entire families for Christ. This is one of the most obvious and challenging areas of need in metropolitan life today. There has not been adequate personnel to tackle this job before, and the area churches have not had leadership or finances to give direction to this work.

Other ministers (from the States) in the Toronto area are the Alan La Rues in Hamilton, the John Clemens family at Willowdale, Richard Wrights at Ottawa, and Les Shell at the Westway church (now self-supporting)

The Luigi Oggiano family of Oria, Italy, immigrated to Toronto in November 1958. When the Guy Mayfields returned on furlough from Italy they visited the Oggianos who urged them to come to Toronto to work with them in establishing a church among the one hundred thousand Italians, most of whom had immigrated from Italy in recent years.

The decision was made and the Mayfields came to Toronto in June 1959. As a means of reaching the Italian people, they began holding English classes and Bible studies. On May 29, 1960 the Italian church of Christ (Chiesa de Cristo Italiana di Toronto) was formed with nine members. An Institute was established and by late August twenty-four were enrolled. Most of the students were young men. Courses in English, typewriting and shorthand were offered and each session closed with a thirty-minute period of songs and Bible study. Bible studies were also held both morning and evening on the Lord's Day. The emphasis of the Mayfields was on the foreign language groups, and upon the Italians in particular. Besides the 100,000 Italians in Toronto, there are over 90,000 Germans who have come since World War II. There are sufficient Chinese, Ukranians, Polish, Hungarians, Yiddish and Latvians for each group to have their own newspapers. The Mayfields have since resumed their witness to the Italians and others in Belgium.

On Prince Edward Island, Kenneth Norris led in the work of two churches at Montague and Murray, as well as broadcasting the Gospel weekly from a station in Charlottetown. On Lord's Day evenings he met with a small group at Truro in Nova Scotia. This required a ferry trip of an hour and a half and a 65-70 mile auto ride (which must be discontinued in the winter time when the strait is frozen and ferry travel is not possible).

By 1960 there were eleven congregations on the Island with a membership of nearly 1,500. The combined totals for Nova Scotia and New Brunswick was about 2,200—none in Newfoundland at that time.

In this area, as in the rest of Canada, there is a great need for the stedfast witness of more workers. Thus it was that the need of Maritime Christian College was realized and became a reality.

Classes began in September 1960 in the building of Central Christian Church, Charlottetown—1,100 miles away from Toronto Christian Seminary.

Completely across the dominion of Canada we come to the city of Vancouver, British Columbia, as did the Don Alberts in September 1958. There was no nucleus for a church of Christ in Burnaby, a suburb of 100,000, chosen for their work. They simply rented a house and began inviting people in for services on the Lord's Day. By February 1960 they had eleven members, with attendance running as high as twenty-eight. In the summer of 1959 students from Ozark Bible College, Rebecca Wilson, Gordon Souder, and Mr. and Mrs. Kent Mechem, assisted the Alberts in the vacation Bible school, calling and camp program. These summer internes have all returned to the work in a full-time ministry.

Gordon and Rebecca Souder were married in 1960 and came to the work at Burnaby. They serve primarily as evangelist and pastor, conducting regular services, VBS, and camps. The work is slow, for the Restoration Movement is not generally well-known in this area. There have been only twelve baptisms in the work at Burnaby, but attendance at services has more than doubled.

In 1965, Gordon made contact with the Russian Christians in Vancouver. He has studied their language and made a three-week tour to Russia and Poland in 1968.

With the Souders' arrival it allowed the Don Albert family to go to Lumby to begin a new church there. The Don Lewis family moved to Lumby in April 1968 to set up a printing ministry for the growing work in British Columbia. Arrangements were made with a school teacher in Cherryville, 14 miles east of Lumby, to begin Sunday School in her area. This is a rural community with no established church. In the fall of that year a Nazarene group in Armstrong sought for leadership which has been given to them by the Alberts, Lewises, and Jim Phillips from Vernon. Other study groups have been conducted in other surrounding communities—all in need of the Gospel message.

To join the work of the Don Lewis family in the Canadian Christian Press is Katy Conklin. Her arrival is scheduled for July 1969. This ministry serves the new churches, tracts for unevangelized areas, and even the College catalog for Alberta Bible College. Requests from missionaries have come for Bible lessons, teaching courses, and other printed helps. Besides assisting in the printing ministry, Katy will be working with the children in the four congregations meeting in the Vernon area, in camps, week-day schools, etc.

The Howard Dillons began witnessing for Christ in British Columbia in 1961. They have been responsible for starting churches in Clearwater, Dunn Lake, Fort Frazier, and Vanderhoof (in 1966). The Dillons moved in 1968 to start a new work in Telkwa (130 miles west of Ft. Frazier), with plans to begin an additional witness in Endako, twenty-five miles away. Three converts from summer camp live in Endako. Brother Dillon is a builder of buildings too, and has contributed much to the making of homes for missionaries and in church buildings.

In 1965, the Lloyd Stricklands went immediately from Ozark Bible College to Clearwater to continue the work the Dillons had begun. They have since added another teaching point in Little Fort, to the south of Clearwater. Lee Midgett, the first student from Alberta Bible College to enter the work in British Columbia, came to Clearwater in June 1968.

The James Mitchells went to Canada in 1967, hoping to work in the new "instant" city of Mackenzie. (Four new government dams have attracted new industry to this area—thus "instant" cities spring up quickly.) Their early efforts for this venture failed, but even this closed door seemed to be God's leading. Within "hours" a home was provided in a country community about ten miles east of Vanderhoof. They were able to teach in a group at the Mapes area, as well as share in the work at Ft. Frazier (thirty miles west of Vanderhoof). There are also Indians living in the area and in remote sections to the north who desperately need His Word. Many have heard only of Roman Catholicism. Another area of work that the Mitchells feel would be beneficial is a radio program offering a visualized correspondence course. Thus far the only radio station in the vicinity has the policy of eliminating all religious programs from the air.

The David Savage family moved to the Vancouver Island in 1963 where they began a new work among the Indians that populate the Island. Their work centers at Nanaimo where a church has been established, with over seventy in attendance. A boat has been purchased to enable them to go among the islands to preach, teach, conduct vacation Bible schools, and camps.

In January 1969 the Paul Walden family arrived in Nanaimo to begin their ministry. They brought with them Linda Gudahl who is now doing the secretarial work for both the Walden and Savage families. She also assists with the services at the church. Larry Walden (Paul's brother) is raising support to form a team with his brother in establishing churches in the islands. The Doug Kendigs (former summer internes) are in Nanaimo seeking employment with the new Junior College, thus enabling them to share in the work there, on a self-supporting basis. With these new workers, plans are being laid to expand the work. The main drawback to the work is the problem of drinking, strongly entrenched in the lives of these Indian people.

The Kent Mechem's first contact with Canada was their summer work in 1959 with the Don Alberts in Vancouver. The following few years were served in a State's ministry and a period of spiritual growth. In the Lord's time (1965) the Mechems reached Vancouver. They served in this area during the Souder's furlough. In September 1966 they moved to the Kamloops area where they have remained. Their worship services are conducted in the public school building. The first year was spent in youth work and with local publicity into the homes in mass mailings. The second year was a time for personal teaching sessions in the homes where contacts had been made, largely through vacation Bible school. Response and receptiveness has been favorable. Since the last of 1967 they have been witnessing in the community called Monte Lake, as well as their work at Westsyde (seven miles from downtown Kamloops). A man from Monte Lake has requested to take the Bible Correspondence Course. This group is made up of Presbyterians, Anglicans, Catholics, and members of the United Church of Canada. A variety of nationalities live in their area too: East Indian, North American Indian, German, French, Italian, Swedish, English and others.

Canada offers a marvelous opportunity for young people from the States to come and serve for a summer, in camps, VBS, and evangelistic efforts, as many have done in the last decade. LeRoy and Karen Riley were two of these summers workers. The challenge they received that summer encouraged them to make plans to join the workers already on the field. They joined the Mechems in the Kamloops area in the summer of 1969. They will also be assisting the Stricklands in the Dunn Lake Bible Camp. They plan to work in this area at least for their first year. The Lord may lead them to open work in a new area in the future.

There are perhaps a number of other New Testament preachers from the United States laboring in Canada, that are not named here (who are raising their own support in order to carry on their Gospel ministry in this mission field). Opportunities for spreading the cause of New Testament Christainity in this vast land are virtually unlimited.

Mexico

"Land of the bull-fight"

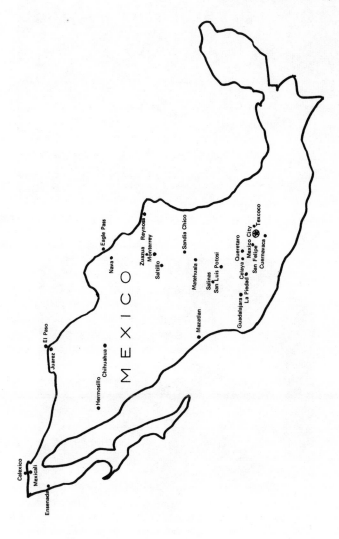

Public school parade in Mexico. Religion is not to be taught in schools, however the national "virgin" of Mexico leads parade.

Many children of Mexico live in poor conditions.

THE LAND . . . .

Mexico is the land of the fiesta, the gateway to Latin-America. Just below the Rio Grande lies this country nearly three times the size of Texas and about one-fourth the size of the United-States. Mexico, or the Republic, as it is referred to by its people, is bounded on the south and southeast by Guatemala and British Honduras.

About six-sevenths of Mexico is a high plateau, bordered by mountains sloping steeply to coastal plains. The western range is the Sierra Madre Occidental, on the east the Sierra Madre Oriental, the south, Sierra del Sur. Varying elevation of the land has given Mexico, broadly speaking, three climatic regions: 1) hot land, from sea level to 3,000 feet. The winters are dry, the summers wet. The temperature rarely falls below sixty degrees and may go as high as one hundred ten degrees; 2) temperate land, from 3,000 feet to 6,500 feet. It is free from extreme heat or cold with a mean annual temperature of seventy-five degrees; 3) cold land, above 6,000 feet. The average temperature is sixty-three degrees. There is never any real heat, nor are the winters so terribly cold, for the heat from the sun at that altitude helps to keep it very livable.

In most of Mexico it is the absence or presence of rain that marks the changing of the seasons, which are two instead of four. The northern half is largely desert, and only about seventeen precent of the population live there. The area below three thousand feet elevation is fertile in places but unhealthful since, due to the amount of rainfall, it is swampy and a breeding place of disease-bearing insects.

The backbone of Mexico's mining industry is gold and silver; lead, zinc, and copper; plus some iron and coal. Most of Mexico's mineral products are exported but the iron and coal are required for home use.

Despite the importance of mining and the growth of manufacturing, agriculture still leads in Mexico's economy. Of the little more than a quarter of a million people, 75% work on the land. Corn, wheat and beans are the principal food crops. The cotton leads all crops in value. Cattle ranching is important in the northern half of the country. Among small farmers methods have changed little. Where the land is level enough the farmer uses and axe and a wooden plow, but in other places he simply punches a hole with a pointed stick, drops in the grains of corn and beans and closes the hole with his foot.

The tropical rain forests of southern Mexico provide valuable hardwoods such as mahogany, rosewood and ebony. About half of the mahogany used in the United States comes from this area.

Mexico is a country of interesting and unusual contrasts. It is a land of modern cities and backward villages, of weathy residences and poor mud houses. The cities are up-to-date, but in the villages of southern Mexico, life goes on in about the same way that it did four or five hundred years ago.

Though Mexico is a rich country, it is a land of poor people.

. . . . THE PEOPLE

Mexico is a people of mixed races in which the Indian element is the strongest, but they have so mingled in blood and customs as to become one people. The Mestizo (mixed) element makes up about seventy per cent of the population. There is probably a little more than one-fourth who are pure Indian and only a small percentage are pure white. American, British, Spanish, German, and French comprise some of the unmixed descent.

Though the standard of living is relatively poor by U.S. standards and despite a variety of diseases caused by low standards of hygiene and nutrition, most Mexicans constitute a contented rural population. They are gracious and friendly, courteous and understanding.

The term Indian is often loosely applied to about half the Mexican population comprised of rural persons who have a relatively low material standard, are generally illiterate, go barefoot or wear sandals, sleep on the ground or in hammocks, wear the modified native dress and eat the common diet. The other half sleep in beds, dress in European-American style, eat wheat breads, and in general consider themselves more "modern".

Male natives of most rural districts wear white cotton trousers, a shirt and a straw hat. A serape, the colors of which vary with the region, is worn or carried except in the warmest areas. A long cotton blouse and a skirt, held to the waist by a sash, constitutes the female attire. The shawl, veil or Spanish mantilla is the most common headgear among all social classes of women; hats seldom being worn. Middle-class and well-to-do Mexicans wear very much the same clothing as is worn in the United States though they are of a more conservative nature.

The peasant's home is of adobe (mud bracks) with a roof of tiles or sheet metal, or even straw. These houses are small, dark and comfortless. There are few, if any, windows. In areas where the rainfall is heavier the buildings have sloping roofs and the walls are made of poles which are sometimes coated with clay.

The basic diet among the Indians is corn (maize), beans, and chile, supplemented by turkeys, boars, rabbits and fowls, and a great variety of fruits, herbs and insects. The most popular drink is pulque, the fermented juice of maguey (a cactus plant), which has a slight alcoholic content. The Indian people rarely drink milk but it is used as a beverage in the cities. According to Spanish tradition, the three meals of the day are breakfast, a large meal about 2:00 p.m. and a light supper at eight or nine in the evening. Many of the middle class have reversed the meals to a lunch and an evening dinner.

Spanish is the official language and perhaps the common language though many may speak one or another of the fifty-four different Indian dialects, which are classified in thirteen different linguistic families. In 1940 less than 7.5% of the people spoke no Spanish and were fluent only in Indian languages. In 1960, only 750,000 Indians did not speak Spanish. However, another million and a half spoke only a little Spanish and understood even less.

In 1940, 51.6% of the adults were illiterate, while in 1950 the rate had dropped to 40%. But in 1964, the rate was still 38%. At this time primary education is free and supposedly compulsory to the age of fifteen. Schooling in Mexico does much more than teach the people to read and write. It also teaches farming, hygiene, marketing and sports. Both public and private religious education in the schools is prohibited. There are twenty-one universities of which the National University in Mexico City is the largest with 72,600 students.

Spanish missionaries converted the Mexicans to the Roman Catholic religion some four hundred years ago. Yet the religion of the country people is still influenced by their ancient beliefs. However, the overwhelming majority of Mexico's population, over 96%, is Roman Catholic, although identification of the rural people with Catholicism is largely nominal. Many pagan practices persist to this time, especially in the Indian villages in the south where they worship ancient gods and still believe in magic.

. . . . THE MISSIONARY . . . .

Brother Enrique Westrup and his wife came into the church of Christ back in 1902, preceded in this action by his parents. He labored with the American missionaries, but was released from the Missionary Society when he found he could not agree to having all his efforts directed by those in Indianapolis. When all the missionary societies among the Christian Churches merged together into the United Christian Missionary Society, the decision was made to leave all of northern Mexico as a mission field in the hands of the Methodist denomination. Through the help of Christian friends in the States, brother Westrup took over active leadership of the work which remained. Though all the buildings were lost into Methodist hands, there were a half dozen teachers of the Christian Institute and several preachers who began laboring under his direction.

A new law which was passed allowing no connection between primary schools and church institutions soon made it necessary for them to drop the work of the school, and devote all efforts to the evangelistic field in the Monterrey area. This brother Westrup faithfully did until his death in 1967 at the age of 87. During his ministry brother Westrup printed many tracts for evangelistic purposes, a Spanish edition of McGarvey's "Commentary on the Acts of the Apostles", and Philip's "Church of Christ".

Pablo Pacheco, a convert of E. T. Westrup, ministers to his own people in a mission work at Monterrey. In 1931 he graduated from Kentucky Christian College and the same year began an eleven year ministry with the Central Christian Church in Monterrey. In 1944, he organized the Tapia Church of Christ, and since that time has carried on a threefold program: preaching, teaching, and printing.

Church at worship in Monterrey.

Brother Pacheco preached at every opportunity, and made of his home the meeting place of the Church and Seminary (Christian Bible Institute). Students who have taken work here are scattered throughout the United States and Mexico. The little printing shop not only was the means of the support of the Pacheco family for many years, but was a tool for the spreading of the Gospel also.

Lonnie Pacheco, son of Pablo Pacheco, and his wife came to assist in the work in 1956. The following year Lonnie began a medical course (paid for by the Mexican government) and received his M.D. degree in 1964.

Property was purchased in late 1957 for permanent buildings for the mission. These buildings housed the chapel, class rooms, clinic, and other mission needs. Bible classes were resumed that same year with nine enrolled. They now also have two small medical offices.

Several tracts and pamphlets have been printed and given for distribution. A paper "El Cristiano" is being spread through the country as fast as possible, and funds permit.

A new church was established in Monterrey in October 1959 with thirty in attendance at the first service. Since 1960 four new congregations have been established—three in the city, and one twenty miles north. A Baptist church was also brought to the New Testament pattern. Most of the eight churches that are meeting regularly through the Pacheco's efforts still meet in homes of the Christians.

Mr. and Mrs. C. Marion Railey (parents of Mrs. Lonnie Pacheco), formerly their forwarding agents, came to join the work to assist where they could. They are leading in the Zuazua work (the one north of Monterrey). As many as forty have gathered to worship here. Eight baptisms were reported recently.

Antonio Medina was born the son of a multimillionaire in Leon, Guanajuato, Mexico. He finished high school in 1915 at the age of fourteen and entered the Seminary to study to be a priest. A year later the revolution closed all the Seminaries and he left it forever.

During the revolution he managed to buy a New Testament which he began reading. Though he laid it aside for a time, its words impressed him very much. In 1918-19 he served with the Mexican delegation to the League of Nations in France, during which time he studied Philosophy and Logic at the University of Paris. Upon his return to Mexico, he studied Commercial Law and Business Administration. It was upon one of the trips for the firm for which he worked following graduation that he visited Charcas, San Luis Potosi. Here, he attended a meeting of the Disciples of Christ and was immersed (in 1926). In 1927 he began preaching around San Luis Potosi, in the state by the same name, and later he moved more and more toward the west.

There became differences in concepts of missions and brother Medina left the Society to preach as a free missionary in Christ Jesus. Doors were closed to him by the churches which still operated under the Missionary Society, so he set out alone to establish churches according to the pattern of the New Testament. One of the largest of these remains today in Estancia, Zacatecas.

In 1932, Antonio Medina married Victoria Infante, who lost her inheritance upon becoming a Christian. Nevertheless, she chose to serve with her husband in Central Mexico. Leaving her fine living behind her, she went into the neglected areas to do medical work, while brother Medina did evangelistic work.

When Antonio Medina first began preaching, his message was unknown and there was little persecution, but as the weeks went by the persecution increased. When forced out of one town, they would preach in another, and so the Gospel found itself extending into towns where there were no evangelical bodies whatsoever. In one town, after he had preached to the people, the Gospel was received with such success that all the brethren (who once were Catholic) brought together all their idols, images, pagan pictures and plaques and burned them in a pile.

Church buildings were constructed in Loreto, Salinas, Las Colonias, and Ojocaliente. In Loreto, the Medinas set up a Christian hospital which later was destroyed by the Catholics. The year of 1947 was a year of great persecution. Seven hundred Romanists stoned the Medinas but, although they nearly died as a result, they continued to preach Christ. As in the days of the early church, Christians were scattered due to the persecution but they witnessed for Christ wherever they went. The Christians who were persecuted in Pastoria, Zacatecas, formed a new village of Colonia Madero, where they could be free in Christ, and the Gospel could be preached in liberty.

The Medina's only daughter, often subjected to the same treatment as her parents, went to the States for Bible training. While in Dallas, Martha Elba met and married Wayne Hayes. In 1954 they came back to the field to assist the Medinas in revivals, workers' institutes and establishing new congregations.

As a result of over thirty years of labor for the Medinas, there were over 4,500 immersions reported by 1957. The estimated number of brethren in the local area that same year was from 1,200 to 1,500.

Central Mexico Christian School was built in which to conduct a four-year primary school and a two-year Bible Institute. English classes were offered to all. Bible courses were given to those preparing for the Christian ministry. Mrs. Medina, unable to do strenuous traveling, as in the past, engaged in more medical work at the home base. She was able to witness for Christ in this ministry to the body's needs.

Two families could not adequately supervise the work in Central Mexico. The Freeman Bumps accepted the challenge and arrived on the field in January 1960. They later moved to Chihuahua.

Moises Saucedo, born in the state of Zacatecas, Mexico, gave his life to the ministry with his own people. Following his training at Colegio Biblico and Ozark Bible College (in the States) he returned to assist Antonio Medina in rural evangelism and worked in camps and conventions with Wayne Hayes and the Ted Murray family. At present he is engaged in new church evangelism in San Luis Potosi, a city of about 200,000 souls.

The Murrays moved to Salinas, in the state of San Luis Potosi, in June of 1964. Immediately they began to care for needy children who were present on every hand. (In the twelve years before going to Mexico they had been foster parents to twenty-three children). In 1965 they were able to purchase, near San Luis Potosi, twenty acres of farm land complete with irrigation systems. This will enable them to train the young boys in good farming methods as well as provide some of their own food. By 1968 their home included fifty children, from ages 3-16, about half of whom have accepted Christ as Savior. The purpose is to train orphaned and abandoned children in the Way of the Lord, that in turn they may in later years seek to establish indigenous churches.

The Bill McCarty family arrived in San Luis Potosi in late summer, 1968, to help with the home established by the Ted Murrays. They hope to also begin a radio broadcast with a follow-up correspondence course. Perhaps later a Christian reading room can be established in the downtown area.

Saltillo Christian Mission serves an area in Mexico of about 180 miles by 60 miles in which there are about five hundred villages, six large towns, and two cities. Of the fourteen congregations and three preaching points in this area in 1957, all but three of them were ministered to by students or faculty of Saltillo Christian School. This school opened in September 1955 and was assisted at that time by the Rodney Northrups, Harold Gibbs, Keith Owenses, and Damon Elletts. The Owenses soon went to share in the work of Colegio Biblico in Eagle Pass and the Elletts began work in a new area of Mexico. Brothers Northrup and Gibbs and families carried on this work with the assistance of some faithful Mexican Christians until 1959 when the Gibbs family went also to serve at Colegio Biblico.

The Northrups continued in village evangelism and church leadership training. The problem was to train leaders as quickly as new fields could be opened for the Gospel. The trade school Bible training plan became important since most congregations are small and cannot support their own ministers. A second such school was established

411

in 1963, known as the Cedars Christian School Project, nearly 150 miles southeast of Saltillo. This was a joint project in conjunction with the Mexican Federal government officials. The government would offer grades 4, 5, and 6,—the mission would provide the Bible training on adjacent ground. By 1968 a full course of night Bible classes was being offered. Village evangelism is emphasized at both schools. In their eighteen years on the field, the Northrups and their co-workers have averaged one and one-half new congregations per year. There have been approximately 450 baptisms reported in the area. More recently church growth camps have been offered for church leaders who are unable to attend the training schools.

In the summer of 1958 Delbert Wilson worked in Mexico on the summer internship plan, spending six weeks with brother Medina and Wayne Hayes and six weeks with Harold Gibbs who was still at Saltillo then. While in that city he met Alice Wantland who was studying the Spanish language in a Saltillo college. Having a mutual interest in the service of Christ in Mexico and in each other, they were married the following summer. When the Gibbs were called to serve at Colegio Biblico, the Wilsons went back to Saltillo to attempt to fill the gap that was left. Progress is slow since they must fight denominationalism and false doctrine on every hand. Their field of service has thus far covered a radius of from thirty miles east of Saltillo to one hundred miles to the west.

Damon Ellett entered Mexico in 1953, beginning a work in Saltillo where he met and married Dr. Leonila Marin in 1955. Brother Ellett had received a short medical course at Platte Valley Bible College and together they operated a Clinic in Saltillo. In May 1957 they went to El Mante, Tamaulipas, Mexico to continue in their mission work.

El Mante is really in the tropics, so the main diseases to be combated physically are tuberculosis and malaria. The people of the area are poor in spirit as well as body. In this region the Roman Church has less influence but the need for Christ is just as great. The Elletts were awarded fifty acres of land in a homesteading project forty miles southwest of El Mante. This is a government sponsored project to build up an agricultural area. It is hoped that income from this land will help to support native Christian workers. Preaching points near El Mante have opened up, thus the work expands.

Just to the west of the Tamaulipas area and at the southern extension of the Northrup's work, new missionaries came to serve in March 1965. The Lord led the Larry Cuylers into His ministry through many unusual means, but lead He did. Mrs. Cuyler became

412

quite ill in 1964 and they were advised to move to a different climate. When they asked the Doctor about north-central Mexico he agreed it would be a better place for her than anywhere in the States. Their first location was 165 miles from a post office or store—a primitive area without doctors, electricity, or means of communication. They began treating the minor ills of the people. By 1966 Mrs. Cuyler found herself delivering babies and many other medical chores. The death rate of children (by age five) was 50% They were able to reduce this in half. This medical assistance began to open doors into villages which were previously closed.

A new highway (fifteen miles away from their present home) has brought them to within 65 miles of the city of Matehuala. They now live on a ranch and hope to eventually make the mission self-supporting through cropping the land. But their basic work is to establish congregations in all the villages of the area. The first village work, begun in the fall of 1965, was left on its own in 1967, averaging 85 in attendance and giving 10% of their income to missions. Three village services were started in 1966 but two were unsuccessful, one because of the severe persecution from the Catholics. Early in 1968 they had started services in four more villages. Three of them had an average attendance over fifty. Other work includes care of unwanted children, Bible schools, intern and recruit programs, and radio evangelism. A children's home is planned for the future.

Baptism at Sandia Chico.

Training classes for Christian workers was begun in 1966 in an informal way. In September 1968 formal training classes began with about ten young men students. These who are taught are preaching in the villages. There were 56 baptisms reported during 1968.

The medical work became so involved that a nurse was necessary to assume the burden of the labor. Susan Ogden arrived in November 1967. The medical work continues to open doors and hearts to the Gospel in the Sandia Chico area. She began her work in the midst of an epidemic of diarrhea, followed by a large breakout of flu. She has been treating forty or more people daily. In August 1969 she will marry Apolinar Calderon, a ministerial student at Colegio Biblico. By early 1968 Karen Kohler had also joined the work with the Cuylers.

A serious auto accident delayed the plans for the Ron Cochrans to enter Mexico to serve their Lord. In June 1968 they moved to McAllen, Texas where they could witness across the border to the Mexicans living in Reynosa. Later in 1969, when funds are sufficient, they will be moving into the market center of Matehuala. Their first work will be to follow up on the contacts that have been made through the radio broadcasts that reach into this area. As quickly as possible a church will be established, from which to reach out to surrounding villages.

In September 1945, in the small village of Nava, Mexico, an incident occurred that changed the whole course of Mexican evangelism. Services were over and a young man approached Harland Cary, American missionary to Mexico, saying, "If you will teach me, I'll be your student". After much prayer and consideration, this challenge was accepted.

The work of Colegio Biblico started in rented buildings in Eagle Pass, while the students lived across the river on the Mexican side of the border and walked to and from classes each day. In 1946, the students were granted visitors' visas to live in Eagle Pass, a privilege that has been enjoyed each year since. In August 1947 an old hospital building was purchased (on time payments) and used until the present 17 lot site was obtained in 1950.

Following the first year of school, Paul and Hazel Rathbern came to assist in the teaching and preaching, where they served until Paul's untimely death in 1961. Mrs. Rathbern now teaches Spanish-speaking people in the San Jose, California area.

The Mexican woman who had helped brother Cary in the beginning left that second year so Miss Vivian Pollock came to the work. Later she married Gordon Thompson and together they served until March 1954. At the present time they are witnessing in Puerto Rico.

Others who served for various periods are: Mrs. Harriet Vester, Theon Bigelow, Glenora Chestnut, and Mrs. Ruthella Clark. Gerald

Bowlin worked with the school from July 1947 to June 1949 when he started Mexican Bible Seminary in western Mexico.

Vincente and Mrs. Aguilar came in June 1947. Being a native himself, brother Aguilar was very important to the teaching program of the school because he not only taught Bible courses but Spanish grammar as well.

Keith and Mrs. Jo Owens served a year among the Mexicans at Saltillo where they operated an extension department of the College before coming to work directly with Colegio Biblico for a few years.

Frank Rairdon, a retired pensioner, gave himself unselfishly to the teaching program of the school. Carroll Langston came with great linguistic ability and a long career in the ministry to prove himself a valuable asset to the School. (He has only recently retired from the work.)

Thomas Martinez was the school evangelist to the Mexican people for many years. Through his untiring efforts many young people were encouraged to dedicate their lives to Christian service.

A more recent addition to the faculty is the Herbert Watkins family. Their first contact with the Mexican work was through migrant workers in Michigan. For five years they made use of every opportunity to reach the summer workers, five to ten thousand strong, who go to Michigan each year. A part of that work was an extensive correspondence Bible study course. They have helped to enlarge the music department of the College. Mexican people love music. The accordian has proved a valuable tool in the field of music, since it is portable and within their power to buy.

With the closing of Southern Christian College in San Antonio, Texas in 1963, Augustine Ortega accepted a call from Colegio Biblico to come serve as their Dean. Though American-born, brother Ortega understands his people and their needs very well. He is filling a great need in the preaching and teaching in the Eagle Pass area.

This Mexican Bible College was the first such center for training Mexican leaders for the churches in Mexico. From the very first it has been a mission work. The students do not pay tuition; for most it would be utterly impossible to do so. By the fall of 1956 twenty-nine students had graduated. By 1960 three-fourths of all the native preachers in Mexico had been trained at Colegio Biblico.

In 1957 Colegio Biblico was responsible for over forty-one services of the New Testament church each week, its students and faculty traveling more than 1,100 miles each week. The influence of the College for Christ continues to spread out as more students enroll in the school. The 1957 enrollment was forty-one, whereas nearly sixty were enrolled in the 1960 fall term. In September 1968 there were seventy students enrolled, the largest number in the history of the school.

Their outreach is unlimited. One graduate is a missionary in Chile. Young peoples' camps have been started throughout Mexico. There is a national youth convention every year. The students reach out to many preaching points every week-end. The young women do an excellent job in teaching children and young people. In July and August they reach as many as 2,000 children in vacation Bible schools. Many of these children have never had any religious training in all their life. During pre-Eeaster week in 1969 students and faculty of Colegio Biblico conducted fifteen revivals and reached between 750-1,000 young people in VBS.

The idea for a Spanish publishing house was conceived by Mary E. (Walden) Gilmer in January 1953. She began working as a missionary to the Mexican people in 1951. There being practically no materials available for Bible schools, VBS, or teacher helps (except from denominational sources) it was necessary for her and every mission to prepare the materials they needed to carry on the teaching program.

While in the States to gain further education and support for such a project, she met Ralph Gilmer to whom she was married in 1955. They had much in common in their purpose of witnessing for Christ, for brother Gilmer was an experienced printer and desired to spread the Gospel through the printed Word. Together they set up the Casa de Publicaciones Cristiana (House of Christian Publications) in Eagle Pass, Texas. Eagle Pass, though in the States, was chosen as the site for this Spanish publishing work because a large part of the missionary work to Spanish-speaking people centers there.

The primary purpose of this work was to take the Gospel to Spanish-speaking people through the printed Word. It provided tracts, teacher training courses, and true-to-the-Bible helps and supplies for Vacation Bible Schools and Spanish Bible Colleges. One of the first projects completed was the 1957 VBS course, "The Promises of God".

The outreach of this work was not limited to the area around Eagle Pass at all, but was of benefit wherever people speak Spanish. In the United States alone there is a Spanish-speaking population of over five hundred thousand. In Mexico, Central America and the western and southern part of South America there are more than 125 million Spanish speaking people, many of whom have never heard or read the Gospel message. In 1960 the location for this work was moved to El Paso, where the Gilmers joined forces with the Eugene Morgans. At present they are associated with Dallas Christian College.

The Gerald Bowlin family came to Mexico in 1950 to set up the Western Mexico Christian Mission. While located in Nogales at the Arizona border five churches were established and five other preaching points were ministered to. One of the major emphasis of the work has been the Mexican Bible Seminary which is now under Mexican leadership.

When brother Bowlin received his immigrant's papers to Mexico in 1955 (the first of our missionaries to do so) the work moved to a new center in Hermosillo which is almost in the center of the state of Sonora. It is felt that the effect of the work has been greatly increased by being in this new location.

Other missionaries who have served with Western Mexico Christian Mission are the Jerry Watkinsons, Jack Gilsons, and Miss Lorene Martin. Miss Martin came in September 1953 to take over the office work but she assisted in the other work as well.

Much of the work is evangelistic in nature, helping the Mexicans to establish new congregations and witnessing everywhere of the love of Christ. The village groups are more ready to accept the Gospel than those in the cities. Typical of the village work is LaMesa. The missionaries were in a neighboring village and were begged to come to LaMesa. When that was possible the message was brought to this village. People responded and the church was established. Now they are making their influence felt in other neighboring villages. There are several hundred such villages in the state of Sonora alone.

The majority of the people of Mexico are a very poor group, having inadequate food, clothing, housing or medical attention. The benevolent work of the mission was unlimited. Mrs. Bowlin, who had had nurses' training, is in charge of the medical work.

In 1961 Lorene Martin and the Jerry Watkinsons moved further west to Ensenada, Baja California, Mexico (a seaport town of some 40,000 population). To their knowledge there had been no one preaching the Gospel after the New Testament pattern in the some 1,100 miles of peninsula, except on the border.

In recent years Lorene Martin has devoted more time to the reproduction of teaching materials in Spanish, especially VBS materials. Some 4,000 workbooks, plus teachers' manuals were printed in one year. These are used not only in Mexico but in South America too.

In 1964 the Watkinsons' work formed a greater association with the work of the Calexico-Mexicali Mission. This Mission, located on the border at the southeastern corner of California, was started in the spring of 1956. In the first three years of existence three congregations were established, one in Calexico where the missionary

417

family, the Joseph Gracianos, lived and two across the border in Mexicali. More than eighty persons were immersed into Christ.

The Calexico Christian College began classes in February 1958 for the purpose of training Mexican young people to take the Gospel message to their own people. In the fall of 1959 twenty students were enrolled, six full-time. The people are generally in dire need since there is not enough work in Mexicali for the multitude of people who live there. Thus the missionaries not only minister to them spiritually, but physically as well, wherever the opportunity presents itself. They are able to distribute used clothing, powdered milk for children and vitamins and medicines for the sick. "When ye have done it unto the least of these my brethren ye have done it unto Me".

Charles and Mrs. Ciangura committed themselves to the work in Mexico. They arrived in 1968 to concentrate their labors in a new orphan's home and training school near Ensenada.

Following two years of work in Hermosillo the Jack Gilsons moved in June 1960 to Colonias, one of the most populous divisions of the city of Culiacan (over 80,000 population). This is located on the west coast (not the Peninsula) on the international highway, nine hundred miles from Calexico-Mexicali, or six hundred and fifty miles from Nogales, Arizona.

A temporary chapel (a simple high "lean-to" of rough poles and roofing) was set up for use until the property could be developed. Various teaching methods were used: the most effective contacts were made through the Life of Christ colored slides. Attendance sometimes ran to several hundred at a showing, though normally the attendance was just under fifty. The church is the only non-Catholic group meeting in the Colonias community. The need is there, but because of Jack's health they moved to Las Cruces in 1966. Here they work with Mexican migrants and immigrants.

Jesus "Chuy" Field saw the need of the area. He was born in Hermosilla and knows the west coast of Mexico well. That is why he chose to return to his home area, following his education in the States. He and his wife plan to reach Mazatlan in 1969. Their work will center around evangelism among the middle and upper class people in the city. However, they will be witnessing to the small mountain villages around Mazatlan as opportunities present themselves. They will be training natives to take over leadership in the churches as they are established. By reaching out to the middle and upper class first they hope to make the work self-supporting.

The work to evangelize north central Mexico began in November 1953 when the Eugene Morgan family left El Paso and came for

418

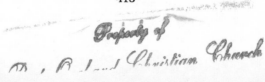

the first time to Chihuahua, 230 miles to the south of El Paso. Having been associated with the Mexican Bible Seminary for one year previous, they were aware of the great needs of the Mexican people. They chose this new section of the country in which to work because it was desolate as far as New Testament Christianity is concerned.

In the spring of 1954 twelve people were immersed and became the nucleus from which to work. As the work grew and its influence was beginning to be felt, outside pressures were brought to bear and eventually this particular group had to meet in another location. About this time another location opened up in the village of Rancheiro Juarez. By March 1955 they were meeting in a building purchased for that purpose. During this time about fifty people were instructed and baptized. Another preaching point was established at Nombre de Dios. As the Lord led, a two-year intensive type of study course was set up to meet the demands of those who already had expressed their desire for such training.

The Morgan's left in 1957 for further training and the work was without much oversight until the Freeman Bumps came in 1961 from central Mexico. They labored here for four years, expanding the exangelistic efforts in six other areas, and the State Penitentiary. The Bill Burr family came to carry on the work at Chihuahua in January 1965. They started a series of weekly classes and have, with the help of native teachers, conducted summer camps, and vacation Bible schools. In 1967 they began a "Voice of Truth" radio program, and conduct a follow-up program. There is also a wide distribution of Christian literature. The historical meeting of the Catholic Archbishop and a Methodist Presbyter, as a part of the Ecumentical Movement, has not brought about scriptural unity, but it has served to remove some of the hostile attitudes between the Catholics and Evangelicals. The soil has become somewhat more fertile. There are four young man from Chihuahua who were attending Colegio Biblico in 1968-69 school year. Though 750 miles away, it was the nearest Bible College in Spanish.

When the Eugene Morgans returned to the Spanish field in 1967 they settled in El Paso and began a weekly Bible study among the Mexican children of the San Juan area. A vacation Bible school conducted in Juarez ended in weekly Bible studies there likewise. In August 1960 the Gilmers, formerly of Eagle Pass, moved to El Paso to consolidate the publishing work with that done by the Morgans. It was felt that by uniting to form one Spanish publishing ministry they could provide more and better material.

Ill health forced the Bill Morgans to leave their new work in

419

Guadalajara and come to the border. Realizing the strategic importance of the El Paso border area, and the need for an evangelistic effort there, they decided to begin working in this neglected city. El Paso has a population of approximately 350,000 and Juarez has over 500,000. A large percentage of those living in El Paso speak Spanish as a native language.

The Bill Morgans immediately set out to establish a New Testament church in El Paso. It began in their rented home on the Lord's Day, Nov. 11, 1964, with twelve people present. On the third Lord's Day, attendance reached forty-two. The congregation was officially organized and incorporated as a non-profit organization in February 1965. The New Testament Christian Church purchased property for a meeting place later in 1965.

The second major project of the Morgan's "Spanish American Evangelism" was the establishment of a Mexican congregation in Juarez, Mexico. A Christian lady, a sister of a Mexican evangelist, was located in Juarez and services were begun in her home on Sunday afternoons in October 1965.

In November of 1965 Freeman and Carolyn Bump joined the work. They had labored for one year in Salinas, and three and a half years in Chihuahua. The work in Juarez began to grow under the fulltime leadership of brother Bump and soon a building was rented.

The third phase of Spanish American Evangelism was then begun. It had long been a desire of the Morgans and the Bumps (and one reason for coming to El Paso) to produce and broadcast a Spanish Gospel radio program that would penetrate deeply into Mexico. The first broadcast was aired in January 1966. It has continued without interruption every other week to the present time. The broadcast tapes are also duplicated and mailed to five other Spanish radio stations where they are heard every Sunday. Time for some of these other stations is paid for by missionaries living in the area of the broadcast range. Various speakers have appeared on the program, but at present Ranulfo Garza (a native evangelist in Chicago) is the program speaker. Freeman Bump and Bill Morgan serve as announcers, and Freeman currently serves as engineer. Special music is recorded. The program is followed up with personal correspondence with all who write in, plus Bible study courses and personal contact when possible.

Each summer vacation Bible schools are held in the churches in El Paso and Juarez, and in several Mexican homes. In 1968 five such schools were held in Mexico and one in El Paso. A Christian camp was conducted in 1968 in El Porvenir, Mexico, for the first time.

The mission staff now includes (besides the Morgans and Bumps)

Cathy McTeer, who came in June 1967, Janet Spencer, who began full-time with the mission in September 1968, and Jenny Sand, who came in June 1968. Besides office work and radio correspondence, the girls work with the youth in Juarez. Jenny will be leaving in the summer of 1969 to be married.

Plans for future expansion include: new congregations on both sides of the border, more stations in Mexico and other Latin American countries carrying the radio broadcast, expansion of the correspondence and personal follow-up program already in operation, the production of filmstrips and silde programs and other visual aids, and continued participation in the various teaching programs of the churches.

The first Christian missionaries to arrive in Guadalajara were Clinton Looney and his family, in September 1961. They immediately enrolled in language study and began investigating possibilities for beginning the Lord's work in this city. Through the language school, contact was made with an American family who had been members of the church in the United States. The two families began holding services in their home.

In November 1961, a Mexican preacher, Mariano Farias, a graduate of Colegio Biblico, moved to Guadalajara to assist in planting the New Testament church there. He became a great help in acting as interpreter, preaching and teaching, and establishing contacts with interested Mexican families. One of these contacts soon led to the beginning of Bible study meetings in a home in San Andres, a suburb of Guadalajara.

In January 1962 the Bill Morgan family arrived and enrolled in language study. They joined in both the English and Spanish work. The Ed Crandells, Roy Webbs, and Allen Moreys assisted with the English work for a period of time.

There are now three Spanish groups meeting regularly in the state of Jalisco, two are in Guadalajara and the third is fifty miles out at San Luis Soyatlan. With a Mexican assistant, brother Looney was able to help establish the first work in the state of Michocan (southeast of Jalisco). There are four locations meeting now around La Piedad, under native leadership.

Marty and Helen Gonzales came to the Mexico City area and spent one year at Tlalnepantla, an industrial city near Mexico City. They worked with Robert Flores who helped them in the language and teaching methods. They moved to the state of Michocan in February 1967. Their work is varied due to the needs of the different places where they serve. Although the state of Michocan is considered fanatic and almost closed to other than Catholicism, they have more invitations for teaching than they are able to accept. Thomas De La Cruz serves with them, living and working in and around San Francisco. The Gonzales will concentrate their efforts on the area around Sabino.

A small bilingual work in Queretaro (a state capital) represents the only efforts of our churches in that state. The Mexican congregation in Celaya, an agricultural center, is the only work in the state of Guanajuato. Brother Looney serves in both these areas which are east of Guadalajara, and north west of Mexico City. The work is slow but rewarding. There have been approximately one hundred baptisms in the state of Jalisco, forty in Michocan, and twenty baptisms in the two new areas of work. The Norman Dungans plan to come to serve at Queretaro later in 1969.

The beginning of our work in the Mexico City area itself is a little uncertain, though apparently the first witness was given by a native evangelist, Jorge Morales, who was laboring there by 1957. However, sometime during that year Theon Biglow and Kathleen Johnson came to witness there, joined six weeks later by Gil Contreras and his wife. By 1961 the church to which Gil Contreras ministered had grown to two hundred and was self-supporting, besides supporting one of their own deacons as a missionary to a new work that sprang up in the jungles of Veracruz. There are at least two congregations there. A short time later Cathy McTeer and Joan Hawkins served with the Contreras family for over a year among the Otomi Indians of San Felipe.

The Robert Flores family came to serve in the Mexico City area in 1964. With the cooperation of other missionaries, a preacher-training school was begun in April 1966. Brother Flores is president of this Instituto Biblico Mexico. He also ministers to the church in Tlalnepantla.

Dean and Julie Cary (eldest son of Harland Cary) began a printing ministry soon after their arrival in Mexico City in November 1965. They are working with the church at Jardin Balbuena, in preaching and teaching. As a pilot with a plane, there are many opportunities of service to and for the missionaries in outlying regions. New landing strips dot many landscapes. One special need arose among the Christians in the state of Oaxaca, where Richard and Leta Atkinson have labored since October 1968 in the village of Zaragoza. Their corn supply was completely gone, and the only corn within their region was out of reach financially. Thus a plane load of corn made its way to these needy people from Mexico City. At the present time the Atkinsons

422

are teaching at the Instituto Biblico Mexico while in Mexico City for an advanced Spanish course.

Another first for the Mexico City work is the joining of a pair of homing pigeons to the missionary staff. The offspring of these racing carrier-homing pigeons will be trained and used to send messages back to Mexico City from outlying areas when unexpected delays necessitate communications. Some areas are three days travel distance to the nearest telegraph office.

Willard and Mary Ann Black were in Mexico City in 1966 engaging in campus evangelism at the University of Mexico.

Glen Hancock has had an unique ministry to Mexico. He conducted an effective ministry-through-the-mails to reach Spanish-speaking people there. Attractively printed study guides on various Bible teachings were prepared and offered to boxholders in selected areas. During one two-month period more than 1,200 new people had requested the first course of study. Some have enrolled in the Instituto Biblico Mexico. He is now a med-student in Mexico City. He plans to go later to work in the state of Oaxaca.

A young man at Ninos de Mexico.　*Oldest boy at the home, a Bible College student and ready to preach.*

Ninos de Mexico (translated children of Mexico) is a home for homeless, abandoned, and unwanted children, located in southern Mexico, near the capital, Mexico City. It is a mission work of faith being carried on by Merlyn and Wanda Beeman. The Beemans were introduced to Mexico during an internship in 1966 with the missionaries in Mexico City. The need of an orphanage was brought to their attention. They arrived back on the field in January 1967 and began their home for children in rented quarters in Mexico City. They have since moved to four acres in the country, 18 miles from the City (six from Texcoco). In the first year twenty-three children were taken into the home. By January 1969 the number had increased to forty-one. Here they found a new life where Christ is the center of all. By mid-'68 twelve of the older children had accepted Christ as their Savior. The oldest boy is going out to preach every week-end.

Children after church in Mexico City.

The first year they worshipped with the Dean Cary family in Mexico City, but as the family grew it became increasingly difficult to transport so many. They now are conducting services at the Home. Visitors from near-by villages are attending. This orphanage (as the one at San Luis Potosi) can be a center of evangelism that will be loved by the people because it is love in action.

In the summer of 1968 Anne DeWelt and Jean Carlton came as "big sisters" to the children of Ninos de Mexico, and share in the heavy load of work involved with caring for the physical and spiritual needs of forty-one children.

The Jim Hosken family arrived in late summer of that year to serve for a few months with the home. They have since returned to Mexico City where they are engaged in a direct evangelism program.

Joaquin Renz worked in the Saltillo area for two years before he returned to the States in 1965 to marry Lisa Keith, and to further his education, especially in the field of journalism.

They entered Mexico in July 1968 and have settled at Cuernavaca, about fifty miles south of Mexico City. There is a particular need here in Mexico for Christian literature for the churches which are already established, both to edify the Christians and to win more to Christ. For this reason, Joaquin, "Buck", studied journalism so that he would be better prepared to produce this needed Christian literature. Since there are already Christian printers in Mexico, he will be working on both the creative and distributive end of the task. Of course, evangelization in Cuernavaca is also an aim, because one produces good literature only as he uses that literature himself. At the present time there are no churches of Christ in Cuernavaca.

South America

1 Ecuador
2 Colombia
3 Venezuela
4 Guyana
5 Surinam
6 French Guiana
7 Brazil
8 Peru
9 Bolivia
10 Paraguay
11 Uruguay
12 Argentina
13 Chile

0 100 200 300 400

Argentina

"Land of the gauchos"

Tucuman •

ARGENTINA

• Mendoza

Buenos Aires ☆

```
0   100   200   300   400
```

THE LAND . . . .

In many ways Argentina resembles the United States. Our own West looks much like the oases and rangeland, the salt flats, and block ranges of inland Argentina. Peoples of both countries still cherish the memory of rugged, independent frontiersmen fighting off bands of Indians in order to gain, step by step, a foothold in the wilderness.

Among the countries of South America, Argentina is generally considered the most modern and the most prosperous. Its population of almost twenty-three million is slightly larger than Canada's, and its area is about one-third that of the United States. It is the largest Latin American republic after Brazil.

The traditional core of the Argentine nation, and the mainstay of its economic life, has been and continues to be the Pampa, the natural prairie that extends in a 350-mile arc around the city of Buenos Aires. Beyond the Pampa the land becomes drier and the vegetation consists mostly of bunch grasses, scrub forests, and deserts.

Large segments of the country have a harsh climate that is either too hot, too cold, or too dry, but the Pampa suffers only occasionally from these extremes, which are brought in from the outlying regions by shifting air masses. At the capital, winters are mild, with an average July temperature of 49 degrees F, and the summers are also pleasant, as is evident from a January average of 73.5 degrees F.

The Pampa, gently rolling in the north but monotonously flat elsewhere (with the exception of two ranges of hills in the far south) has an adequate rainfall of between twenty to forty inches a year. Its tall natural grasses were well suited for cattle grazing; and its rich soils were turned to good account when mechanized grain farming was introduced.

Buenos Aires and its suburbs make up the overwhelmingly dominant industrial center of the country, specializing in meat packing, milling, shipbuilding and petroleum refining; shoes and leather goods; chemical, textile, brewing, paper, automotive, and metallurgical industries. This is a diversification equaled in few other places. Buenos Aires is also the leading port of the country.

It is the production of the Pampa especially which dominates the country's exports. About 55% of the total exports are animal products: meat (mostly frozen), hides, wool, and dairy products. Another 40% comes from the fields: wheat, other grains, linseed oil, and flour (to name the most important ones).

Argentina must ship abroad the yield from its land so that it may buy the many things which, as a farming and ranching nation, it does not produce at home.

. . . . THE PEOPLE

The inhabitants of Argentina, as of other Spanish-American republics, first developed from a combination of aborigines, Spanish colonists, and African slaves. The early inhabitants of the country were wandering tribes who developed few permanent centers of life.

The governing and intellectual classes maintained their Spanish traditions and family life, developing a highly cultured civilization. Inter-marriage with Indian women produced the mestizo, who constituted a large segment of the population. The transformation of Argentina from a mestizo country into a predominately white one took place in the late 19th century when the "gauchos" were pushed back, to become peons on the great estates. Less than 3% are of the indigenous Indian races today.

In few countries is the population so clearly divided as it is in Argentina, between the residents of Buenos Aires, who are known as "people of the port", and those living in the rural sections and small towns. Industrial development is bringing about a closer bond in some respects. Many of rural laborers have moved to the industrial suburbs of Buenos Aires to live in the slums, known as "villas miserias"—where a social division still exists.

The national language of the country is Spanish, though it has developed many differences from the pure Castilian. Italian, French, German and Portuguese are also widely spoken due to the number of immigrants who have come here to work.

Argentina has one of the lowest illiteracy rates in Latin America, less than 11%. Education is free, secular, and compulsory for children aged six to fourteen. Secondary education is similar to that of the English preparatory school. Eight national universities provide ample opportunity for higher learning. The public role of women in the country's society has been growing in recent decades. They were given the right to vote for the first time in the late 1940's.

Urban health in Argentina has been greatly improved in recent years. A long-term program for improving rural health is being developed for in these areas disease is still an imposing problem. Tuberculosis remains among the five principal causes of death, and leprosy is still fairly prevalent, especially in the hot northern section. Housing is the country's most backward sector from the standpoint of social development.

The Roman Catholic Church does not have as influential a hold on education in Argentina as it does in other Latin American countries, although it is a strong factor in the national life. Almost 99% of the population is Roman Catholic, at least in name. Authorities insist that Roman Catholicism is not the official religion, although the President must be a Roman Catholic and the state pays for the construction and maintenance of church buildings, supports the clergy, and names the bishops and maintains almost complete control over ecclesiastical matters. However, full religious freedom is guaranteed and practiced. The Socialist Party is anticlerical, and many intellectuals and labor union members profess no religion. The Jews, who number near 400,000 constitute the second largest concentration in the Americas. Protestants number around 200,000 and have churches in all the principal towns. Spiritualism and Oriental cults have a considerable following in the cities.

. . . . THE MISSIONARY . . . .

Everett Easley and his family are preparing to leave for Buenos Aires by August 1969. The Easley's work will be the first new work of the restoration churches in Argentina since the thriving work of the Disciples was turned over to others in comity arrangements in the early 1920's. They plan to work among the English-speaking people in Buenos Aires while in language preparation.

They hope later to be able to set up a Christian Information Center, and produce a radio work that can be followed-up with correspondence Bible study courses—all to the end that souls may be saved and the church established.

Bolivia

"In the heart of the Andes"

THE LAND . . . .

Bolivia, an inland republic, ranks fifth in size among the South American countries. It is a land of color, contrast, and change. The land is as diversified in nature as is any on earth. In one way or another, in large areas or small, virtually every climate in the world is found within its boundaries.

In Bolivia the Andes attain their greatest width of some four hundred miles and occupy one-third of the country. As in all mountainous countries in the tropics, one is wholly aware not only of distances north and south of the equator, but of those up and down. Bolivia lies entirely within the south tropical zone but its altitudes range from about three hundred feet in the east to well over 21,000 in the west. On the tops of the high mountains, caps of eternal snow grow smaller in summer and bigger in winter but never quite disappear. Just below the ice caps is the bare semidesert area, wind-swept and stormy, with hardy Alpine vegetation and bunch grass, used largely for grazing. Sheep, alpacas and llamas graze on the high plateau. Farther down is their "cold country", resembling what we refer to as temperate. Blustering cold winds sweep the land and snow and hail are common during the winter rainy season. Though a harsh climate, the farmers can grow potatoes, oats, wheat, apples and other crops. Further down the slopes lies the area the South Americans call "temperate". The weather here is subtropical, warm but not too warm, with no really cool temperatures throughout the year. Coffee and citrus fruits do well in this belt. From 3,000 feet down is the "hot country" where orchids and tropical fruits thrive in the uniformly warm and moist climate.

Bolivia has rich natural resources and yet its people are poor. Little of the great potential agricultural, forest, and mineral wealth has been developed. Although agriculture employs two-thirds of the people it produces little above subsistence level. By 1965 it was self-sufficient in sugar and rice. Only about 10% of the farm equipment is mechanized.

The economy of Bolivia has always been dependent on mineral exports, principally of tin. Manufacturing is very limited, and most Bolivians, particularly the Indians, are still not in the market for factory-made goods.

Bolivia is potentially one of the world's most important forest nations. More than half of the total area is held as public lands by the state. After Brazil, Bolivia is South America's leading rubber exporter. Brazil nuts are also gathered in the northeast and exported in quantity. Many trees are used for fuel and charcoal.

Since 1952 all the principal towns and cities have been connected by railroads, highways, or both. This will help to improve the economy of the land since it will increase the possibility of reaching out to greater market areas. Outside the main cities most buying and selling is carried on at weekly markets and village fairs. In less accessible areas barter transactions are still more common than the use of money.

. . . . THE PEOPLE

Almost all Bolivians have Indian blood in their veins and a great majority still speak the Indian tongues of Aymara or Quechua, rather than Spanish, the official language. Only 15% are whites, mostly descendents from the early Spanish settlers. Most women still wear brightly colored Indian costumes, topped by fantastic "stovepipe" hats.

The cities are neat little European islands, reminiscent of their Spanish colonial past. Most of the 3,900,000 people, however, live in the bleak, high Andean third of the country, while only a minority (about one-fourth) live in the large, potentially wealthy eastern plains.

The Spanish that is spoken here differs less from standard Castilian than do the dialects of many regions in Spain itself. When the Indian learns to speak Spanish he is classified (by his people) as a cholo (mixed blood) though rather than a racial distinction it is cultural. An increasing number of Indians are learning to speak Spanish, though most Indian peasants lack the ambition as well as the opportunity to make fundamental changes in their social status. Rural education programs since 1953 have emphasized the teaching of Spanish and its use is spreading rapidly among young Indians who are in accessible areas.

About 70% of the total population over five years of age is illiterate. Education is free and supposedly compulsory through the seventh grade; many regions however, have no schools whatsoever. In 1963 United States aid funds helped to launch a ten-year program for improvement of education.

Health conditions are notably poor in Bolivia, owing to both the lack of hygenic conditions and medical facilities. Infant mortality is particularly high. The most common diseases are malaria, influenza, dysentery, tuberculosis, and veneral diseases. Malnutrition is a serious problem.

The predominntly native rural dwelling consists of a one-room (or two sometimes) hut of adobe with thatched roof, dirt floor, and no window or smoke vent. There are no heating, running water, or sanitary facilities. Housing units in urban areas are increasing but 73% of urban population is still ill-housed.

Although the 1961 constitution abolished state support of the Catholic Church (thus formally separating church and state) the majority of the city-dwelling Bolivians are at least formally members of the Roman Catholic faith. The majority of the Indians, although nominally Roman Catholic, are in reality pagans and worship the gods of their ancestors, though these gods may have been given the names of Christian saints. All religions and beliefs are tolerated. There are a number of Protestant churches as well as several Jewish synagogues.

. . . . THE MISSIONARY . . . .

Preliminary surveys into the new field of Bolivia were made by William E. Loft, a missionary in Brazil who also pioneered opening of areas there. The area selected for this beginning was at Cochabamba, where some contacts had already been made.

The Ed Knowles' family, from Brazil, turned over their work there to a new missionary family, when they made the move to Bolivia in the middle of 1968. It was anticipated that a work here might assist in opening other Spanish-speaking countries in South America to the Gospel.

Plans were laid for evangelization for the establishment of the church; a baby-rescue mission; and a reception and culture-training center for new missionaries. Having spoken Portuguese in their Brazil work, their first job was to learn Spanish. Early in 1969 circumstances necessitated their return from this new effort.

Brazil

"Home of the inland capital"

Rural housing in central Brazil.

Bricks are made of mud and sun-dried.

THE LAND . . . .

Brazil is the land of the Amazon; the first of the Latin-Americas named for its forest, and the only one of whose people do not speak Spanish. In area, Brazil is the fifth greatest country in the world, following Russia, China, Canada, and the United States. It occupies forty-seven percent of the South American continent yet has only a population of eighty-one million (est. in 1965), not counting the Indian jungle population. It is a "young" country. In 1960, over forty-two percent were under fifteen, while fifty-three percent were between the ages of fifteen and sixty.

Most of the population is found on a comparatively narrow strip of land extending southward along the Atlantic coast, below the mouth of the Amazon to the line of Uruguay, or on the banks of the Amazon. The Amazon River is the largest in the world, exceeded in length only by the Nile.

Rainfall in the Amazon area averages 79 inches annually, the average temperature is 79 degrees. The humidity is high and the major part of this area is only a few hundred feet above sea level. The highest recorded temperature of 96.0 was reported only a few degrees from the equator at Santarim on the Amazon. It is sub-tropic and temperate in large parts of the great Brazilian plateau and three southern states of the republic. Frost and snow may sometimes be seen in these states during July and August. On the plateau the sun temperatures are high but the nights are cool and refreshing. The tableland of Minas Gerais, Sao Paulo and Rio de Janeiro in the heart of Brazil claims 40% of the total inhabitants due to its favored weather conditions. Summer rains and a winter dry season are characteristic of most of Brazil, but in the south they have no dry season—just less rainfall.

Health conditions vary widely due to wide differences in race and cultural and economic levels. Large cities rate about the same as similarily located cities in the United States. However, in rural and interior areas the death rate is high; the most serious diseases being tuberculosis, malaria, intestinal parasites, leprosy, trachoma, waterborne diseases including typhoid and dysenteries, plague and yellow fever. Smallpox remains a menace in some districts. There is also a high infant mortality rate.

Agriculture has always been the basic industry of Brazil. Though only 10% of the area is actually cultivated it is officially estimated that 60% of all workers are engaged in the pursuit of farming. Coffee growing has dominated agriculture since 1835. Cotton ranks second, although the importance of sugar is increasing. Brazil is the world's third largest producer of cacao (from which cocoa is obtained), and probably is the best source of vegetable oils.

Brazil's stock-raising industry is one of the largest in the world, the southern states having a vast abundance of grazing lands. The high plains of the interior have never been of economic importance, but the building of the new capital, Brasila, in the central area of Goias, may bring about some change in that respect.

Throughout 1963 political turmoil increased and culminated in a revolt. Constitutional government was seriously modified in 1964 when a military coup d'etat forced the incumbent president from office. Certain persons were barred from political office for ten-year periods. The constitution of 1967 strengthened the presidency and increased the power of the central government at the expense of the states. For example, the president now can even appoint the state governor. Following the coup d'etat of 1964, Communists and many persons accused of being leftists were arrested or removed from positions of influence in government, the trade unions and other fields.

. . . . THE PEOPLE

Brazil was discovered and settled by the Portuguese who gave the country its language, the one common thing that the population has, basic racial type, and Catholic faith.

The pure Indian, which now numbers 150,000, exist only in certain isolated areas of the interior along the Amazon; the mixed (mestizo) are found in a few instances in the north. Whites predominate in the southern states; Mulattoes and Negroes in the central and northern coast states. The Portuguese, Italian, and Spaniards have been readily absorbed. The German settlement of over 400,000 was not so easily assimilated. Of the more recent immigrants to the country about 8% are Japanese.

Since Brazil is a varied country its people live in various ways. The upper class prosper. For the increasing middle class, life is hard, and for the poor it is pitiable. The typical hut of the Amazon's lower valley is built of bamboo strips, with mud filling the chinks. The average farm worker is a laborer on a big plantation or a share-cropper whose cottage is provided by the owner. These frontier families move on to new grounds every two or three years. The favorite foods of the farm worker are beans, rice, sweet potatoes, fresh meat, and dried beef.

Primary education is free and compulsory up to the age of fourteen, although primary schooling is for five years—with only four years in some rural areas. Yet the proportion of illiteracy of persons over fifteen is 50%. The educational system is still mainly based on European models. According to Article 168, religious instruction is provided as "part of the teaching schedule of public schools and shall be administered according to the religious confession of the pupil".

Under the empire the Roman Catholic Church was state supported but since Brazil has become a republic the church and state have been entirely separated thus allowing a certain religious freedom. In fact according to Article 31 the government is forbidden "to establish or subsidize religious sects or embarrass their exercise". Yet the overwhelming majority of Brazilians (93%), and immigrants as well, are at least nominally Catholic, but Protestantism has made some progress especially in the field of education. By 1962 there were probably four million Protestants who were attempting to create national religious leaders. In rural sections African ceremonies are often mixed with Roman Catholic worship.

. . . . THE MISSIONARY . . . .

While still in Bible College, Lloyd David Sanders determined to go to the "uttermost parts" of the world carrying the gospel of Christ as a foreign missionary. In March of 1948 he and his wife, Ruth, began the first missionary work of the New Testament church in Brazil. For several months they remained in Rio de Janeiro for language study while making exploratory trips and careful investigations of the surrounding areas. It was determined that the state of Goias, in the heart of Brazil, offered the greatest possibilities, thus the Brazil Christian Mission began operations in the strategic capital, Goiania. (Since that time the national capital has been moved to Brasilia, 105 miles northeast of this city, placing even greater importance to the area.)

Immediately the Sanders began a school for the underprivileged children of the small villages around the city. Teaching the children to read and write their native language, Portuguese, they used as their chief text, the Bible. Thus began the Gospel ministry in Brazil.

The Sanders were joined in 1950 by the Dick Ewing family and Miss Ruth Spurgeon, who, after nine months of language study and orientation, took over the work while the Sanders family returned to the States for a furlough. Following a year of language study, Miss Ellen Case began active service at the mission in 1952, having had practical experience in home Mexican and Negro missions.

Out of these first efforts of the mission grew two major projects: 1) the Vila Nova congregation, 2) the "Escola Biblica", a state registered Christian Day School, which offered Christian training to the lower grades. By 1960 there were three such schools with a total enrollment of 190.

Approaching the field primarily as a Christian evangelist and teacher, Miss Spurgeon, who is a registered nurse, found many opportunities to heal the sick and gain a hearing for Christ through that ministry.

Early in 1953 the Sanders opened a second field in the town of Silvania, about sixty miles southeast of Goiania. Missionaries Dick Ewing and Lloyd Sanders were the first to break the tradition that 'no Protestant has stayed here (Silvania) after sundown'. The early efforts were met with opposition but seed was sown that soon began to grow. In later years the work died out, but in more recent months the church has been reopened.

One of the major goals of the Brazil Christian Mission was to set up a school for the training of national evangelists. "Instituto Cristao de Goiania" was the fulfillment of that goal. The first session was held in the spring of 1953 with twelve students; thirty enrolled for the first full term. The first building for the school was not completed until 1955 and an intensive building program continued. The school offered general education adapted to the academic achievements of the students to supplement the Bible training and was aimed at giving a well-rounded foundation to religious workers, preachers, teachers, and evangelists. (This school has since been discontinued.)

From necessity a trade school was operated so that students might learn to do a job that would help support them, not only while in school but, as they ministered to their own people. Short-term Bible training courses were taken to the areas where national ministers requested such training.

A rural and village evangelism program was set up under the leadership of brother Ewing. Being a pilot, and possessing a Brazilian license, he was able to cover much more territory with the use of a plane (when one was available). Students from the Institute received valuable training by assisting in this program of evangelism.

There had long been a real need for the printing of Restoration materials, as well as more teachers at the preacher-training school; the coming of the Kenneth Mathis family in 1956 was an answer to prayer in this matter. Brother Mathis had been interested for some time in the training of a national ministry for Brazil, and during school days had maintained a small business in off-set printing. His hobby in carpentry and cabinet making enabled him to assist in the trade school as well. He also labored in rural evangelism with a team of Institute students until he resigned from the Mission to take up a ministry in Indiana.

Along with the Mathis family, the Edwin Knowles family began language study in the state of Sao Paulo, coming on to Goiania in May 1957. Too much emphasis cannot be given to the important phase of language study. To reach the Brazilians you must know their language well. Having served with Intermountain Bible College in Colorado, the Knowles came experienced in the field of education, ready to assist in the training of young nationals in Brazil. He also was a printer and was used in this department. After serving for three years they resigned and in February 1960 returned to Brazil to work independently in Goias, specializing in the production of Christian literature in Portuguese. There is no medium which takes the place of the printed Word. As the door opened, they moved to Bolivia for a period before returning to the States.

The Merlin Shields first became interested in the work of Brazil Christian Mission in March of 1955. Since then their only desire was to equip themselves in all ways so as to more effectively serve the Lord in this most opportune and needy land. They arrived in Campinas, Sao Paulo in late 1957, and following the language and orientation schooling they went on to Goias in the latter part of 1959. They served faithfully and well in the evangelistic efforts of the Mission. In the summer of 1968 they resigned from Brazil Christian Mission. They plan to continue to work in Brazil, but in an area and with a type of program that is out of range of the present scope of activities of the Mission.

In the "fullness of time" the capital city of Brasilia was launched. This has been Brazil's dream for over a century, but somehow the Lord arranged for the dream to become a reality only when New Testament Christianity was ready and willing to launch out too. The missionaries to Brazil were prepared for this advancement. (The city is set upon a high plateau in the central part of the country, its importance is as the city spoken of by Jesus when He said that "a city that is set on a high hill cannot be hid".)

The move to Brasilia started as early as January 1957 when four hundred people moved there. One hundred thousand lived there by 1960, but by 1967 there were 400,000 inhabitants. In November 1958, less than two years after the first settlement began, the Bill Loft family moved from the Belem area to the capital city. They became the first foreign missionaries (of any religion) to set up permanent residence in Brasilia. They also erected the first permanent building of any religious group. By October 1959 preaching was being carried on in two different locations. The Christian primary school was started in Taguatinga, a suburban community of Brasilia. This area is planned to house workers and by 1961 had 85,000 residents.

Elders of Taguatinga church.

Some young people of Taguatinga church.

Bill and Lora Metz came in 1961 to assist in the Taguatinga work. They spent the preceding six months in Belem, studying the language and customs of the people. They had planned to work on Marajo Island, but conditions were not favorable and the time was right in Brasilia and additional workers were needed. In 1962 they moved to the Gama section of Brasilia. Later in the year another Bible school was started in another section of Gama, called Gaminha. There were 115 baptisms in these areas in the first two years. By 1966 they had a primary school in operation. By 1967 they were helping in nightly services, plus nine on the Lord's Day. There had been 427 decisions for Christ in the Gama church by early 1968, and it was soon to become self-supporting.

Betty Cole also came in 1961 to work with the mission school in Taguatinga. The primary school began in 1961 with the first five grades and at the end of five years became, more or less, self-supporting. That year they had 300 students enrolled.

Partly because of the school, the church of Christ had gained a reputation for being progressive, evangelistic, interested in youth and children, and the general good of Brazil. The children are taught to study and learn, as cheating on tests is not allowed as it is in most Brazilian schools. Because of this, out of those who take entrance exams to get into high schools, a larger percentage of the students from the school in Taguatinga are accepted. These students are going out with some Bible knowledge, higher morality, and a better sense of values.

Jennie Lee Titus arrived in May 1962 to teach the missionary children in an English session daily, and to work in general church activities.

By 1964 a third Sunday school was being conducted in another section of the city. Jerry Hall and his family reached Brazil late in 1966 and settled in Taguatinga for language study with the Wycliffe Bible Translators' course in Portuguese. They were plagued with illness for several months, but were eventually able to share in the witness in the area.

The Lynn Cleaveland family arrived in 1967 to assist in the work in central Brazil.

During a missionary rally in Detroit in 1966, Wade Pope was challenged by Bill Loft to go to the Brazilian mission field. The guidance of the Holy Spirit led them to the field in 1968 where they worked with the Lofts during their period of language study and cultural adjustment. Early in 1969 the Pope family moved to Rio de Janeiro area to begin a new work in the northern section of this state of some 7-9 million people. Several have signed up to study with them in a Bible correspondence course.

The Harry Douglass family, who arrived on the field about the same time as the Popes, studied language in Taguatinga too, and moved to Rio to share in the work there. They plan a three-pronged

449

attack: 1) the first will be the ministry to the suburban areas of Nova Iquacu, San Joao de Merito, and Duque de Caxias, which are similar to the Taguatinga area with which they are familiar. 2) The second approach is to form a "School of the Bible". This will be located in Rio proper, with the thrust toward the middle-class, through radio programs, correspondence courses, and classes in the school itself. 3) The third approach will be to reach the English-speaking Brazilian community. It is hard to imagine the desire of these people to learn English. Many of their books in the University courses and in business are written in English. Very quickly English-speaking services were started on the Lord's Day with some Brazilians and some Americans attending regularly.

The newest recruits to Rio is the Earl Haubner family, who will add their witness to this needy area.

In 1960, the Lloyd Sanders' family, with other representatives of Brazil Christian Mission, began laboring in the residential area of downtown Brasilia. A new church building to seat 600 (now nearly completed) was built in an unique neighborhood apartment area where 10,000 persons live within about 1,500 ft. radius. The work progresses, though rather slowly at times. An annual youth convention hosted by the Brasilia church in November 1968 had 175 in attendance. Twelve young people dedicated their lives to the ministry of the Gospel during the convention.

The Harry Scates family arrived in Brazil in January 1963 to serve with Brazil Christian Mission until September 1968. In November they moved to Uberlandia, a city of 110,000, located around 300 miles south of Brasilia. This is a key city in a developing agricultural region of Brazil. We have had no previous witness in this area at all. The Lynn Cleavelands are now working with them in this area. They plan to have a Christian Information Center downtown and will be conducting Bible studies in various homes.

Dale and Carol McAfee conducted a trip into the Ceres, Goias area at the end of 1965 and were impressed of the need of workers in this area. They located in Ceres in late February 1966 to help evangelism efforts that were originally established as early as the middle and late 50's by David Sanders and Dick Ewing. To assist in the outreach, a Bible bookstore was officially opened in October 1967.

This center of Ceres is 160 miles north of the state capital, Gioania. They have evangelized out from the city as far as 520 miles north at Paraiso do Norte, and several areas northeast of Ceres on the Brasilia-Belem highway. Over one hundred baptisms have been reported in all these areas, many are folk in rural areas who have been found to

450

be warmly receptive. In February 1969 services were started in the McAfee home in Ceres: English communion service in the afternoon and Portuguese preaching at night.

Baptismal at Sao Luiz do Norte.

Everyone helps to build church building at Sao Luiz do Norte.

Tom and Libby Fife and their children came to labor with the Brazil Christian Mission in 1964. Their work included evangelism, home teaching, work in camps, and various other realms of service. They are now no longer affiliated organizationally with the Mission since they have been selected to oversee the work of APLIC, an organization to promote and produce religious literature in Portuguese.

Gerald and Mary Holmquist arrived in Campinas, Sao Paulo in

1960 to engage themselves in the study of the Portuguese language. In 1961 they moved to Anapolis, Goias and built a home in which services were first conducted in July of that year. By December the average attendance was 45. They built their first church building in 1962 (a new one was begun in 1968). This church maintains a full program of teaching and witnessing. These are led by the Brazilians themselves. Average Sunday school attendance in 1968 was about 130; evening service was 160. Prayer meeting attendance averaged seventy. Over fifty youth are active in the work also. Several of the church men are able preachers and are great students of the Word. A second church in Anapolis was begun in 1966 under native leadership—attendance averaging over ninety. Another work was opened up at Ouro Verde, twenty miles northwest of Anapolis. There have been 450-500 baptisms reported in these areas.

When the Holmquists return to Brazil in 1969 they will be holding revivals in the churches in and around Anapolis. After they dispose of their mission home they will be serving in a new area as the Lord leads.

The work of the Amazon Valley Christian Mission was born in 1949 when Bill and Ginny Loft, upon graduation from Bible College, came to the realization of the lack of New Testament teaching in Brazil, especially among the Indian tribes along the mighty Amazon River.

The Lofts reached Brazil in the summer of 1952. In the following year they continued on in Belem in language (Portuguese) study. In spite of the opposition from the Roman Church, most of their work that year was done through the Children's Home where they had received the first child as early as November 1952. Through witness at the Home and the regular church services they were able to baptize twenty-six people. Fifty-seven were immersed during their first term on the field. The Kenneth Foxes were also here assisting in this work for a brief period of time during its beginning.

The Richard Robinson family sailed to Brazil in the summer of 1954 to assume the responsibility of the Children's Home which had, by this time, been moved from Belem to some property purchased near Icoaraci, twelve miles away. This enabled the Lofts to proceed more definitely into plans for evangelism of the Brazilian people.

Besides the Children's Home, which provided loving care for the child who is poor, orphaned, or abandoned, there was established a Primary School. This was almost necessary since there were no other schools for the children to attend except the Catholic ones in the community. The Robinsons also began to supervise the activities at the church that met near the Home.

In 1956, along with their labor at Icoaraci, the Robinsons were able to establish three river preaching points where Dick was assisted by two of the faithful Christians who were studying to prepare for the ministry to their own people. A small boat, 'The Evangelista', was purchased to be used for river evangelism. Following their own furlough period the Robinsons served in Macapa in the absence of the Clint Thomas family.

Mr. and Mrs. Ed Bartlebaugh came to work in the Children's Home in 1955, for a period of one year during Loft's furlough. They found great opportunities for service; actually they were doing for Brazilians what they had previously done for Americans, having labored at the East Tennessee Christian Home. Although they left when the year was up, they left a part of themselves in the lives of the children with whom they worked.

It was to this work that the Bartlebaughs returned in 1958, at which time they took over the responsibilities of the Home. By 1959 there were forty-one children in the Home. The children in the neighborhood, as well as the Home, attended school at the Mission Home. There were 95 enrolled for the 1960 school year, twenty-two of them from the Home. VBS attendance was as high as 102. The Home teaches the children that work is honorable, regardless of how menial the task. It teaches them in their play that they must show good sportsmanship; it teaches the Bible in order that they may learn to serve Jesus. The Home is a key witness of practical doing.

Challenged by the Robinsons on their last furlough, the Frank Horns, former classmates of the Robinsons, began their work in Brazil with the Home in the fall of 1960. Frank was a farm boy and used his knowledge to utilize the land around the Home in farming. They also taught and helped in the construction program. They served in the Home and witnessed to the children until the Home was closed in December 1966. They served a small congregation in the Barreiro section of Belem before they returned to the States in late summer of 1967.

The city of Belem is unique to the Amazon Valley; it is the gateway to the Amazon and its largest city. The population of 500,000 people offers great opportunities for the preaching of the Gospel. Belem is one of the most Catholic cities in Brazil. Though there is a slight turning away from the Catholic religion, the influence is still strongly felt. From all indication the fastest growing religion is spiritualism.

453

Besides the obvious work of evangelism, a supply service from Belem was offered to all the missionaries in the Valley. This phase of the work became known under the title of Belem Area Evangelism. One of the results of this program of evangelism was the establishment of a New Testament church in Marambaia, a Belem suburb. By summer of 1957 they had twenty-six active members. The opportunities of this area are unlimited; the importance of it unmatched.

Since the Loft's arrival on the field for the first time they felt the need for literature in the Portuguese language. Thus, through the guidance and blessing of God, late in 1956 there was the beginning of the Amazon Valley Christian Literature Service. By the first of 1957 several tracts had been printed and a bi-monthly religious paper was started in February of that year. Over two thousand copies of the Life of Christ Visualized booklets were distributed by 1957. Experience proved the need for this special ministry. Can you imagine what it would be like if we had not religious magazines, teacher study courses, or preacher training material in English? This literature service was the planting and the cultivating in the long-range program of evangelism, and it must be done to reap the best harvest.

In 1959 the Amazon Valley was dropped from the Christian Literature Service, because the work reached far beyond the Valley. In due time it became known as APLIC. Charles and Ann Kent went to Brazil in 1964 to work with the Association for Christian Literature. Following a period of language study and the departure of the Knowles family, the Kents assumed complete responsibility of the printing work. The printing is mostly Bible school material. A Primary course, a Junior course, and an advanced Youth course are being used by the Brazilian churches. A new course for Junior High is being printed and other material is being prepared. Carol and Barbara Lowe directed the work in 1968 during the furlough of the Kent family. The Kents do not minister to any of the churches but worship and serve at the Vila Nova congregation. There are four congregations in Goiania whose combined Bible school attendance averages about 200. These churches are under native leadership. The Lowes left Goiana to begin their language study in Sao Paulo.

In a recent meeting it was decided that Tom Fife, the newly elected president of APLIC, will prepare all the material. Charles Kent will be in charge of promotion, sales and distribution. Carol Lowe will be in charge of the actual production of the work. They plan to increase and upgrade material and expand production.

Lew Cass became a recruit to the Amazon Valley work in 1956. In April of that year he was injured in an automobile accident but made a marvelous recovery. Feeling that he was spared by God, brother Cass was more determined than ever to be used of God. He arrived on the field in late summer (our season) 1957 to assist in the Belem area evangelism, especialy among the youth. Later he helped the Lofts in the beginning of the work in Brasilia and supervised it during their furlough. In August 1960 he returned to the States for furlough. On September the first, he and Vida Stewart, missionary nurse from Kulpahar, India, (whom he had met during his recovery period in 1956) were united in marriage. They returned in 1961 to serve in various areas of Brazil, not only in Brasilia, but in Belo Horizonte during the Art Carter furlough (due to illness). He also taught in Goiania Bible College, while it was still in operation. They left the field in 1966 to make plans to enter Indonesia.

Mr. and Mrs. Art Carter arrived on the field in August 1957 to also help relieve the work of the Lofts. Their plans for work were: 1) to help establish a preacher-training school, 2) to assist in the evangelistic efforts, and 3) to work among the poor people where Art's short medical course could prove of some value. A traveling medical clinic to help cure the people's diseases offered a way of contact for the preaching of Christ.

The missionaries believe in the necessity of training Brazilians to evangelize this country, thus Belem Bible Seminary became a reality. In 1959 the Pan-Americano High School became a part of the training program.

Besides teaching in the Seminary, the Carters were kept busy in the building program at the Seminary and among the churches. They were also instrumental in starting two Christian Day Schools. Part of their effort has been in translation and printing; one major work was the Christian Doctrine Workbook (in Portuguese). Art has been a builder, teacher, service agent, and diplomat. He acted as forwarding correspondent for the workers in Brasilia when the work first started. The Carters gave invaluable aid to missionaries just arriving or leaving the field.

They began a totally new witness in Belo Horizonte, but were forced to come home in 1964 due to severe illness of Art. Although still in the States they continue to work on behalf of the Brazilian witness and financially assist with the work in Belo Horizonte. When the Carters were forced to leave the field the Robert Smiths moved to have oversight of the work.

The Jerry Halls came to Belo Horizonte to relieve the Smiths for furlough. On the Smith's return, the Halls will concentrate their efforts with the Bea Vista church in suburban Belo Horizonte.

David Bayless, young student at Ozark Bible College, interested in the missionary possibilities of Brazil, came to the Amazon Valley to labor in the summer of 1957. Immediately he began to share in the labor. Knowing Spanish, he was able to pick up some of the Portuguese language quite rapidly. His experience was a blessing not only to himself but to those with whom he worked.

In 1958, back in the States, David married, and together, he and his wife made preparation for service in Brazil, arriving in the fall of 1959. Along with language study they worked at teacher training in the church. When Belem Bible Seminary, later called Para Bible Institute, began in 1961, David was one of the teachers. When the Institute did not produce the leadership hoped for, it was discontinued (in 1964). At this time the missionaries in the area formed an evangelizing association, called SEVIC. This group produced a 10-lesson Bible correspondence course, which eventually enrolled 850 through 1967. This correspondence course was advertised not only by newspaper but through the weekly gospel radio broadcast which has been on the air since 1966. Dick Robinson was in charge of the broadcast, but has now trained men of the church to have complete charge of programming. The Robinsons arrived in the States in 1969 on an extended "educational" furlough.

In connection with the SEVIC, a religious library and study center was opened downtown in Belem. New churches were opened up, largely through the trained Brazilian leadership. A church was begun in the center of Belem in 1967 which began to reach middle and upper class for the first time. The Bayless family returned from furlough in June 1969 and will work with the new "downtown" church in particular. By mid-68 there were five churches and seven preaching points in this area of Brazil.

The Paul Lanham family entered Belem in December 1959 and engaged in language study. At the end of this study they took charge of the work at Sacramenta (suburb of Belem) in 1960 while teaching at the Bible Institute. A Christian Day School was established here too. Education is an important instrument in evangelism.

The Stan Wohlenhaus family arrived in the Belem area in 1963 to witness through the Bible Institute during the remaining time it existed. Then they witnessed through the evangelistic efforts of SEVIC until their return to the States in 1966. Within a few months of their arrival in the States, Mrs. Wohlenhaus was killed in an auto accident, leaving three small children without a mother. Stan has since remarried and is teaching at Ozark Bible College, lending his influence for recruits to enter the mission field.

James C. Jones and family arrived in the Belem area in April 1967. They made their residence in Icoaraci and began the study of the language.

The Norman Maddux family reached the Belem area in 1968 to set up the print shop to turn out the immediate needs of the area, in correspondence lessons, tracts, pamphlets and booklets. This will not be in competition with the work of APLIC.

The Allen Kisner family plan a two-year internship with the workers in the Belem area, beginning in the summer of 1969. Bill Moreland and his family plan to be in Belem in 1969 and will stay in the area during their language study during the first year. The Gary Meyers' family plan to join the work in the fall of 1969.

In the fall of 1953, Bill Loft and Bob Smith, who, with his family, had only recently arrived in Belem, made a survey trip up north of the Amazon River to the territory of Amapa where they found excellent possibilities in the capital city of Macapa, some two hundred air miles from Belem. It was at this new location that the Smiths opened up a work in 1954. Macapa was the answer to the Smith's prayer for a place of service. Here there were many natives of British West Indies (English-speaking Negroes) and thousands of Portuguese speaking natives, thus a double opportunity to witness for Christ. This was a previously unentered field and the possibilities were unlimited. The Amazon Valley contains more unexplored territory than any other area on the earth's surface. But everywhere there is always the influence of the priest, it seems. At times it appears that the only hope is for the newer generation, who do not follow so superstitiously the traditional religion. However, several invitations came from various small villages near Macapa, and plans were made for a 'circuit preaching' venture. At the mouth of each of the smaller rivers emptying into the Amazon there is a village or trading post where the people from the interior buy and sell supplies. By going to these key centers people from up each river can be reached. When Bob Smith accepted the Presidency of Belem Bible Seminary it left this phase of the river evangelism program not fully developed.

Marlin and LaVonna McNeil accepted the call of God to take the message to the thousands of native tribesmen along the upper reaches of the Amazon River. Many of them have never heard the Gospel of Christ; many also have no written language. They reached the field in February 1960 and came to Macapa to study Portuguese, build a houseboat for transportation and living quarters, and make other preparations to carry the Gospel in this needed program of river evangelism. However, they were not able to fulfill their plans since

457

they were forced to return to the States in June 1961, due to health problems.

When the Jim Morelands arrived in Brazil in 1961 they came to Macapa to fill the McNeil's place in the river evangelism among the West Indians. In 1966 they moved to the Araguaina area, over 400 miles south of Belem (in the northern part of the state of Goias). They are also teaching in two other areas near Araguaina. In 1967 they were living in a tent on the church lot, to be near the work.

Clint Thomas spent the summer of 1954 in the Amazon Valley and was challenged with the opening door for evangelism. After completing his Bible training in the States, he returned, with his wife, to Brazil in June 1956. A farming background helped the adjustment that had to be made to the adverse condition in Valley living. By September they were settled with the Smith family in Macapa. Much of their earlier months were spent in necessary language study. Not until early 1957 were they able to actually begin their teaching work. Due to the Roman influence, they found the work with the adult men to be most fruitful, for children could be removed from the missionary's influence and women ordered by husbands to leave the church. But everyone was given the opportunity to hear, as far out as they could reach.

In 1965 the Clint Thomas family moved to Urucara on the Amazon River where no evangelism has been carried on before.

Main street of Urucara.

The Dale Mason family arrived in Belem in late 1967 where they spent their first year in language study. During this period they were able to help establish a new congregation and Dale used his

458

limited medical knowledge with the poor in the city. They plan to spend this year, at least, with the Thomas family on the River, and will then go elsewhere on the Amazon to work.

In Southern Brazil the first mission work to be planned by direct-support missionaries was the Sao Paulo Christian Mission with John and Bettie Nichols the missionaries. John, the son of missionary parents, is well acquainted with the cause of New Testament evangelism, and has been provided an excellent background for the work that was planned for the Sao Paulo area. Sao Paulo, the capital of a state of well over ten million people, is the largest city of Brazil, and probably the fastest growing large city of the world. There has not been a land of more opportunities since the early days of our own country. Truly the need is great and the potential unlimited.

The Nichols arrived in June 1959 and immediately entered language school in Campinas. Though they witnessed for a brief period they were unable to carry out their intended plans and returned to the States in 1961. Two families from Christian Missionary Fellowship have labored here over a period of time. The church of Christ (anti-instrument) brethren have some work also in this state. It apparently has been quite effective.

The John Bush family arrived in Recife, Brazil in January 1969 to begin a new ministry under the title "Northeast Brazil Christian Mission". The name locates the area in which their work will be.

Gary and Pam Burrell plan to enter Brazil by January 1970. For nine years they have been preparing in Latin American studies for such a time as this. Their area of service is still unknown but they plan to serve where they can evangelize through the pulpit and in the homes, and by means of distribution of literature.

Brazil has changed greatly since the arrival of our first missionary on the field. Although Catholicism is still the pre-dominant religion, and is as totalitarian and oppressive as ever, there is not a general climate which permits extreme persecution. Still, bureaucratic obstacles and every possible difficulty are created for non-Catholics. Yet in the hearts of many of the common people is the search for the truth in God's Word, a truth they have never known before. May God's servants be equal to the task!

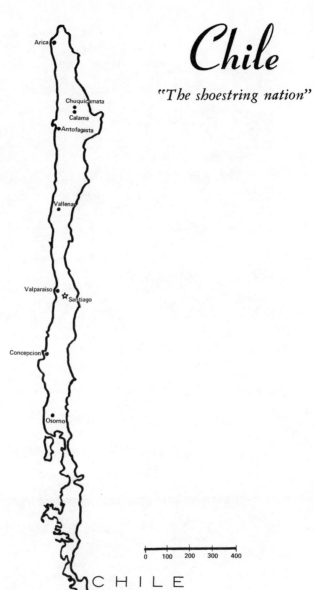

Chile

"The shoestring nation"

Arica

Chuquicamata
Calama
Antofagasta

Vallenar

Valparaiso
Santiago

Concepcion

Osorno

0   100   200   300   400

C H I L E

Preparing lumber for a building in southern Chile.

Team of oxen pulling modern vehicle out of mud.

THE LAND . . . .

Chile is situated on the South American continent's southwestern coast between the Andes Mountains and the Pacific Ocean. It is a narrow ribbon-like country (a shoestring republic) whose length along the coast is 2,653 miles. The width varies from 221 to 50 miles. It is often said that its head is burning while its feet are freezing. This vast difference comes because it stretches across half of the southern hemisphere. It is divided into three sections from the long strip of tropical desert in the north through the temperate zone to the bleak and rocky island shores in the south. Generally speaking the northern section is hot and arid, the southern is wet and cold. The northern desert area may go for years without rain which makes it one of the driest places on earth, while rain is abundant in the Central Valley and very heavy in the southern region. The interior area varies some from the coastal conditions. Not many countries have the climatic extremes of Chile.

Among the South American countries Chile is perhaps the richest in mineral resources. They account for 70% of the value of Chilean exports. The northern part depends almost entirely on mining industries, being rich in copper ore and deposits of sodium chloride, radium nitrate and iodine salts. Copper is Chile's most important industrial metal and its leading export. Chile is one of the leading industrial nations in South America. It leads the world in production of iodine, a by-product of the nitrate industry.

The Central Valley offers mild wet winters and cool dry summers (the temperature seldom freezes or rises above 77 degrees), which makes it ideal for human comfort. In fact 90% of the people live in this area. The principal agricutural region extends from slightly north of Valparaiso to Valdivia in the south central part which includes this Central Valley, one of the garden spots of the world. However, only about 8% of the land is used for agricultural purposes. Three leading crops are wheat, barley, and oats. Principal fruits are apples, melons, and grapes, from which comes the well-known wines of Chile. Also in this area the livestock business is an important one.

Chile's main forested area lies in the south, almost totally uninhabited except for the nomads and herders, for there is an abundance of grazing land for sheep whose fleece is long and of high quality. This forest area is one of the stormiest regions on earth. Though most of these resources of the forest region are unexploited, Chile is now self-sufficient in lumber and exports beech, pine, and laurel.

Unlike most Latin-American countries, Chile has no wildlife to speak of. There are few birds or animals, and scarcely any snakes.

. . . . THE PEOPLE

While the majority of the eight and one-half million Chileans are of European (chiefly Spanish and Basque) origin, there is considerable infusion of Indian blood especially in the laboring class. British, Irish, German, and other European nationalities have mixed with the largely Spanish upper and middle classes, the latter class representing over half of the Chilean population. Nomads live in the extreme south; the Changos live in the north coast region. Araucanians live along the Andes slopes. They have a fierce love of liberty and struggled long against the invading whites. These Indians live chiefly by hunting and fishing, and are good at handicrafts. Their background is rich in musical folklore.

The population is divided into two classes (not of race but of social position), those who do not and those who do possess material and cultural wealth. The laborer is nominally independent but lacks vision or initiative. The landlord, who profits by the laborers' work, cares little for the condition of his tenants who live in thatched huts and other humble type dwellings and whom he used to pay about 12c a day. However the landlord does supply his own requirements and standards of living, residing in fabulous haciendas or city dwellings, even to educating his children abroad. Wages in Santiago in 1966 were about $52 per month for salaried employees, and 10c an hour for blue-collar workers.

The people in general are hardy and vigorous and fond of strenuous sports. Soccor is the most popular game and polo is a favorite with the wealthy. The Indians are adept at a hockey game played with a stone.

Chilean women have been liberated from their former subordinate position and are allowed to vote; they are very active and influential politically.

Primary education is free and nonsectarian, and compulsory from the ages of seven to fifteen. Public and private kindergartens are available for children ages four to six. Secondary schools are also both public and private. There are five institutions of higher learning. Illiteracy was 26.5 per cent back in 1940 but it has since continued to fall at a steady rate. In 1964 it was reduced to 16%. The official language is Spanish, although Mapuche is still spoken by some of the Araucanian Indians.

The Roman Catholic Church and the state under the Chilean constitution were very close until the new constitution was adopted in 1925. At present Catholicism is far more liberal in Chile than in any other Latin-American country though nearly 90% of the people are Roman Catholics. Due largely to the fact that the majority of the people are Catholics there is no divorce in the country. Protestantism, much in the minority, is tolerated and has gained power due to British influence and educational facilities provided by the North American churches.

. . . . THE MISSIONARY . . . .

Nearly forty years ago Bertrand Smith began his preparation for a ministry to the people of South America. During the early years of his college training he became acquainted with a former missionary to Uruguay, and found himself definitely interested in South America. Though hardly more than a hobby he began the study of the Spanish language. While through the years he served in the States his eyes would turn again and again toward the harvest fields of Latin America.

In the winter of 1947 brother Smith made a special trip to Colombia to effect a permanent entry visa, but this was denied. Only later did the Smith family see the guiding hand of a living Lord, closing the door of Colombia to them. For it was there that evangelical Christians suffered fanatical persecution at the hands of the Catholics which resulted in many deaths and much destruction of property. And in the very city of Cali, where they had planned to settle, a tragic explosion laid waste a vast portion of the heart of the city, killing more than a thousand people.

Not long after returning from the futile attempt to enter Colombia, it occurred to brother Smith to try to obtain a visa to Chile. Here the door was open—and soon the way was prepared. Brother Smith, with his family, arrived on July 10, 1949 (mid-winter in Chile) in the harbor of Valparaiso.

The Smiths found that a religious revolution was quietly taking place as the people gradually were throwing off the yoke of Rome; sometimes, however, only to be yoked again to Protestant sectarianism. So the task began—to walk beside these people, struggling and groping their way out of an age-long darkness, and to point them to the true way of simple New Testament Christianity.

It took nearly two months to become acquainted with the city and lay the ground work for future missionary activities. The first public services were held on September 14 with thirty people in attendance. The first convert, Enrique Santamaria, an Argentinian, was baptized October 3, 1949.

For fourteen years the Smiths labored alone, often with discouragements and insufficient funds. But in spite of the handicaps they accomplished a remarkable work establishing churches and preaching points in the central zone, carrying out a weekly radio ministry since 1952, and using other special efforts, such as vacation Bible schools, camps, and special meetings. Along with this ministry was felt the need of adequate reliable literature. In March 1955 the Smiths printed a 4-page weekly folder which included Bible school lesson text, a study outline and other good material. Early in 1956, however, this publication was changed into a monthly magazine of 16-20 pages, containing some of the same material as the weekly magazine, plus a Bible story, doctrinal articles and news. It was designed as an all-purpose religious periodical and does occupy an important place in the life of the churches.

A number of tracts have also been printed in quantity and distributed. The tract most used is the one entitled "The Church of Christ, What it is and What it Teaches". Although it has not been possible to establish a Bible College, home study courses are offered to those desiring to train for the ministry or for special work of some other type in the church.

An interesting and encouraging aspect of the work has been the discovery of various congregations seeking to dispense with denominational allegiance and to pattern themselves after the church in the New Testament. Disciples striving to be Christians only have been found in Vallenar, Concepcion, the Osorno area, and in other parts of Chile. The churches in the Osorno area seem to be closer to the New Testament ideal. These brethren, through the study of their leaders, have been led out of a Pentecostal denomination and call themselves the Evangelical Church of Christ. They have discovered many important truths through their own study. Seeing the opportunity to learn more rapidly they have repeatedly extended the invitation for missionaries to come and live and work among them.

Gale Smith, oldest son of the Bertrand Smiths, assumed his share of the missionary responsibilities as he became a young man. In 1963 he moved to the desert area of the north to minister to the existing churches in Chuquicamota and Calama. The young Chilean woman, Ana Reyes, through whose efforts these congregations were started, moved in 1964 to Ovalle, at the south edge of the northern desert area. She planned to help establish a new work there. In 1964 Gale led in efforts to bring a new work in Antofagosta. The following year he married the daughter of a Chilean policeman. They have since returned to the States to further their college education.

The Mark Huntleys were the first recruits to come to the assistance of the Smiths' witness in Chile. Their arrival in 1963 made it possible for the evangelistic effort to be extended. They were joined by the James Mick family in 1964 (who spent their first year in language study). Miss Alta Tanner reached Chile in 1965 to begin helping in the task of teaching the Gospel. Having had experience with the Spanish language in Mexico she was able to immediately begin work with the women and children. These two families and Miss Tanner moved to the Osorno area to work in personal and radio evangelism in the southern part of Chile.

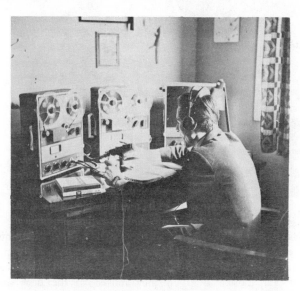

Alberto Gonzales taping radio sermon.

In May 1967 Alberto and Maria Gonzales arrived in Osorno, Chile intent on starting a Gospel radio ministry. The first broadcast began toward the middle of December that year on the island of Chiloe. Other broadcasts began in Osorno and Valparaiso in the following weeks. A fifth station, in Calama, was added by the fall of 1968. At that time 160 students had enrolled in the Bible correspondence course offered on the program. Brother Bertrand Smith oversees these courses. Since the requests come in from numerous areas it may well be the means through which to extend the work into new fields.

467

Since Spanish is their native tongue, they are doing some translation work. They also witness through teaching and preaching, not only in Osorno but in neighboring areas of Puerto Octay and Rio Negro. Maria is able to work in the medical field too. Many poor people, especially on the island of Chiloe, cannot afford proper medical attention.

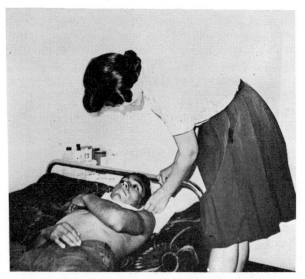

Maria treating patient for serious skin infection.

The Harvey Beasley family arrived in Chile at the beginning of 1965 with plans to preach Christ over the air with a follow-up Bible correspondence course. They first studied language in Vina del Mar, a suburb of Valparaiso. In 1966 they moved to the new work at Antofagasta where they were able to start the radio ministry. Attendance was averaging 50-60 at the church by the end of 1967. Jeff and Judy Myers began working with the Antofagasta work in 1968. The Beasleys are in the States now and upon advice of doctors will remain here, as a result of arsenic poisoning received on the field. They hope to continue to witness to the Chileans through translation and printing work.

Carl and Debbie Paschal assumed responsibility of the work at Chuquicamata on their arrival to the field. Early in 1968 they opened a new work in Tocconao, which is seventy miles away (ten miles from Argentina border). There are hundreds of small towns and villages such as Toccanao in which they hope to evangelize eventually. Vacation Bible School reached ninety-five children in 1968 in the Chuquicamata work. They assisted too in the Calama work until early in 1969 when national workers took over the guidance of this work. The vacation Bible school at Calama in 1969 enrolled 175 students. The Paschals joined the Myers' family in Antofagasta in preparation for starting two other churches in that city.

Response in Chile is often slow in coming, for when a Chilean accepts Christ he sometimes chooses self-exile as well—or he may lose his job, or friends. A student may be ostracized at school for refusing to take part in a Catholic service.

Colombia

"King of the coffee growers"

THE LAND . . . .

Colombia, named for Christopher Columbus, is the fourth largest country of South America. About as large as Texas, Oklahoma and New Mexico put together, it had an estimated population in 1965 of 18,068,000. With nine cities exceeding the 100,000 mark, Colombia has a greater portion of truly urban dwellers than any of the other west coast countries.

The surface of the land is uneven, ranging from sea level plains to mountain peaks almost 20,000 feet high. The Great Andes Mountains enter at the southwest edge and fan out into three fairly distinct ranges whose peaks are high and valleys sharp and deep. This presents a most serious obstacle in constructing a unified transportation system that will provide outlets for products and thus push forward economic development.

The climate varies from extremely tropical heat to steady, biting cold. In the highlands the climate is healthful and pleasant, very springlike, but in the forests, where rainfall is heavy and almost never stops, it is unhealthful. Almost 150 million acres, nearly half the country, are covered with trees. A treasure in forests exists, yet, due to the transportation problem, too little has been done commercially.

Farming is the chief industry, although only 2% of the land is cultivated. It is a country of small farmers with a few exceptions in the banana plantations and cattle ranches. The working of the land by these small farmers has been by the most primitive methods. However, much must be imported due to the low per-acre yield. A program to increase production, put more acreage in cultivation and improve methods, is underway.

Colombia ranks next to Venezuela and Argentina in oil production in South America. The country is almost self-sufficient in refined products. It ranks first in gold, though that is fifth in value of exports from the country. It is also the world's chief source of emeralds and platinum. Uranium has been found as well. Coffee alone provides livelihood for one-fourth of the population, and the country ranks second in world coffee production.

. . . . THE PEOPLE

The people of Colombia are a mixture of races, including Spanish, Negro and Indian. The latter group now numbers about 2% since most have intermarried with the whites and are included in the 70% Mestizos. It is more truly a white-man's country than any of the other Andean countries, except Chile. A 1964 census counted 20% of the population pure white.

The high interior cities have kept traces of early Spanish civilization. The plains in the south and southeast are the homes of the Indians, however, there still exists in the north one mountain tribe of savage Indians. Negroes live largely in the coastal lowlands, by hunting and fishing, and a little primitive farming.

Colombia has one of the lowest standards of living for the common people of any country in the western hemisphere, though there is some cause for optimism. Most rural areas and urban slums lack adequate water and sewage facilities, and such diseases as malaria and typhoid fever are still serious health problems in the lowlands. Housing for the poor, particularly urban housing, is miserable. Yellow fever is still endemic in some forest zones. The majority of the people suffer from intestinal parasites. Malnutrition is another serious health problem, with nutritional goiter, anemia, scurvy, and pellagra frequent. Respiratory and venereal diseases, and hookworm also, are among Colombia's most serious health problems.

On the occupied islands given to Colombia in 1928 live some 6,000 English speaking and Protestant Negroes; the descendants of slaves. However, most of the people on the mainland are Roman Catholic, about 96%, that religion being established there in 1525. The present government, while not friendly to missionaries, is not hostile, though there have been encounters of serious opposition and some persecution. Other religions are permitted by law as long as they are not practiced "contrary to Christian morals or to the law".

Primary education is free everywhere, and compulsory where schools are available, but facilities are limited. Illiteracy is therefore close to 40%. Spanish is the official language, and only a few isolated Indian tribes do not speak it. Spanish, as spoken and written by Colombians, is generally considered to be the purest in all Latin America.

One of the most popular spectator sports in Colombia is bullfighting. Tejo, a game in which flat stones are tossed at explosive caps, is very popular in the highlands. Along the coast, baseball is popular. Horse racing attracts great crowds, but soccer is the sport with the largest following.

. . . . THE MISSIONARY . . . .

While there were ten years of violence and persecution in Colombia until the mid-50's, it has since been comparatively quiet and persecution continues only in isolated instances. Many missionary organizations have workers on the field and are sending more. Many areas completely closed during the years of violence are now open.

Groups presently in the country use the influence of their converts in government positions to help in bringing new missionaries into the country. The fact that we have no previous work established there presented a problem, but that very fact was challenge enough to the Warren Sanders who felt God led them to labor in this needy field.

To offset the possible difficulties, the Sanders entered Colombia as students in one of the Universities. As students they would have opportunity for travel and survey work which is invaluable to the establishment of a permanent work with the Colombian people. As students they could witness to the young people who will some day be the leaders in the country.

For this type of ministry a year of language study was expedient, which the Sanders took at San Jose, Costa Rica. Residence in Colombia began in February 1962 on student visas. Their early efforts were met with opposition, from Catholics who gave warning to some, and indifference on the part of others.

Shortly after their arrival, Mrs. Sanders was offered a job teaching English in a private institute. They found this left more time for calling than did Warren's studies. Thus their official status was changed from student to teacher. This prepared them for the new phase of mission work—the operation of an elementary day school in the city of Bogota.

With the help of Bertrand Smith, missionary to Chile, a new project of Bible correspondence courses was begun in 1966. In May 1967 there were fifty-five enrolled in the course, though it is not expected that all will complete the work.

A nucleous for a church in the large city of Cali has been uncovered through these courses.

Mark and Barbara Stringer arrived in Colombia in January 1966 and immediately began language study in the University of the Andes. Upon completion of the course of study in early 1967 they moved to Villavicencio, eighty miles from Bogota.

Upon their arrival they became temporary directors of a children's home (24 children) that was started by two registered nurses who operate under an independent evangelical mission. Through this contact, the Stringers were able to become friends of the bank president, the governor of the state, and many others of the middle and upper class. From this area they plan to go out to help strengthen some of the existing churches in the Llanos.

Evangelism in small towns around their area could be accomplished partly through Christian Day schools. Teachers are welcome because illiteracy is high. A mobile Bible institute could go to the remote areas to train preachers, as many of these people are too poor to go away to school.

When the Stringers left the Home in 1967 they moved into the city to continue Bible teaching, teaching English, uring reforms in the church's way of doing things, preaching, and taking occasional trips into the country. Their section of the city has 30,000 population. A church building was built in 1969 and a Christian Day school is being operated by two native Christians, giving fifty youngsters a Christ-oriented education. A Bible Bookstore was set up to help distribute the Word. By 1968 the Stringers were holding Bible classes in Acacias, preparing for the founding of the first non-Catholic church in that city of 25,000 souls.

Carl Hines left the States in June 1969 to join the workers in Colombia. Difficulties with the immigration authorities in Bogota had delayed his departure several weeks.

There are many isolated Indian tribes in the rugged mountain areas of Colombia, most of which do not have a written language. Nearly one hundred linguists of the Wycliffe Bible Translators are working among these tribes so that eventually they will have the Bible in their own language. Harvest time is coming, but there is much work to be done to be ready for that period of reaping.

BIBLIOGRAPHY

The American People's Encyclopedia, 1950
Franklin J. Meine, Editor
Spencer Press, Inc.
Chicago, Illinois

Collier's Encyclopedia, 1952, 1968
William T. Couch, Editor
Crowell-Collier Pub. Co.
New York, New York

The Encyclopedia Americana
Lavinia P. Dudley, Editor
Americana Corp.
New York, New York

Encyclopedia Britiannica, 1956
Walter Yust, Editor
Werner Co.
Chicago, Illinois

Grolier Encyclopedia, 1952
Kenneth D. Sultzer, Editor
Grolier Society
New York, New York

The World Book Encyclopedia, 1955, 1960
J. Morris Jones, Editor
Field Enterprises, Inc.
Chicago, Illinois

Worldmark Encyclopedia of the Nations, 1968
Worldmark Press
Harper and Row
New York, New York

American Geographical Society
Around the World Program
Nelson Doubleday, Inc.
Garden City, New York

ADDRESSES

Mailing addresses for most of the missionaries referred to in this book may be obtained from:

Mission Services
Box 968
Joliet, Illinois 60434

or

A Directory of the Ministry
Box 825
Springfield, Illinois 62705

For information regarding missionaries who work under the auspices of the United Christian Missionary Society, please write:

United Christian Missionary Society
222 South Downey Avenue
Indianapolis, Indiana 46219

Information about missionaries who work with the Christian Missionary Fellowship may be obtained by writing:

Christian Missionary Fellowship
Box 26306
Indianapolis, Indiana 46226